PAROCHIAL AND PLAIN SERMONS

By JOHN HENRY NEWMAN, B.D.

FORMERLY VICAR OF ST. MARY'S, OXFORD

IN EIGHT VOLUMES

VOL. II.

NEW EDITION

RIVINGTONS

WATERLOO PLACE, LONDON

Oxford and Cambridge

MDCCCLXXX

TO

JOHN WILLIAM BOWDEN, ESQ.

ETC. ETC.

IN THE CHEERFUL CONVICTION

THAT THE ENGLISH CHURCH AMID MANY DEFECTIONS

STILL HOLDS HER INFLUENCE

OVER AN ATTACHED AND ZEALOUS LAITY,

THIS VOLUME

IS INSCRIBED,

BY HIS AFFECTIONATE FRIEND,

J. H. N.

Feb. 21st, 1835.

CONTENTS.

'

SERMON I.

The World's Benefactors.

(THE FEAST OF ST. ANDREW THE APOSTLE.)

" One of the two which heard John speak, and followed Him, was Andrew, Simon Peter's brother."—JOHN i. 40.

WITH this Festival we begin our year,—thus usher-
ing in, with a few weeks of preparation, the day
of Christ's Nativity. St. Andrew, whom we now commemorate, has been placed first of the Apostles, because
(as far as Scripture informs us) he was the first among
them who found the Messiah, and sought to be His
disciple. The circumstances which preceded his call
are related in the passage of the Gospel from which
the text is taken. We are there informed that it was
John the Baptist who pointed out to him his Saviour.
It was fitting that the forerunner of Christ should be
the instrument of leading to Him the first-fruits of his
Apostles.

St. Andrew, who was already one of St. John's
disciples, was attending on his master with another,
when, as it happened, Jesus passed by. The Baptist,

who had from the first declared his own subordinate place in the dispensation which was then opening, took this occasion of pointing out to his two disciples Him in whom it centred. He said, "Behold the Lamb of God;" this is He of whom I spake, whom the Father has chosen and sent, the true sacrificial Lamb, by whose sufferings the sins of the world will be expiated. On hearing this, the two disciples (Andrew, I say, being one of them) straightway left John and followed Christ. He turned round and asked them, "What seek ye?" They expressed their desire to be allowed to wait upon His teaching; and He suffered them to accompany Him home, and to pass that day with Him. What He said to them is not told us; but St. Andrew received such confirmation of the truth of the Baptist's words, that in consequence he went after his own brother to tell him what he had found. "He first findeth his own brother Simon, and saith unto him, We have found the Messias . . . . and he brought him to Jesus."

St. John the Evangelist, who has been guided to preserve various notices concerning the separate Apostles which are not contained in the first three Gospels, speaks of Andrew in two other places; and introduces him under circumstances which show that, little as is known of this Apostle now, he was, in fact, very high in the favour and confidence of his Lord. In his twelfth chapter he describes Andrew as bringing to Christ certain Greeks who came up to Jerusalem to worship and who were desirous of seeing Him. And, what is remarkable, these strangers · had first applied to St. *Philip, who,* though an Apostle himself, instead of taking upon him to introduce them, had recourse to his fellow-townsman, St. Andrew, as if, whether from age or intimacy with Christ, a more suitable channel for furthering their petition. " Philip cometh, and telleth Andrew ; and again, Andrew and Philip tell Jesus."

These two Apostles are also mentioned together in the sixth chapter of the same Gospel, at the consultation which preceded the miracle of the loaves and fishes ; and there again Andrew is engaged, as before, in the office of introducing strangers to Christ. " There is a lad here," he says to his Lord, a lad who, perhaps, had not courage to come forward of himself, " which hath five barley loaves and two small fishes."

The information afforded by these passages, of St. Andrew's especial acceptableness to Christ among the Apostles, is confirmed by the only place in the other Gospels, beside the catalogue, in which his name occurs. After our Lord had predicted the ruin of the Temple, " Peter, James, John, and *Andrew* asked Him privately, Tell us when shall these things be?"[1] and it was to these four that our Saviour revealed the signs of His coming, and of the end of the world. Here St. Andrew is represented as in the especial confidence of Christ ; and associated too with those Apostles whom He is known to have selected from the Twelve, on various occasions, by tokens of His peculiar favour.

Little is known of St. Andrew in addition to these inspired notices of him. He is said to have preached the Gospel in Scythia ; and he was at length martyred

---

[1] *Mark* xiii. 3.

in Achaia. His death was by crucifixion; that kind of cross being used, according to the tradition, which still goes by his name.

Yet, little as Scripture tells us concerning him, it affords us enough for a lesson, and that an important one. These are the facts before us. St. Andrew was the first convert among the Apostles; he was especially in our Lord's confidence; thrice is he described as introducing others to Him; lastly, he is little known in history, while the place of dignity and the name of highest renown have been allotted to his brother Simon, whom he was the means of bringing to the knowledge of his Saviour.

Our lesson, then, is this; that those men are not necessarily the most useful men in their generation, nor the most favoured by God, who make the most noise in the world, and who seem to be principals in the great changes and events recorded in history; on the contrary, that even when we are able to point to a certain number of men as the real instruments of any great blessings vouchsafed to mankind, our relative estimate of them, one with another, is often very erroneous: so that, on the whole, if we would trace truly the hand of God in human affairs, and pursue His bounty as displayed in the world to its original sources, we must unlearn our admiration of the powerful and distinguished, our reliance on the opinion of society, our respect for the decisions of the learned or the multitude, and turn our eyes to private life, watching in all we read or witness for the true signs of God's presence, *the graces of* personal holiness manifested in His elect;

which, weak as they may seem to mankind, are mighty through God, and have an influence upon the course of His Providence, and bring about great events in the world at large, when the wisdom and strength of the natural man are of no avail.

Now, first, observe the operation of this law of God's government, in respect to the introduction of those temporal blessings which are of the first importance in securing our well-being and comfort in the present life. For example, who was the first cultivator of corn? Who first tamed and domesticated the animals whose strength we use, and whom we make our food? Or who first discovered the medicinal herbs which, from the earliest times, have been our resource against disease? If it was mortal man, who thus looked through the vegetable and animal worlds, and discriminated between the useful and the worthless, his name is unknown to the millions whom he has benefited. It is notorious, that those who first suggest the most happy inventions, and open a way to the secret stores of nature,—those who weary themselves in the search after Truth, who strike out momentous principles of action, who painfully force upon their contemporaries the adoption of beneficial measures, or, again, who are the original cause of the chief events in national history, are commonly supplanted, as regards celebrity and reward, by inferior men. Their works are not called after them; nor the arts and systems which they have given the world. Their schools are usurped by strangers; and their maxims of wisdom circulate among the children of their *people,* forming, perhaps, a nation's

character, but not embalming in their own immortality
the names of their original authors.

Such is the history of the social and political world;
and the rule discernible in it is still more clearly
established in the world of morals and religion. Who
taught the Doctors and Saints of the Church, who,
in their day, or in after times, have been the most
illustrious expounders of the precepts of right and
wrong, and, by word and deed, are the guides of our
conduct? Did Almighty Wisdom speak to them
through the operation of their own minds, or rather,
did it not subject them to instructors unknown to fame,
wiser perhaps even than themselves? Andrew followed
John the Baptist, while Simon remained at his nets.
Andrew first recognised the Messiah among the inhabitants of despised Nazareth; and he brought his brother
to Him. Yet to Andrew Christ spake no word of
commendation which has been allowed to continue on
record; whereas to Simon, even on his first coming,
He gave the honourable name by which he is now
designated, and afterwards put him forward as the
typical foundation of His Church. Nothing indeed can
hence be inferred, one way or the other, concerning
the relative excellence of the two brothers; so far only
appears, that, in the providential course of events, the
one was the secret beginner, and the other the public
instrument, of a great divine work. St. Paul, again, was
honoured with the distinction of a miraculous conversion,
and was called to be the chief agent of the propagation
of the Gospel among the heathen; yet to Ananias, an
otherwise unknown saint, dwelling at Damascus, was

committed the high office of conveying the gifts of pardon
and the Holy Ghost to the Apostle of the Gentiles.

Providence thus acts daily. The early life of all men
is private; it is as children, generally, that their characters are formed to good or evil; and those who form
them to good, their truest and chief benefactors, are
unknown to the world. It has been remarked, that
some of the most eminent Christians have been blessed
with religious mothers, and have in after life referred
their own graces to the instrumentality of their teaching.
Augustine has preserved to the Church the history of
his mother Monica; but in the case of others, even the
name is denied to us of our great benefactress, whosoever she was, and sometimes, doubtless, the circumstance
of her service altogether.

When we look at the history of inspiration, the same
rule still holds. Consider the Old Testament, which
"makes us wise unto salvation." How great a part of
it is written by authors unknown! The book of Judges,
the second of Samuel, the books of Kings, Chronicles,
Esther, and Job, and great part of the book of Psalms.
The last instance is the most remarkable of these.
" Profitable" beyond words as is the instruction conveyed to us in every word of Scripture, yet the Psalms
have been the most directly and visibly useful part of
the whole volume, having been the prayer-book of the
Church ever since they were written; and have done
more (as far as we dare judge) to prepare souls for
heaven, than any of the inspired books, except the
Gospels. Yet the authors of a large portion of them
are altogether *unknown.* And so with the Liturgies

which have been the possession of the Christian Church
from the beginning; who were those matured and
exalted Saints who left them to us? Nay, in the whole
system of our worship, who are the authors of each
decorous provision and each edifying custom? Who
found out the musical tunes, in which our praises are
offered up to God, and in which resides so wondrous a
persuasion "to worship and fall down, and kneel before
the Lord our Maker?" Who were those religious men,
our spiritual fathers in the "Catholic faith," who raised
of old time the excellent fabrics all over the country,
in which we worship, though with less of grateful reverence for their memory than we might piously express?
Of these greatest men in every age, there is "no memorial;" they "are perished as though they had never
been, and become as though they had never been
born."

Now I know that reflections of this kind are apt
to sadden and vex us; and such of us particularly. as
are gifted with ardent and enthusiastic minds, with a
generous love of what is great and good, and a noble
hatred of injustice. These men find it difficult to
reconcile themselves to the notion that the triumph of
the Truth, in all its forms, is postponed to the next
world. They would fain anticipate the coming of the
righteous Judge: nay, perhaps they are somewhat too
favourably disposed towards the present world, to
acquiesce without resistance in a doctrine which tes-
tifies to the corruption of its decisions, and the worthlessness of its honours. But that it is a truth, has
already been showed almost as matter of fact, putting

the evidence of Scripture out of consideration; and if it be such, it is our wisdom, as it will become our privilege, to accustom our minds to it, and to receive it, not in word merely, but in seriousness.

Why indeed should we shrink from this gracious law of God's present providence in our own case, or in the case of those we love, when our subjection to it does but associate us with the best and noblest of our race, and with beings of nature and condition superior to our own? Andrew is scarcely known except by name; while Peter has ever held the place of honour all over the Church; yet Andrew brought Peter to Christ. And are not the blessed Angels unknown to the world? and is not God Himself, the Author of all good, hid from mankind at large, partially manifested and poorly glorified, in a few scattered servants here and there? and His Spirit, do we know whence It cometh, and whither It goeth? and though He has taught men whatever there has been of wisdom among them from the beginning, yet when He came on earth in visible form, even then it was said of Him, "The world knew Him not." His marvellous providence works beneath a veil, which speaks but an untrue language; and to see Him who is the Truth and the Life, we must stoop underneath it, and so in our turn hide ourselves from the world. They who present themselves at kings' courts, pass on to the inner chambers, where the gaze of the rude multitude cannot pierce; and we, if we would see the King of kings in His glory, must be content to disappear from the things that are seen. Hid are the saints of God; if they are known *to men*, it is accidentally, in their temporal offices, as holding some high earthly station, or effecting some mere civil work, not as saints. St Peter has a place in history, far more as a chief instrument of a strange revolution in human affairs, than in his true character, as a self-denying follower of his Lord, to whom truths were revealed which flesh and blood could not discern.

How poor spirited are we, and what dishonour we put upon the capabilities and the true excellence of our nature, when we subject it to the judgment and disposal of all its baser specimens, to the rude and ignorant praise, and poor recompensing of carnal and transgressing man! How shall the flesh be at all a judge of the spirit? or the sinner of God's elect? Are we to look downwards, not upwards? Shall we basely acknowledge the right of the Many, who tread the broad way, to be the judges of holiness, which comes from God, and appeals to Him? And does not the eye of faith discern witnesses of our conduct, ever present, and far worthier of our respect, than even a world of the ungodly? Is man the noblest being in the creation? Surely we, as well as our Divine Lord, are "seen of Angels;" nay, and ministered unto by them, much as they excel us in strength! St. Paul plainly tells us, that it is God's purpose that "His manifold wisdom should be known to the heavenly principalities and powers, through the Church."[1] When we are made Christians, we are baptized "into that within the veil," we are brought near to an innumerable company of Angels; and, resembling them in their hidden con-

1 Eph. iii. 10.

dition, share their sympathy and their services. Therefore, the same Apostle exhorts Timothy to persevere in
obedience, not only by the thought of God, but by that
of the Angels; and surely we ought to cultivate the
habitual feeling, that they see us in our most private
deeds, and most carefully guarded solitudes.

It is more than enough for a sinful mortal to be
made a fellow-worker and fellow-worshipper with the
Blessed Spirits, and the servant and the son of God
Most High. Rather let us try to realize our privilege,
and withal humble ourselves at our want of faith.
We are the elect of God, and have entrance "through
the gates into the" heavenly " City," while we " do His
commandments,"[1] following Christ as Andrew did,
when pointed out to us by His preachers and ministers.
To those who thus "follow on to know" Him, He
manifests Himself, while He is hid from the world.
They are near Him, as His confidential servants, and
are the real agents in the various providences which
occur in the history of nations, though overlooked by
their annalists and sages. They bring before Him the
temporal wants of men, witnessing His marvellous
doings with the barley loaves and fishes; they, too,
lead strangers before Him for His favourable notice,
and for His teaching. And, when He brings trouble
and distress upon a sinful people, they have truest
knowledge of His will, and can best interpret His
works; for they had lived in contemplation and prayer,
and while others praise the goodly stones and buildings
of the external Temple, have heard from Him in secret

[1] *Rev.* xxii. 14.

how the end shall be. Thus they live; and when they die, the world knows nothing of its loss, and soon lets slip what it might have retained of their history; but the Church of Christ does what she can, gathering together their relics, and honouring their name, even when their works cannot be found. But those works have followed them; and, at the appearing of their Lord in judgment, will be at length displayed before all the world, and for His merits eternally rewarded in His heavenly kingdom.

SERMON II.

Faith without Sight.

(THE FEAST OF ST. THOMAS THE APOSTLE.)

" Thomas, because thou hast seen Me, thou hast believed ; blessed are they that have not seen, and yet have believed."—JOHN xx. 29.

ST. THOMAS is the Apostle who doubted of our Lord's resurrection. This want of faith has given him a sort of character in the minds of most people, which is referred to in the Collect for the day. Yet we must not suppose that he differed greatly from the other Apostles. They all, more or less, mistrusted Christ's promises when they saw Him led away to be crucified. When He was buried, their hopes were buried with Him; and when the news was brought them, that He was risen again, they all disbelieved it. On His appearing to them, He "upbraided them with their unbelief and hardness of heart."[1] But, as St. Thomas was not present at this time, and only heard from his fellow Apostles that they had seen the Lord, his time of perplexity and darkness lasted longer than theirs.

[1] *Mark* xvi. 14.

At the news of this great miracle, he expressed his determination not to believe unless he himself saw Christ, and was allowed to touch Him. And thus, by an apparently accidental circumstance, Thomas is singled out from his brethren, who at first disbelieved as well as he, as if he were an especial instance of unbelief. None of them believed till they saw Christ, except St. John, and he too hesitated at first. Thomas was convinced latest, because he saw Christ latest. On the other hand, it is certain that, though he disbelieved the good news of Christ's resurrection at first, he was no cold-hearted follower of his Lord, as appears from his conduct on a previous occasion, when he expressed a desire to share danger, and to suffer with Him. When Christ was setting out for Judæa to raise Lazarus from the dead, the disciples said, "Master, the Jews of late sought to stone Thee, and goest Thou thither again?"[1] When He remained in His intention, Thomas said to the rest, "Let us also go, that we may die with Him." This journey ended, as His Apostles foreboded, in their Lord's death; they indeed escaped, but it was at the instance of Thomas that they hazarded their lives with Him.

St. Thomas then loved his Master, as became an Apostle, and was devoted to His service; but when He saw Him crucified, his faith failed for a season with that of the rest. At the same time we need not deny that his especial doubts of Christ's resurrection were not altogether owing to circumstances, but in a measure arose from some faulty state of mind. St. John's narrative itself, and our Saviour's speech to him, convey

[1] John xi. 8

an impression that he was more to blame than the rest. His standing out alone, not against one witness only, but against his ten fellow disciples, besides Mary Magdalene and the other women, is evidence of this; and his very strong words, " Except I shall see in His hands the print of the nails, and put my finger into the print of the nails, and thrust my hand into His side, I will not believe."[1] And it is observable that, little as we know of St. Thomas, yet the one remaining recorded speech of his (before Christ's crucifixion), intimates something of the same doubting perplexed state of mind. When Christ said He was going to His Father, and by a way which they all knew, Thomas interposed with an argument: " Lord, we know not whither Thou goest, and how can we know the way?"[2] that is, we do not see heaven, or the God of heaven, how can we know the way thither? He seems to have required some sensible insight into the unseen state, some infallible sign from heaven, a ladder of Angels like Jacob's, which would remove anxiety by showing him the end of the journey at the time he set out. Some such secret craving after certainty beset him. And a like desire arose within him on the news of Christ's resurrection. Being weak in faith, he suspended his judgment, and seemed resolved not to believe anything, till he was told everything. Accordingly, when our Saviour appeared to him, eight days after His appearance to the rest, while He allowed Thomas his wish, and satisfied his senses that He was really alive, He accompanied the permission with a

[1] *John xx. 25.*   [2] John xiv 5.

rebuke, and intimated that by yielding to his weakness, He was withdrawing from him what was a real blessedness. " Reach hither thy finger, and behold my hands; and reach hither thy hand, and thrust it into my side : and be not faithless, but believing. And Thomas answered and said unto Him, My Lord and my God. Jesus saith unto him, Thomas, because thou hast seen Me, thou hast believed : blessed are they that have not seen, and yet have believed."[1]

However, after all, we are not so much concerned with considerations respecting the natural disposition and temper of the Blessed Apostle, whom we to-day commemorate, as with the particular circumstance in which his name occurs, and with our Saviour's comment upon it. All His disciples minister to Him; and, as in other ways, so also in giving occasion for the words of grace which proceed from His mouth. They minister to Him even in their weaknesses, which are often brought to light in Scripture, not hidden as Christian friends would hide in piety, that so He may convert them into instruction and comfort for His Church. Thus Martha's over-earnestness in household duties had drawn from Him a sanction for a life of contemplation and prayer; and so, in the history before us, the over-caution of St. Thomas has gained for us His promise of especial blessing on those who believe without having seen. I proceed to make some remarks on the nature of this believing temper, and why it is blessed.

It is scarcely necessary to observe, that what our Saviour says to Thomas so clearly and impressively, He

[1] John xx. 27—29.

has implied, in one way or other, all through His ministry; the blessedness of a mind that believes readily.
His demand and trial of faith in the case of those who
came for His miraculous aid, His praise of it where
found, His sorrow where it was wanting, His warnings
against hardness of heart; all are evidence of this.
"Verily I say unto you, I have not found so great faith,
no, not in Israel." "Daughter, be of good comfort; thy
faith hath made thee whole." "Thy faith hath saved
thee; go in peace." "An evil and adulterous generation
seeketh after a sign." "O fools, and slow of heart to
believe all that the prophets have spoken."[1] These will
remind us of a multitude of similar passages in especial
praise of faith. St. Paul pursues the line of doctrine
thus begun by his Lord. In three Epistles he sets
before us the peculiar place faith holds among the evidences of a religious mind: and each time refers to a
passage in the Prophets, in order to show that he was
bringing in no new doctrine, but only teaching that
which had been promulged from the beginning. In
consequence, in our ordinary language we speak of
religion being built upon faith, not upon reason; on the
other hand, it is as common for those who scoff at
religion to object this very doctrine against us; as if,
in so saying, we had almost admitted that Christianity
was not true. Let us then consider how the case
stands.

Every religious mind, under every dispensation of
Providence, will be in the habit of looking out of and

[1] Matt. viii. 10 ; ix. 22.   Luke vii. 50.   Matt. xii. 39.
Luke xxiv. 25.

beyond self, as regards all matters connected with its highest good. For a man of religious mind is he who attends to the rule of conscience, which is born with him, which he did not make for himself, and to which he feels bound in duty to submit. And conscience immediately directs his thoughts to some Being exterior to himself, who gave it, and who evidently is superior to him; for a law implies a lawgiver, and a command implies a superior. Thus a man is at once thrown out of himself, by the very Voice which speaks within him; and while he rules his heart and conduct by his inward sense of right and wrong, not by the maxims of the external world, still that inward sense does not allow him to rest in itself, but sends him forth again from home to seek abroad for Him who has put His Word in him. He looks forth into the world to seek Him who is not of the world, to find behind the shadows and deceits of this shifting scene of time and sense, Him whose Word is eternal, and whose Presence is spiritual. He looks out of himself for that Living Word to which he may attribute what has echoed in his heart; and being sure that it is to be found somewhere, he is predisposed to find it, and often thinks he has found it when he has not. Hence, if truth is not at hand, he is apt to mistake error for truth, to consider as the presence and especial work of God what is not so; and thinking anything preferable to scepticism, he becomes (what is sometimes imputed to him by way of reproach) superstitious. This, you may suppose, is the state of the better sort of persons in a heathen country. They are *not vouchsafed* the truer tokens of God's power and will, which we possess; so they fancy where they cannot find, and, having consciences more acute than their reasoning powers, they pervert and misuse even those indications of God which are provided for them in nature. This is one cause of the false divinities of pagan worship, which are tokens of guilt in the worshipper, not (as we trust) when they could know no better, but when they have turned from the light, not liking "to retain God in their knowledge." And if this is the course of a religious mind, even when it is not blessed with the news of divine truth, much more will it welcome and gladly commit itself to the hand of God, when allowed to discern it in the Gospel. Such is faith as it exists in the multitude of those who believe, arising from their sense of the presence of God, originally certified to them by the inward voice of conscience.

On the other hand, such persons as prefer this world to the leadings of God's Spirit within them, soon lose their perception of the latter, and lean upon the world as a god. Having no presentiment of any Invisible Guide, who has a claim to be followed in matters of conduct, they consider nothing to have a substance but what meets their senses, are contented with this, and draw their rules of life from it. They truly are in no danger of being superstitious or credulous; for they feel no antecedent desire or persuasion that God may have made a revelation of Himself in the world; and when they hear of events supernatural, they come to the examination of them as calmly and dispassionately as if they were judges in a court of law, or inquiring into *points of science.* They acknowledge no especial interest in the question proposed to them; and they find it no effort to use their intellect upon it as rigidly as if it were some external instrument which could not be swayed. Here then we see two opposite characters of mind, the one credulous (as it would be commonly called), the latter candid, well-judging, and sagacious; and it is clear that the former of the two is the religious temper rather than the latter. In this way then, if in no other, faith and reason are opposed; and to believe much is more blessed than to believe little.

But this is not all. Everyone who tries to do God's will, is sure to find he cannot do it perfectly. He will feel himself to be full of imperfection and sin; and the more he succeeds in regulating his heart, the more he will discern its original bitterness and guilt. Here is an additional cause of a religious man's looking out of himself. He knows the evil of his nature, and forebodes God's wrath as its consequence; and when he looks around him, he sees it reflected from within upon the face of the world. He fears; and, in consequence, seeks about for some means of propitiating his Maker, for some token, if so be, of God's relenting. He cannot stay at home; he cannot rest in himself; he wanders about from very anxiety; he needs some one to speak peace to his soul. Should a man come to him professing to be a messenger from heaven, he is at once arrested and listens; and, whether such profession be actually true or false, yet his first desire is that it may be true. Those, on the contrary, who are without this sense of sin, can bear the first news of God's having *spoken to man*, without being startled. They can patiently wait till the body of evidence is brought out before them, and then receive or reject, as reason may determine for them.

Further still, let us suppose two persons of strong mind, not easily excitable, sound judging and cautious; and let them be equally endowed in these respects. Now there is an additional reason why, of these two, he who is religious will believe more and reason less than the irreligious; that is, if a man's acting upon a message is the measure of his believing it, as the common sense of the world will determine. For in any matter so momentous and practical as the welfare of the soul, a wise man will not wait for the fullest evidence before he acts; and will show his caution, not in remaining uninfluenced by the existing report of a divine message, but by obeying it though it might be more clearly attested. If it is but fairly probable that rejection of the Gospel will involve his eternal ruin, it is safest and wisest to act as if it were certain. On the other hand, when a man does not make the truth of Christianity a practical concern, but a mere matter of philosophical or historical research, he will feel himself at leisure (and reasonably on his own grounds) to find fault with the evidence. When we inquire into a point of history, or investigate an opinion of science, we do demand decisive evidence; we consider it allowable to wait till we obtain it, to remain undecided; in a word, to be *sceptical.* If religion be not a practical matter, it is right and philosophical in us to be sceptics. Assuredly higher and fuller evidence of its truth might be given us; *and, after all,* there are a number of deep questions concerning the laws of nature, the constitution of the human mind, and the like, which must be solved before we can feel perfectly satisfied. And those whose hearts are not " tender,"[1] as Scripture expresses it,—that is, who have not a vivid perception of the Divine Voice within them, and of the necessity of His existence from whom it issues,—do not feel Christianity as a practical matter, and let it pass accordingly. They are accustomed to say that death will soon come upon them, and solve the great secret for them without their trouble,—that is, they wait for sight : not understanding, or being able to be made to comprehend, that their solving this great problem without sight is the very end and business of their mortal life : according to St. Paul's decision, that faith is " the substance," or the realizing, " of things hoped for," " the evidence," or the making trial of, the acting on, the belief of " things not seen."[2] What the Apostle says of Abraham is a description of all true faith ; it goes out not knowing *whither* it goes. It does not crave or bargain to see the end of the journey ; it does not argue with St. Thomas, in the days of his ignorance, " we know not whither, and how can we know the way ?" it is persuaded that it has quite enough light to walk by, far more than sinful man has a right to expect, if it sees one step in advance ; and it leaves all knowledge of the country over which it is journeying, to Him who calls it on.

And this blessed temper of mind, which influences religious men in the greater matter of choosing or rejecting the Gospel, extends itself also into their reception of

---

[1] *2 Kings* xxii. 19.　　　　　[2] Heb. xi. 1.

it in all its parts. As faith is content with but a little light to begin its journey by, and makes it much by acting upon it, so also it reads, as it were, by twilight, the message of truth in its various details. It does not stipulate that the text of Scripture should admit of rigid and laboured proofs of its doctrines; it has the practical wisdom to consider that the Word of God must have mainly one, and one only sense, and to try, as well as may be, to find out what that sense is, whether the evidence of it be great or little, and not to quarrel with it if it is not overpowering. It keeps steadily in view that Christ *speaks* in Scripture, and receives His words as if it *heard* them, as if some superior and friend spoke them, one whom it wished to please; not as if it were engaged upon the dead letter of a document, which admitted of rude handling, of criticism and exception. It looks off from self to Christ; and instead of seeking impatiently for some personal assurance, is set by obedience, saying, " Here am I; send me." And in like manner towards every institution of Christ, His Church, His Sacraments, and His Ministers, it acts not as a disputer of this world, but as the disciple of Him who appointed them. Lastly, it rests contented with the revelation made to it; it has " found the Messias," and that is enough. The very principle of its former rest-lessness now keeps it from wandering. When " the Son of God is come, and hath given us an understanding to know the true God," wavering, fearfulness, superstitious trust in the creature, pursuit of novelties, are signs, not of faith, but of unbelief.[1]

[1] *Vide Cant.* iii. 1—2.

Much might be added in conclusion, by way of applying what has been said to the temper of our own day,
in which men around us are apt almost to make it a
boast that "theirs is a rational religion." Doubtless,
this happens to be the case; but it is no necessary mark
of a true religion that it is rational in the common sense
of the word; nor is it any credit to a man to have
resolved only to take up with what he considers rational.
The true religion is in part altogether above reason, as in
its Mysteries; and so again, it might have been introduced into the world without that array of Evidences,
as they are called, which our reason is able, and delights
to draw out; yet it would not on that account have been
less true. As far as it is above reason, as far as it has
extended into any countries without sufficient proof of
its divinity, so far it cannot be called rational. Indeed,
that it is at all level to the reason, is rather a privilege
granted by Almighty God, than a point which may be
insisted on by man; and unless received as an un-
merited boon, may become hurtful to us. If this remark
be in any measure true, we know what to think of
arguing against the doctrines of the Gospel on the
ground of their being irrational, or of attempting to
refute the creed of others by ridiculing articles of it
as unaccountable and absurd, or of thinking that the
superstitious have advanced a step towards the truth
when they have plunged into infidelity, or of accounting
it wrong to educate children in the Catholic faith, lest
they should not have the opportunity of choosing for
themselves in mature years. Dismissing such thoughts
from the mind, let us rather be content with the words

of the Apostle. "The preaching of the cross," he says, "is to them that perish, foolishness; but unto us which are saved, it is the power of God. For it is written, I will destroy the wisdom of the wise, and will bring to nought the understanding of the prudent. Where is the wise? where is the scribe? where is the disputer of this world? Hath not God made foolish the wisdom of this world? For after that in the wisdom of God the world by wisdom knew not God, it pleased God, by the foolishness of preaching, to save them that believe." [1]

[1] 1 Cor. i. 18—21.

SERMON III.

The Incarnation.

(THE FEAST OF THE NATIVITY OF OUR LORD.)

" The Word was made flesh, and dwelt among us."—JOHN i. 14.

THUS does the favoured Apostle and Evangelist announce to us that Sacred Mystery, which we this day especially commemorate, the incarnation of the Eternal Word. Thus briefly and simply does he speak as if fearing he should fail in fitting reverence. If any there was who might seem to have permission to indulge in words on this subject, it was the beloved disciple, who had heard and seen, and looked upon, and handled the Word of Life; yet, in proportion to the height of his privilege, was his discernment of the infinite distance between him and his Creator. Such too was the temper of the Holy Angels, when the Father " brought in the First-begotten into the world:"[1] they straightway worshipped Him. And such was the feeling of awe and love mingled together, which re-

---

[1] Heb. i. 6.

mained for a while in the Church after Angels had announced His coming, and Evangelists had recorded His
sojourn here, and His departure; "there was silence as
it were for half an hour."[1]   Around the Church, indeed,
the voices of blasphemy were heard, even as when He
hung on the cross; but in the Church there was light
and peace, fear, joy, and holy meditation. Lawless
doubtings, importunate inquirings, confident reasonings
were not. An heartfelt adoration, a practical devotion
to the Ever-blessed Son, precluded difficulties in faith,
and sheltered the Church from the necessity of speaking.

He who had seen the Lord Jesus with a pure mind,
attending Him from the Lake of Gennesareth to Calvary, and from the Sepulchre to Mount Olivet, where
He left this scene of His humiliation; he who had
been put in charge with His Virgin Mother, and heard
from her what she alone could tell of the Mystery to
which she had ministered; and they who had heard it
from his mouth, and those again whom these had
taught, the first generations of the Church, needed no
explicit declarations concerning His Sacred Person.
Sight and hearing superseded the multitude of words;
faith dispensed with the aid of lengthened Creeds and
Confessions. There was silence. "The Word was made
flesh;" "I believe in Jesus Christ His only Son our
Lord;" sentences such as these conveyed everything,
yet were officious in nothing. But when the light of
His advent faded, and love waxed cold, then there was
an opening for objection and discussion, and a difficulty
in answering. Then misconceptions had to be explained,

[1] *Rev. viii. 1.*

doubts allayed, questions set at rest, innovators silenced. Christians were forced to speak against their will, lest heretics should speak instead of them.

Such is the difference between our own state and that of the early Church, which the present Festival especially brings to mind. In the New Testament we find the doctrine of the Incarnation announced clearly indeed, but with a reverent brevity. " The Word was made flesh." " God was manifest in the flesh." " God was in Christ." " Unto us a Child is born,—the mighty God." " Christ, over all, God, blessed for ever." " My Lord and my God." " I am Alpha and Omega, the beginning and the ending,—the Almighty." " The Son of God, the brightness of His glory, and the express image of His person."[1] But we are obliged to speak more at length in the Creeds and in our teaching, to meet the perverse ingenuity of those who, when the Apostles were removed, could with impunity insult and misinterpret the letter of their writings.

Nay, further, so circumstanced are we, as to be obliged not only thus to guard the Truth, but even to give the reason of our guarding it. For they who would steal away the Lord from us, not content with forcing us to measures of protection, even go on to bring us to account for adopting them; and demand that we should put aside whatever stands between them and their heretical purposes. Therefore it is necessary to state clearly, as I have already done, why the Church has lengthened her statements of Christian doctrine. Another

[1] 1 Tim. iii. 16.   2 Cor. v. 19.   Isa. ix. 6.   Rom. ix. 5.
    John xx. 28.   Rev. i. 8.   Heb. i. 2, 3.

reason of these statements is as follows: time having proceeded, and·the true traditions of our Lord's ministry being lost to us, the Object of our faith is but faintly reflected on our minds, compared with the vivid picture which His presence impressed upon the early Christians. True is it the Gospels will do very much by way of realizing for us the incarnation of the Son of God, if studied in faith and love. But the Creeds are an additional help this way. The declarations made in them, the distinctions, cautions, and the like, supported and illuminated by Scripture, draw down, as it were, from heaven, the image of Him who is on God's right hand, preserve us from an indolent use of words without apprehending them, and rouse in us those mingled feelings of fear and confidence, affection and devotion towards Him, which are implied in the belief of a personal advent of God in our nature, and which were originally derived to the Church from the very sight of Him.

And we may say further still, these statements—such, for instance, as occur in the Te Deum and Athanasian Creed—are especially suitable in divine worship, inasmuch as they kindle and elevate the religious affections. They are hymns of praise and thanksgiving; they give glory to God as revealed in the Gospel, just as David's Psalms magnify His Attributes as displayed in nature, His wonderful works in the creation of the world, and His mercies towards the house of Israel.

With these objects, then, it may be useful, on to-day's Festival, to call your attention to the Catholic doctrine of the Incarnation.

The Word *was from the* beginning, the Only-begotten

Son of God. Before all worlds were created, while as yet time was not, He was in existence, in the bosom of the Eternal Father, God from God, and Light from Light, supremely blessed in knowing and being known of Him, and receiving all divine perfections from Him, yet ever One with Him who begat Him. As it is said in the opening of the Gospel: "In the beginning was the Word, and the Word was with God, and the Word was God." If we may dare conjecture, He is called the Word of God, as mediating between the Father and all creatures; bringing them into being, fashioning them, giving the world its laws, imparting reason and conscience to creatures of a higher order, and revealing to them in due season the knowledge of God's will. And to us Christians He is especially the Word in that great mystery commemorated to-day, whereby He became flesh, and redeemed us from a state of sin.

He, indeed, when man fell, might have remained in the glory which He had with the Father before the world was. But that unsearchable Love, which showed itself in our original creation, rested not content with a frustrated work, but brought Him down again from His Father's bosom to do His will, and repair the evil which sin had caused. And with a wonderful condescension He came, not as before in power, but in weakness, in the form of a servant, in the likeness of that fallen creature whom He purposed to restore. So He humbled Himself; suffering all the infirmities of our nature in the likeness of sinful flesh, all but a sinner,—pure from all sin, yet subjected to all temptation,—and at length *becoming obedient* unto death, even the death of the cross.

1 have said that when the Only-begotten Son stooped to take upon Him our nature, He had no fellowship with sin. It was impossible that He should. Therefore, since our nature was corrupt since Adam's fall, He did not come in the way of nature, He did not clothe Himself in that corrupt flesh which Adam's race inherits. He came by miracle, so as to take on Him our imperfection without having any share in our sinfulness. He was not born as other men are; for "that which is born of the flesh is flesh."[1]

All Adam's children are children of wrath; so our Lord came as the Son of Man, but not the son of sinful Adam. He had no earthly father; He abhorred to have one. The thought may not be suffered that He should have been the son of shame and guilt. He came by a new and living way; not, indeed, formed out of the ground, as Adam was at the first, lest He should miss the participation of our nature, but selecting and purifying unto Himself a tabernacle out of that which existed. As in the beginning, woman was formed out of man by Almighty power, so now, by a like mystery, but a reverse order, the new Adam was fashioned from the woman. He was, as had been foretold, the immaculate " seed of the woman," deriving His manhood from the substance of the Virgin Mary; as it is expressed in the articles of the Creed, "conceived by the Holy Ghost, born of the Virgin Mary."

Thus the Son of God became the Son of Man; mortal, but not a sinner; heir of our infirmities, not of our guiltiness; the offspring of the old race, yet

[1] *John iii. 6.*

"the beginning of the" new "creation of God."
Mary, His mother, was a sinner as others, and born
of sinners; but she was set apart, "as a garden in-
closed, a spring shut up, a fountain sealed," to yield
a created nature to Him who was her Creator. Thus
He came into this world, not in the clouds of heaven,
but born into it, born of a woman; He, the Son of
Mary, and she (if it may be said), the mother of God.
Thus He came, selecting and setting apart for Himself
the elements of body and soul; then, uniting them to
Himself from their first origin of existence, pervading
them, hallowing them by His own Divinity, spiritualiz-
ing them, and filling them with light and purity, the
while they continued to be human, and for a time
mortal and exposed to infirmity. And, as they grew
from day to day in their holy union, His Eternal
Essence still was one with them, exalting them, acting
in them, manifesting Itself through them, so that He
was truly God and Man, One Person,—as we are soul
and body, yet one man, so truly God and man are not
two, but One Christ. Thus did the Son of God enter
this mortal world; and when He had reached man's
estate, He began His ministry, preached the Gospel,
chose His Apostles, suffered on the cross, died, and was
buried, rose again and ascended on high, there to reign
till the day when He comes again to judge the world.
This is the All-gracious Mystery of the Incarnation,
good to look into, good to adore; according to the
saying in the text, "The Word was made flesh,—and
dwelt among us."

The brief account thus given of the Catholic doctrine

of the Incarnation of the Eternal Word, may be made more distinct by referring to some of those modes mentioned in Scripture, in which God has at divers times condescended to manifest Himself in His creatures, which come short of it.

1. God was in the Prophets, but not as He was in Christ. The divine authority, and in one sense, name, may be given to His Ministers, considered as His representatives. Moses says to the Israelites, "Your murmurings are not against us, but against the Lord." And St. Paul, "He therefore that despiseth, despiseth not man, but God."[1] In this sense, Rulers and Judges are sometimes called gods, as our Lord Himself says.

And further, the Prophets were inspired. Thus John the Baptist is said to have been filled with the Holy Ghost from his mother's womb. Zacharias was filled with the Holy Ghost, and prophesied. In like manner the Holy Ghost came on the Apostles at Pentecost and at other times; and so wonderfully gifted was St. Paul, that "from his body were brought unto the sick handkerchiefs or aprons, and the diseases departed from them, and the evil spirits went out of them."[2] Now the characteristic of this miraculous inspiration was, that the presence of God came and went. Thus we read, in the afore-mentioned and similar narratives, of the Prophet or Apostle being *filled* with the Spirit on particular occasions; as again of " the Spirit of the Lord departing from Saul," and an evil spirit troubling him. Thus this divine inspiration was so far parallel to demoniacal possession. We find in the Gospels the

[1] *Exod. xvi. 8.*   *1 Thess. iv. 8.*   [2] Acts xix. 12.

devil speaking with the voice of his victim, so that
the tormentor and the tormented could not be distinguished from each other. They seemed to be one and
the same, though they were not; as appeared when
Christ and His Apostles cast the devil out. And so
again the Jewish Temple was in one sense inhabited by
the presence of God, which came down upon it at
Solomon's Prayer. This was a type of our Lord's manhood dwelt in by the Word of God as a Temple; still,
with this essential difference, that the Jewish Temple
was perishable, and again the Divine Presence might
recede from it. There was no real unity between the
one and the other; they were separable. But Christ
says to the Jews of His own body, "Destroy this Temple
and I will raise it in three days;" implying in these
words such an unity between the Godhead and the
manhood, that there could be no real separation, no
dissolution. Even when His body was dead, the Divine
Nature was one with it; in like manner it was one
with His soul in paradise. Soul and body were really
one with the Eternal Word,—not one in name only,—
one never to be divided. Therefore Scripture says that
He rose again " according to the Spirit of holiness;"
and "that it was not possible that He should be holden
of death."[1]

2. Again, the Gospel teaches us another mode in
which man may be said to be united with Almighty
God. It is the peculiar blessedness of the Christian,
as St. Peter tells us, to be "partaker of the Divine
Nature."[2] We believe, and have joy in believing, that

[1] *Rom. i. 4.*   Acts ii. 24.   [2] 2 Pet. i. 4.

the grace of Christ renews our carnal souls, repairing the effects of Adam's fall. Where Adam brought in impurity and unbelief, the power of God infuses faith and holiness. Thus we have God's perfections communicated to us anew, and, as being under immediate heavenly influences, are said to be one with God. And further, we are assured of some real though mystical fellowship with the Father, Son, and Holy Spirit, in order to this: so that both by a real presence in the soul, and by the fruits of grace, God is one with every believer, as in a consecrated Temple. But still, inexpressible as is this gift of Divine Mercy, it were blasphemy not to say that the indwelling of the Father in the Son is infinitely above this, being quite different in kind; for He is not merely of a divine nature, divine by participation of holiness and perfection, but Life and Holiness itself, such as the Father is,—the Co-eternal Son incarnate, God clothed with our nature, the Word made flesh.

3. And lastly, we read in the Patriarchal History of various appearances of Angels so remarkable that we can scarcely hesitate to suppose them to be gracious visions of the Eternal Son. For instance; it is said that "the Angel of the Lord appeared unto" Moses "in a flame of fire out of the midst of a bush;" yet presently this supernatural Presence is called "the Lord," and afterwards reveals His name to Moses, as the God of Abraham, Isaac, and Jacob." On the other hand, St. Stephen speaks of Him as "the Angel which appeared to Moses in the bush." Again, he says soon after, that Moses was "*in the Church* in the wilderness with the

Angel which spake to him in the mount Sinai;" yet in the book of Exodus we read, "Moses went up unto God, and the Lord called unto him out of the mountain;" "God spake all these words saying;" and the like. Now, assuming, as we seem to have reason to assume, that the Son of God is herein revealed to us as graciously ministering to the Patriarchs, Moses, and others, in angelic form, the question arises, what was the nature of this appearance? We are not informed, nor may we venture to determine; still, any how, the Angel was but the temporary outward form which the Eternal Word assumed, whether it was of a material nature, or a vision. Whether or no it was really an Angel, or but an appearance existing only for the immediate purpose, still, any how, we could not with propriety say that our Lord " took upon Him the nature of Angels."

Now these instances of the indwelling of Almighty God in a created substance, which I have given by way of contrast to that infinitely higher and mysterious union which is called the Incarnation, actually supply the senses in which heretics at various times have perverted our holy and comfortable doctrine, and which have obliged us to have recourse to Creeds and Confessions. Rejecting the teaching of the Church, and dealing rudely with the Word of God, they have ventured to deny that "Jesus Christ is come in the flesh," pretending He merely showed Himself as a vision or phantom;—or they have said that the Word of God merely dwelt in the man Christ Jesus, as the

---

[1] Exod. iii. 2.   Acts vii. 35—38.   Exod. xix. 3; xx. 1.

Shechinah in the Temple, having no real union with the Son of Mary (as if there were two distinct Beings, the Word and Jesus, even as the blessed Spirit is distinct from a man's soul) ;—or that Christ was called God for His great spiritual perfections, and that He gradually attained them by long practice. All these are words not to be uttered, except to show what the true doctrine is, and what is the meaning of the language of the Church concerning it. For instance, the Athanasian Creed confesses that Christ is " God of the substance of the Father, begotten before the worlds, perfect God," lest we should consider His Divine Nature, like ours, as merely a nature resembling God's holiness: that He is " Man of the substance of His Mother, born in the world, perfect man," lest we should think of Him as "not come in the flesh," a mere Angelic vision ; and that " although He be God and man, yet He is not two, but one Christ," lest we should fancy that the Word of God entered into Him and then departed, as the Holy Ghost in the Prophets.

Such are the terms in which we are constrained to speak of our Lord and Saviour, by the craftiness of His enemies and our own infirmity ; and we intreat His leave to do so. We intreat His leave, not as if forgetting that a reverent silence is best on so sacred a subject ; but, when evil men and seducers abound on every side, and our own apprehensions of the Truth are dull, using zealous David's argument, " Is there not a cause" for words? We intreat His leave, and we humbly pray that what was first our defence against pride and indolence, may become an outlet of devotion.

a service of worship. Nay, we surely trust that He will accept mercifully what we offer in faith, "doing what we can;" though the ointment of spikenard which we pour out is nothing to that true Divine Glory which manifested itself in Him, when the Holy Ghost singled Him out from other men, and the Father's voice acknowledged Him as His dearly beloved Son. Surely He will mercifully accept it, if faith offers what the intellect provides; if love kindles the sacrifice, zeal fans it, and reverence guards it. He will illuminate our earthly words from His own Divine Holiness, till they become saving truths to the souls which trust in Him. He who turned water into wine, and (did He so choose) could make bread of the hard stone, will sustain us for a brief season on this mortal fare. And we, while we make use of it, will never so forget its imperfection, as not to look out constantly for the True Beatific Vision; never so perversely remember that imperfection as to reject what is necessary for our present need. The time will come, if we be found worthy, when we, who now see in a glass darkly, shall see our Lord and Saviour face to face; shall behold His countenance beaming with the fulness of Divine Perfections, and bearing its own witness that He is the Son of God. We shall see Him as He is.

Let us then, according to the light given us, praise and bless Him in the Church below, whom Angels in heaven see and adore. Let us bless Him for His surpassing loving-kindness in taking upon Him our infirmities to redeem us, when He dwelt in the inner-most love of the Everlasting Father, in the glory which

He had with Him before the world was. He came in lowliness and want; born amid the tumults of a mixed and busy multitude, cast aside into the outhouse of a crowded inn, laid to His first rest among the brute cattle. He grew up, as if the native of a despised city, and was bred to a humble craft. He bore to live in a world that slighted Him, for He lived in it, in order in due time to die for it. He came as the appointed Priest, to offer sacrifice for those who took no part in the act of worship; He came to offer up for sinners that precious blood which was meritorious by virtue of His Divine Anointing. He died, to rise again the third day, the Sun of Righteousness, fully displaying that splendour which had hitherto been concealed by the morning clouds. He rose again, to ascend to the right hand of God, there to plead His sacred wounds in token of our forgiveness, to rule and guide His ransomed people, and from His pierced side to pour forth His choicest blessings upon them. He ascended, thence to descend again in due season to judge the world which He has redeemed.—Great is our Lord, and great is His power, Jesus the Son of God and Son of man. Ten thousand times more dazzling bright than the highest Archangel, is our Lord and Christ. By birth the Only-begotten and Express Image of God ; and in taking our flesh, not sullied thereby, but raising human nature with Him, as He rose from the lowly manger to the right hand of power,—raising human nature, for Man has redeemed us, Man is set above all creatures, as one with the Creator, Man shall judge man at the last day. So *honoured is this* earth, that no stranger shall judge us, but He who is our fellow, who will sustain our interests, and has full sympathy in all our imperfections. He who loved us, even to die for us, is graciously appointed to assign the final measurement and price upon His own work. He who best knows by infirmity to take the part of the infirm, He who would fain reap the full fruit of His passion, He will separate the wheat from the chaff, so that not a grain shall fall to the ground. He who has given us to share His own spiritual nature, He from whom we have drawn the life's blood of our souls, He our brother will decide about His brethren. In that His second coming, may He in His grace and loving pity remember us, who is our only hope, our only salvation !

SERMON IV.

Martyrdom.

(THE FEAST OF ST. STEPHEN THE MARTYR.)

" They were stoned, they were sawn asunder, were tempted, were slain with the sword."—HEB. xi. 37.

ST. STEPHEN, who was one of the seven Deacons, is called the Protomartyr, as having first suffered death in the cause of the Gospel. Let me take the opportunity of his festival to make some remarks upon martyrdom generally.

The word Martyr properly means "a *witness*," but is used to denote exclusively one who has suffered *death* for the Christian faith. Those who have witnessed for Christ without suffering death, are called *Confessors;* a title which the early Martyrs often made their own, before their last solemn confession unto death, or Martyrdom. Our Lord Jesus Christ is the chief and most glorious of Martyrs, as having "before Pontius Pilate witnessed a good confession;"[1] but we do not call Him a Martyr, as being much more than a Martyr.

---

[1] 1 Tim. vi. 13.

True it is, He died for the Truth; but that was not the chief purpose of his death. He died to save us sinners from the wrath of God. He was not only a Martyr; He was an Atoning Sacrifice.

He is the supreme object of our love, gratitude, and reverence. Next to Him we honour the noble army of Martyrs; not indeed comparing them with Him, "who is above all, God blessed for ever," or as if they in suffering had any part in the work of reconciliation, but because they have approached most closely to His pattern of all His servants. They have shed their blood for the Church, fulfilling the text, "He laid down His life for us, and we ought to lay down our lives for the brethren."[1] They have followed His steps, and claim our grateful remembrance. Had St. Stephen shrunk from the trial put upon him, and recanted to save his life, no one can estimate the consequences of such a defection. Perhaps (humanly speaking) the cause of the Gospel would have been lost; the Church might have perished; and, though Christ had died for the world, the world might not have received the knowledge or the benefits of His death. The channels of grace might have been destroyed, the Sacraments withdrawn from the feeble and corrupt race which has such need of them.

Now it may be said, that many men suffer pain, as great as Martyrdom, from disease, and in other ways: again, that it does not follow that those who happened to be martyred were always the most useful and active defenders of the faith; and therefore, that in honouring

[1] 1 John iii. 16.

the Martyrs, we are honouring with especial honour those to whom indeed we *may* be peculiarly indebted (as in the case of Apostles), but nevertheless who may have been but ordinary men, who happened to stand in the most exposed place, in the way of persecution, and were slain as if by chance, because the sword met them first. But this, it is plain, would be a strange way of reasoning in any parallel case. We are grateful to those who have done us favours, rather than to those who might or would, if it had so happened. We have no concern with the question, whether the Martyrs were the best of men or not, or whether others would have been Martyrs too, had it been allowed them. We are grateful to those who were such, from the plain matter of fact that they were such, that they did go through much suffering, in order that the world might gain an inestimable benefit, the light of the Gospel.

But in truth, if we could view the matter considerately, we shall find that (as far as human judgment can decide on such a point), the Martyrs of the primitive times were, as such, men of a very elevated faith ; not only our benefactors, but far our superiors. The utmost to which any such objection as that I have stated, goes, is this ; to show that others who were not martyred, might be equal to them (St. Philip the Deacon, for instance, equal to his associate St. Stephen), not that those who were martyred were not men eminently gifted with the Spirit of Christ. For let us consider what it was then to be a Martyr.

1. First, it was to be a *voluntary* sufferer. Men, perhaps, suffer *in various diseases* more than the martyrs

did, but they cannot help themselves. Again, it has frequently happened that men have been persecuted for their religion without having expected it, or being able to avert it. These in one sense indeed are martyrs; and we naturally think affectionately of those who have suffered in our cause, whether voluntarily or not. But this was not the case with the primitive martyrs. They knew beforehand clearly enough the consequences of preaching the Gospel; they had frequent warnings brought home to them of the sufferings in store for them, if they persevered in their labours of brotherly love. Their Lord and Master had suffered before them; and, besides suffering Himself, had expressly *foretold their* sufferings; "If they have persecuted Me, they will also persecute you."[1] They were repeatedly warned and strictly charged by the chief priests and rulers, not to preach in Christ's name. They had experience of lesser punishments from their adversaries in earnest of the greater; and at length they saw their brethren, one by one, slain for persevering in their faithfulness to Christ. Yet they continued to keep the faith, though they might be victims of their obedience any day.

All this must be considered when we speak of their sufferings. They lived under a continual trial, a daily exercise of faith, which we, living in peaceable times, can scarcely understand. Christ had said to His Apostles, "Satan hath desired to have you, that he may sift you as wheat."[2] Consider what is meant by sifting, which is a continued agitation, a shaking about to separate the mass of corn into two parts. Such was

---

[1] John xv. 20.   [2] Luke xxii. 31.

the early discipline inflicted on the Church. No mere
sudden stroke came upon it; but it was solicited day
by day, in all its members, by every argument of hope
and fear, by threats and inducements, to desert Christ.
This was the lot of the martyrs. Death, their final
suffering, was but the consummation of a life of anticipated death. Consider how distressing anxiety is; how
irritating and wearing it is to be in constant excitement,
with the duty of maintaining calmness and steadiness
in the midst of it; and how especially inviting any
prospect of tranquillity would appear in such circumstances; and then we shall have some notion of a
Christian's condition, under a persecuting heathen
government. I put aside for the present the peculiar
reproach and contempt which was the lot of the
primitive Church, and their actual privations. Let us
merely consider them as *harassed*, shaken as wheat in a
sieve. Under such circumstances, the stoutest hearts
are in danger of failing. They could steel themselves
against certain definite sufferings, or prepare themselves
to meet one expected crisis; but they yield to the
incessant annoyance which the apprehension of persecution, and the importunity of friends inflict on them.
They sigh for peace; they gradually come to believe
that the world is not so wrong as some men say it is,
and that it is possible to be over-strict and over-nice.
They learn to temporize and to be double-minded. First
one falls, then another; and such instances come as an
additional argument for concession to those that remain
firm as yet, who of course feel dispirited, lonely, and
begin to *doubt the correctness* of their own judgment;

while, on the other hand, those who have fallen, in self-defence become their tempters. Thus the Church is sifted, the cowardly falling off, the faithful continuing firm, though in dejection and perplexity. Among these latter are the martyrs ; not accidental victims, taken at random, but the picked and choice ones, the elect remnant, a sacrifice well pleasing to God, because a costly gift, the finest wheat flour of the Church : men who have been warned what to expect from their profession, and have had many opportunities of relinquishing it, but have " borne and had patience, and for Christ's name sake have laboured, and have not fainted."[1] Such was St. Stephen, not entrapped into a confession and slain (as it were) in ambuscade, but boldly confronting his persecutors, and, in spite of circumstances that foreboded death, awaiting their fury. And if martyrdom in early times was not the chance and unexpected death of those who happened to profess the Christian faith, much less is it to be compared to the sufferings of disease, be they greater or not. No one is maintaining that the mere undergoing pain is a great thing. A man cannot help himself when in pain ; he cannot escape from it, be he as desirous to do so as he may. The devils bear pain against their will. But to be a martyr, is to feel the storm coming, and willingly to endure it at the call of duty, for Christ's sake, and for the good of the brethren ; and this is a kind of firmness which we have no means of displaying at the present day, though our deficiency in it may be, and is continually evidenced, as often as we

[1] Rev. ii. 3.

yield (which is not seldom) to inferior and ordinary temptations.

2. But, in the next place, the suffering itself of Martyrdom was in some respects peculiar. It was a death, cruel in itself, publicly inflicted: and heightened by the fierce exultation of a malevolent populace. When we are in pain, we can lie in peace by ourselves. We receive the sympathy and kind services of those about us ; and if we like it, we can retire altogether from the sight of others, and suffer without a witness to interrupt us. But the sufferings of martyrdom were for the most part public, attended with every circumstance of ignominy and popular triumph, as well as with torture. Criminals indeed are put to death without kindly thoughts from bystanders ; still, for the most part, even criminals receive commiseration and a sort of respect. But the early Christians had to endure "the shame" after their Master's pattern. They had to die in the midst of enemies who reviled them, and in mockery, bid them (as in Christ's case) come down from the cross. They were supported on no easy couch, soothed by no attentive friends ; and considering how much the depressing power of pain depends on the imagination, this circumstance alone at once separates their sufferings widely from all instances of pain in disease. The unseen God alone was their Comforter, and this invests the scene of their suffering with supernatural majesty, and awes us when we think of them. "Yea, though I walk through the valley of the shadow of death, I will fear no evil; *for Thou art with me.*"[1] A Martyrdom is

[1] Psalm xxiii. 4.

a season of God's especial power in the eye of faith, as great as if a miracle were visibly wrought. It is a fellowship of Christ's sufferings, a commemoration of His death, a representation filling up in figure, "that which is behind of His afflictions, for his Body's sake, which is the Church."[1] And thus, being an august solemnity in itself, and a kind of sacrament, a baptism of blood, it worthily finishes that long searching trial which I have already described as being its usual fore-runner in primitive times.

I have spoken only of the early martyrs, because this Festival leads me to do so ; and besides, because, though there have been martyrs among us since, yet, from the time that kings have become nursing fathers to the Church, the history of confessors and martyrs is so implicated with state affairs, that their conduct is not so easily separable *by us* from the world around them, nor are we given to know them so clearly : though this difficulty of discerning them should invest their memory with peculiar interest when we do discern them, and their connexion with civil matters, far from diminishing the high spiritual excellence of such true sons of the Church, in some respects even increases it.

To conclude.—It is useful to reflect on subjects such as that I have now laid before you, in order to humble ourselves. "We have not resisted unto blood, striving against sin."[2] What are our petty sufferings, which we make so much of, to their pains and sorrows, who lost their friends, and then their own lives for Christ's sake ; who were assaulted by all kinds of temptations, the

---

[1] Col. i. 24.   [2] Heb. xii. 4.

sophistry of Antichrist, the blandishments of the world, the terrors of the sword, the weariness of suspense, and yet fainted not? How far above ours are both their afflictions, and their consolations under them! Now I know that such reflections are at once, and with far deeper reason, raised by the thought of the sufferings of Christ Himself; but commonly, His transcendent holiness and His depth of woe do not immediately affect us, from their very greatness. We sum them up in a few words, and we speak without understanding. On the other hand, we rise somewhat towards the comprehension of them, when we make use of that heavenly ladder by which His saints have made their way towards Him. By contemplating the lowest of His true servants, and seeing how far any one of them surpasses ourselves, we learn to shrink before His ineffable purity, who is infinitely holier than the holiest of His creatures; and to confess ourselves with a sincere mind to be unworthy of the least of all His mercies. Thus His Martyrs lead us to Himself, the chief of Martyrs and the King of Saints.

May God give us grace to receive these thoughts into our hearts, and to display the fruit of them in our conduct! What are we but sinful dust and ashes, grovellers who are creeping on to heaven, not with any noble sacrifice for Christ's cause, but without pain, without trouble, in the midst of worldly blessings! Well;—but He can save in the humblest paths of life, and in the most tranquil times. There is enough for us to do, far more than we fulfil, in our own ordinary course. Let *us strive to* be more humble, faithful,

merciful, meek, self-denying than we are. Let us
" crucify the flesh with the affections and lusts."[1] This,
to be sure, is sorry martyrdom; yet God accepts it for
His Son's sake. Notwithstanding, after all, if we get to
heaven, surely we shall be the lowest of the saints there
assembled; and if all are unprofitable servants, we
verily shall be the most unprofitable of all.

[1] Gal. v. 24.

SERMON V.

Love of Relations and Friends.

" Beloved, let us love one another, for love is of God."— 1 JOHN iv. 7

ST. JOHN the Apostle and Evangelist is chiefly and most familiarly known to us as " the disciple whom Jesus loved." He was one of the three or four who always attended our Blessed Lord, and had the privilege of the most intimate intercourse with Him ; and, more favoured than Peter, James, and Andrew, he was His bosom friend, as we commonly express ourselves. At the solemn supper before Christ suffered, he took his place next Him, and leaned on His breast. As the other three communicated between the multitude and Christ, so St. John communicated between Christ and them. At that Last Supper, Peter dared not ask Jesus a question himself, but bade John put it to Him,—who it was that should betray Him. Thus St. John was the private and intimate friend of Christ. Again, it was to St. John that *our Lord* committed His Mother, when

He was dying on the cross; it was to St. John that He revealed in vision after His departure the fortunes of His Church.

Much might be said on this remarkable circumstance. I say *remarkable,* because it might be supposed that the Son of God Most High could not have loved one man more than another; or again, if so, that He would not have had only one friend, but, as being All-holy, He would have loved all men more or less, in proportion to their holiness. Yet we find our Saviour had a private friend; and this shows us, first, how entirely He was a man, as much as any of us, in His wants and feelings; and next, that there is nothing contrary to the spirit of the Gospel, nothing inconsistent with the fulness of Christian love, in having our affections directed in an especial way towards certain objects, towards those whom the circumstances of our past life, or some peculiarities of character, have endeared to us.

There have been men before now, who have supposed Christian love was so diffusive as not to admit of concentration upon individuals; so that we ought to love all men equally. And many there are, who, without bringing forward any theory, yet consider practically that the love of many is something superior to the love of one or two; and neglect the charities of private life, while busy in the schemes of an expansive benevolence, or of effecting a general union and conciliation among Christians. Now I shall here maintain, in opposition to such notions of Christian love, and with our Saviour's pattern before me, that the best preparation for loving *the world* at large, and loving it duly and wisely, is to cultivate an intimate friendship and affection towards those who are immediately about us.

It has been the plan of Divine Providence to ground what is good and true in religion and morals, on the basis of our good natural feelings. What we are towards our earthly friends in the instincts and wishes of our infancy, such we are to become at length towards God and man in the extended field of our duties as accountable beings. To honour our parents is the first step towards honouring God; to love our brethren according to the flesh, the first step towards considering all men our brethren. Hence our Lord says, we must become as little children, if we would be saved; we must become in His Church, as men, what we were once in the small circle of our youthful homes.—Consider how many other virtues are grafted upon natural feelings. What is Christian high-mindedness, generous self-denial, contempt of wealth, endurance of suffering, and earnest striving after perfection, but an improvement and transformation, under the influence of the Holy Spirit, of that natural character of mind which we call romantic? On the other hand, what is the instinctive hatred and abomination of sin (which confirmed Christians possess), their dissatisfaction with themselves, their general refinement, discrimination, and caution, but an improvement, under the same Spirit, of their natural sensitiveness and delicacy, fear of pain, and sense of shame? They have been chastised into self-government, by a fitting discipline, and now associate an acute sense of discomfort and annoyance with the notion of sinning. And so of the love of our fellow Christians and of the world at large, it is the love of kindred and friends in a fresh shape; which has this use, if it had no other, that it is the natural branch on which a spiritual fruit is grafted.

But again, the love of our private friends is the only preparatory exercise for the love of all men. The love of God is not the same thing as the love of our parents, though parallel to it; but the love of mankind in general should be in the main the same habit as the love of our friends, only exercised towards different objects. The great difficulty in our religious duties is their extent. This frightens and perplexes men,—naturally; those especially, who have neglected religion for a while, and on whom its obligations disclose themselves all at once. This, for example, is the great misery of leaving repentance till a man is in weakness or sickness; he does not know how to set about it. Now God's merciful Providence has in the natural course of things narrowed for us at first this large field of duty; He has given us a clue. We are to begin with loving our friends about us, and gradually to enlarge the circle of our affections, till it reaches all Christians, and then all men. Besides, it is obviously impossible to love all men in any strict and true sense. What is meant by loving all men, is, to feel well-disposed to all men, to be ready to assist them, and to act towards those who come in our way, as if we loved them. We cannot love those about whom we know nothing; except indeed we view them in Christ, as the objects of His Atonement, that is, rather in faith than in love. And love, besides, is a habit, and cannot be attained without actual *practice*, which on so *large a scale is* impossible We see then how absurd it is, when writers (as is the manner of some who slight the Gospel) talk magnificently about loving the whole human race with a comprehensive affection, of being the friends of all mankind, and the like. Such vaunting professions, what do they come to? that such men have certain benevolent *feelings* towards the world,—feelings and nothing more;—nothing more than unstable feelings, the mere offspring of an indulged imagination, which exist only when their minds are wrought upon, and are sure to fail them in the hour of need. This is not to love men, it is but to talk about love.—The real love of man *must* depend on practice, and therefore, must begin by exercising itself on our friends around us, otherwise it will have no existence. By trying to love our relations and friends, by submitting to their wishes, though contrary to our own, by bearing with their infirmities, by overcoming their occasional way-wardness by kindness, by dwelling on their excellences, and trying to copy them, thus it is that we form in our hearts that root of charity, which, though small at first, may, like the mustard seed, at last even overshadow the earth. The vain talkers about philanthropy, just spoken of, usually show the emptiness of their pro-fession, by being morose and cruel in the private rela-tions of life, which they seem to account as subjects beneath their notice. Far different indeed, far different (unless it be a sort of irreverence to contrast such dreamers with the great Apostle, whose memory we are to-day celebrating), utterly the reverse of this fictitious benevolence was his elevated and enlightened sym-pathy for all men. We know he is celebrated for his declarations about Christian love. "Beloved, let us love one another, for love is of God. If we love one another, God dwelleth in us, and His love is perfected in us. God is love, and he that dwelleth in love dwelleth in God, and God in him."[1] Now did he begin with some vast effort at loving on a large scale? Nay, he had the unspeakable privilege of being the *friend of Christ.* Thus he was taught to love others; first his affection was concentrated, then it was expanded. Next he had the solemn and comfortable charge of tending our Lord's Mother, the Blessed Virgin, after His departure. Do we not here discern the secret sources of his especial love of the brethren? Could he, who first was favoured with his Saviour's affection, then trusted with a son's office towards His Mother, could he be other than a memorial and pattern (as far as man can be), of love, deep, contemplative, fervent, unruffled, unbounded?

Further, that love of friends and relations, which nature prescribes, is also of use to the Christian, in giving form and direction to his love of mankind at large, and making it intelligent and discriminating. A man, who would fain begin by a general love of all men, necessarily puts them all on a level, and, instead of being cautious, prudent, and sympathising in his benevolence, is hasty and rude; does harm, perhaps, when he means to do good, discourages the virtuous and well-meaning, and wounds the feelings of the gentle. Men of ambitious and ardent minds, for example, desirous of doing good on a large scale, are especially exposed to the temptation of sacrificing individual to

[1] 1 John iv. 7, 12, 16.

general good in their plans of charity. Ill-instructed men, who have strong abstract notions about the necessity of showing generosity and candour towards opponents, often forget to take any thought of those who are associated with themselves; and commence their (so-called) liberal treatment of their enemies by an unkind desertion of their friends. This can hardly be the case, when men cultivate the private charities, as an introduction to more enlarged ones. By laying a foundation of social amiableness, we insensibly learn to observe a due harmony and order in our charity; we learn that all men are not on a level; that the interests of truth and holiness must be religiously observed; and that the Church has claims on us before the world. We can easily afford to be liberal on a large scale, when we have no affections to stand in the way. Those who have not accustomed themselves to love their neighbours whom they have seen, will have nothing to lose or gain, nothing to grieve at or rejoice in, in their larger plans of benevolence. They will take no interest in them for their own sake; rather, they will engage in them, because expedience demands, or credit is gained, or an excuse found for being busy. Hence too we discern how it is, that private virtue is the only sure foundation of public virtue; and that no national good is to be expected (though it may now and then accrue), from men who have not the fear of God before their eyes.

I have hitherto considered the cultivation of domestic affections as the *source* of more extended Christian love. Did time permit, I might now go on to show, besides, that they involve a real and difficult exercise of it. Nothing is more likely to engender selfish habits (which is the direct opposite and negation of charity), than *independence* in our worldly circumstances. Men who have no tie on them, who have no calls on their daily sympathy and tenderness, who have no one's comfort to consult, who can move about as they please, and indulge the love of variety and the restless humours which are so congenial to the minds of most men, are very unfavourably situated for obtaining that heavenly gift, which is described in our Liturgy, as being "the very bond of peace and of all virtues." On the other hand, I cannot fancy any state of life more favourable for the exercise of high Christian principle, and the matured and refined Christian spirit (that is, where the parties really seek to do their duty), than that of persons who differ in tastes and general character, being obliged by circumstances to live together, and mutually to accommodate to each other their respective wishes and pursuits.—And this is one among the many providential benefits (to those who will receive them) arising out of the Holy Estate of Matrimony ; which not only calls out the tenderest and gentlest feelings of our nature, but, where persons do their duty, must be in various ways more or less a state of self-denial.

Or, again, I might go on to consider the private charities, which have been my subject, not only as the sources and as the discipline of Christian love, but further, as the *perfection of it ;* which they are in some cases. The Ancients thought so much of friendship, *that they* made it a *virtue.* In a Christian view, it is

not quite this ; but it is often accidentally a special *test*
of our virtue.   For consider :—let us say that this man,
and that, not bound by any very necessary tie, find
their greatest pleasure in living together : say that this
continues for years, and that they love each other's
society the more, the longer they enjoy it.   Now observe
what is implied in this.   Young people, indeed, readily
love each other, for they are cheerful and innocent ;
more easily yield to each other, and are full of hope ;
—types, as Christ says, of His true converts.   But this
happiness does not last ; their tastes change.   Again,
grown persons go on for years as friends ; but these do
not live together ; and, if any accident throws them into
familiarity for a while, they find it difficult to restrain
their tempers and keep on terms, and discover that they
are best friends at a distance.   But what is it that can
bind two friends together in intimate converse for a
course of years, but the participation in something that
is Unchangeable and essentially Good, and what is this
but religion ?   Religious tastes alone are unalterable.
The Saints of God continue in one way, while the
fashions of the world change ; and a faithful indestructible friendship may thus be a test of the parties, so
loving each other, having the love of God seated deep
in their hearts.   Not an infallible test certainly : for
they may have dispositions remarkably the same, or
some engrossing object of this world, literary or other ;
they may be removed from the temptation to change, or
they may have a natural sobriety of temper, which
remains contented wherever it finds itself.   However,
under certain *circumstances*, it is a lively token of the

presence of divine grace in them; and it is always a sort of symbol of it, for there is at first sight something of the nature of virtue in the very notion of constancy, dislike of change being not only the characteristic of a virtuous mind, but in some sense a virtue itself.

And now I have suggested to you a subject of thought for to-day's Festival,—and surely a very practical subject, when we consider how large a portion of our duties lies at home. Should God call upon us to preach to the world, surely we must obey His call; but at present, let us do what lies before us. Little children, let us love one another. Let us be meek and gentle; let us think before we speak; let us try to improve our talents in private life; let us do good, not hoping for a return, and avoiding all display before men. Well may I so exhort you at this season, when we have so lately partaken together the Blessed Sacrament which binds us to mutual love, and gives us strength to practise it. Let us not forget the promise we then made, or the grace we then received. We are not our own; we are bought with the blood of Christ; we are consecrated to be temples of the Holy Spirit, an unutterable privilege, which is weighty enough to sink us with shame at our unworthiness, did it not the while strengthen us by the aid itself imparts, to bear its extreme costliness. May we live worthy of our calling, and realize in our own persons the Church's prayers and professions for us !

SERMON VI.

The Mind of Little Children.

(THE FEAST OF THE HOLY INNOCENTS.)

" Except ye be converted, and become as little children, ye shall not enter into the kingdom of Heaven."—MATT. xviii. 3.

THE longer we live in the world, and the further removed we are from the feelings and remembrances of childhood (and especially if removed from the sight of children), the more reason we have to recollect our Lord's impressive action and word, when He called a little child unto Him, and set him in the midst of His disciples, and said, "Verily I say unto you, Except ye be converted, and become as little children, ye shall not enter into the kingdom of Heaven. Whosoever, therefore, shall humble himself as this little child, the same is greatest in the kingdom of Heaven." And in order to remind us of this our Saviour's judgment, the Church, like a careful teacher, calls us back year by year upon this day from the bustle and fever of the world. She takes advantage of the Massacre of the Innocents recorded in St. Matthew's Gospel, to bring

before us a truth which else we might think little of;
to sober our wishes and hopes of this world, our high
ambitious thoughts, or our anxious fears, jealousies,
and cares, by the picture of the purity, peace, and contentment which are the characteristics of little children.

And, independently of the benefit thus accruing to
us, it is surely right and meet thus to celebrate the
death of the Holy Innocents : for it was a blessed one.
To be brought near to Christ, and to suffer for Christ,
is surely an unspeakable privilege; to suffer anyhow,
even unconsciously. The little children whom He took
up in his arms, were not conscious of His loving condescension; but was it no privilege when He blessed
them? Surely this massacre had in it the nature
of a Sacrament; it was a pledge of the love of the
Son of God towards those who were included in it.
All who came near Him, more or less suffered by
approaching Him, just as if earthly pain and trouble
went out of Him, as some precious virtue for the good
of their souls;—and these infants in the number.
Surely His very presence was a Sacrament; every
motion, look, and word of His conveying grace to
those who would receive it: and much more was fellowship with Him. And hence in ancient times such
barbarous murders or Martyrdoms were considered as a
kind of baptism, a baptism of blood, with a sacramental
charm in it, which stood in the place of the appointed
Laver of regeneration. Let us then take these little
children as in some sense Martyrs, and see what
instruction we may gain from the pattern of their
innocence.

There is very great danger of our becoming cold-hearted, as life goes on : afflictions which happen to us, cares, disappointments, all tend to blunt our affections and make our feelings callous. That necessary self-discipline, too, which St. Paul enjoins Timothy to prac-tise, tends the same way. And, again, the pursuit of wealth especially ; and much more, if men so far openly transgress the word of Almighty God, as to yield to the temptations of sensuality. The glutton and the drunkard brutalize their minds, as is evident. And then further, we are often smit with a notion of our having become greater and more considerable persons than we were. If we are prosperous, for instance, in worldly matters, if we rise in the scale of (what is called) society, if we gain a name, if we change our state by marriage, or in any other way, so as to create a secret envy in the minds of our companions, in all these cases we shall be exposed to the temptation of *pride.* The deference paid to wealth or talent commonly makes the possessor arti-ficial, and difficult to reach ; glossing over his mind with a spurious refinement, which deadens feeling and heartiness. Now, after all, there is in most men's minds a secret instinct of reverence and affection towards the days of their childhood. They cannot help sighing with regret and tenderness when they think of it ; and it is graciously done by our Lord and Saviour, to avail Himself (so to say) of this principle of our nature, and, as He employs all that belongs to it, so to turn this also to the real health of the soul. And it is dutifully done on the part of the Church to follow the intimation *given her by her* Redeemer, and to hallow one day every year, as if for the contemplation of His word and deed.

If we wish to affect a person, and (if so be) humble him, what can we do better than appeal to the memory of times past, and above all to his childhood ! Then it was that he came out of the hands of God, with all lessons and thoughts of Heaven freshly marked upon him. Who can tell how God makes the soul, or how He new-makes it? We know not. We know that, besides His part in the work, it comes into the world with the taint of sin upon it; and that even regeneration, which removes the curse, does not extirpate the root of evil. Whether it is created in Heaven or hell, how Adam's sin is breathed into it, together with the breath of life, and how the Spirit dwells in it, who shall inform us? But this we know full well,—we know it from our own recollection of ourselves, and our experience of children,—that there is in the infant soul, in the first years of its regenerate state, a discernment of the unseen world in the things that are seen, a realization of what is Sovereign and Adorable, and an incredulity and ignorance about what is transient and changeable, which mark it as the fit emblem of the matured Christian, when weaned from things temporal, and living in the intimate conviction of the Divine Presence. I do not mean of course that a child has any formed principle in his heart, any habits of obedience, any true discrimination between the visible and the unseen, such as God promises to reward for Christ's sake, in those who come to years of discretion. Never *must we forget* that, in spite of his new birth, evil is within him, though in its seed only; but he has this one great gift, that he seems to have lately come from God's presence, and not to understand the language of this visible scene, or how it is a temptation, how it is a veil interposing itself between the soul and God. The simplicity of a child's ways and notions, his ready belief of everything he is told, his artless love, his frank confidence, his confession of helplessness, his ignorance of evil, his inability to conceal his thoughts, his contentment, his prompt forgetfulness of trouble, his admiring without coveting; and, above all, his reverential spirit, looking at all things about him as wonderful, as tokens and types of the One Invisible, are all evidence of his being lately (as it were) a visitant in a higher state of things. I would only have a person reflect on the earnestness and awe with which a child listens to any description or tale; or again, his freedom from that spirit of proud independence, which discovers itself in the soul as time goes on. And though, doubtless, children are generally of a weak and irritable nature, and all are not equally amiable, yet their passions go and are over like a shower; not interfering with the lesson we may gain to our own profit from their ready faith and guilelessness.

The distinctness with which the conscience of a child tells him the difference between right and wrong should also be mentioned. As persons advance in life, and yield to the temptations which come upon them, they lose this original endowment, and are obliged to grope about by the mere reason. If they debate whether they should *act in this* way or that, and there are many

n]

considerations of duty and interest involved in the decision, they feel altogether perplexed. Really, and truly, not from self-deception, but really, they do not know how they ought to act; and they are obliged to draw out arguments, and take a great deal of pains to come to a conclusion. And all this, in many cases at least, because they have lost, through sinning, a guide which they originally had from God. Hence it is that St. John, in the Epistle for the day, speaks of Christ's undefiled servants as "following the Lamb whithersoever He goeth." They have the minds of children, and are able by the light within them to decide questions of duty at once, undisturbed by the perplexity of discordant arguments.

In what has already been said, it has been implied how striking a pattern a child's mind gives us of what may be called a church temper. Christ has so willed it, that we should get at the Truth, not by ingenious speculations, reasonings, or investigations of our own, but by teaching. The Holy Church has been set up from the beginning as a solemn religious fact, so to call it,—as a picture, a revelation of the next world, as itself the Christian Dispensation, and so in one sense the witness of its own divinity, as is the Natural World. Now those who in the first place receive her words, have the minds of children, who do not reason, but obey their mother; and those who from the first refuse, as clearly fall short of children, in that they trust their own powers for arriving at truth, rather than informants which are external to them.

In conclusion, I shall but remind you of the

difference, on the other hand, between the state of a child and that of a matured Christian ; though this difference is almost too obvious to be noticed. St. John says, " He that *doeth* righteousness is righteous, even as He is righteous ;" and again, "Every one that doeth righteousness is born of Him."[1] Now, it is plain a child's innocence has no share in this higher blessedness. He is but a type of what is at length to be fulfilled in him. The chief beauty of his mind is on its mere surface ; and when, as time goes on, he attempts to act (as is his duty to do), instantly it disappears. It is only while he is still, that he is like a tranquil water, reflecting heaven. Therefore, we must not lament that our youthful days are gone, or sigh over the remembrances of pure pleasures and contemplations which we cannot recall ; rather, what we were when children, is a blessed *intimation*, given for our comfort, of what God will make us, if we surrender our hearts to the guidance of His Holy Spirit,—a prophecy of good to come,—a foretaste of what will be fulfilled in heaven. And thus it is that a child is a pledge of immortality ; for he bears upon him in figure those high and eternal excellences in which the joy of heaven consists, and which would not be thus shadowed forth by the All-gracious Creator, were they not one day to be realized. Accordingly, our Church, for the Epistle for this Festival, selects St. John's description of the Saints in glory.

As then we would one day reign with them, let us in this world learn the mind of little children, as the same

[1] *1 John* iii. 7; ii. 29.

Apostle describes it: "My little children, let us not love in word, neither in tongue; but in deed and in truth." "Beloved, let us love one another: for love is of God; and every one that loveth is born of God, and knoweth God. He that loveth not knoweth not God; for God is love."[1]

[1] 1 John iii. 18; iv. 7, R.

SERMON VII.

Ceremonies of the Church.

(THE FEAST OF THE CIRCUMCISION OF OUR LORD.)

"Suffer it to be so now: for thus it becometh us to fulfil all righteousness."—MATT. iii. 15.

WHEN our Lord came to John to be baptized, He gave this reason for it, "Thus it becometh us to fulfil all righteousness;" which seems to mean,—"It is becoming in Me, the expected Christ, to conform in all respects to all the rites and ceremonies of Judaism, to everything hitherto accounted sacred and binding." Hence it was that He came to be baptized, to show that it was not His intention in any way to dishonour the Established Religion, but to fulfil it even in those parts of it (such as Baptism) which were later than the time of Moses; and especially to acknowledge thereby the mission of John the Baptist, His forerunner. And those ordinances which Moses himself was commissioned to appoint, had still greater claim to be respected and observed. It was on this account that He was circumcised, *as we this day* commemorate; in order, that is, to show that He did not renounce the religion of Abraham, to whom God gave circumcision, or of Moses, by whom it was embodied in the Jewish Law.

We have other instances in our Lord's history, besides those of His circumcision and baptism, to show the reverence with which He regarded the religion which He came to fulfil. St. Paul speaks of Him as " born of a woman, born under the Law,"[1] and it was His custom to observe that Law, like any other Jew. For instance, He went up for the feasts to Jerusalem; He sent the persons He had cured to the priests, to offer the sin-offering commanded by Moses; He paid the Temple-tax; and again, He attended as "a custom" the worship of the synagogue, though this had been introduced in an age long after Moses; and He even bade the multitudes obey the Scribes and Pharisees in all lawful things, as those who sat in Moses' place.[2]

Such was our Saviour's dutiful attention to the religious system under which He was born; and that, not only so far as it was directly divine, but further, where it was the ordinance of uninspired though pious men, where it was but founded on ecclesiastical authority. His Apostles followed His pattern; and this is still more remarkable,—because after the Holy Spirit had descended, at first sight it would have appeared that all the Jewish ordinances ought at once to cease. But this was far from being the doctrine of the Apostles. They taught, indeed, that the Jewish rites were no longer of any use in obtaining God's favour; that Christ's death was now set forth as the full and

[1] *Gal. iv. 4.*　　　　[2] *Matt. xxiii. 2, 3.*

sufficient Atonement for sin, by that Infinite Mercy who had hitherto appointed the blood of the sacrifices as in some sort means of propitiation : and, besides, that every convert who turned from Christ back to Moses, or who imposed the Jewish rites upon his brethren as necessary to salvation, was grievously erring against the Truth. But they neither abandoned the Jewish rites themselves, nor obliged any others to do so who were used to them. Custom was quite a sufficient reason for retaining them ; every Christian was to remain in the state in which he was called ; and in the case of the Jew, the practice of them did not necessarily interfere with a true and full trust in the Atonement which Christ had offered for sin.

St. Paul, we know, was the most strenuous opposer of those who would oblige the Gentiles to become Jews, as a previous step to their becoming Christians. Yet, decisive as he is against all attempts to force the Gentiles under the rites of Law, he never bids the Jews renounce them, rather he would have them retain them ; leaving it for a fresh generation, who had not been born under them, to discontinue them, so that the use of them might gradually die away. Nay, he himself circumcised Timothy, when he chose him for his associate ; in order that no offence might be given to the Jews.[1] And how fully he adhered to the Law in his own person, we learn from the same inspired history ; for instance, we hear of his shaving his head, as having been under a vow,[2] according to the Jewish custom.

Now from this obedience to the Jewish Law, enjoined

[1] *Acts xvi. 1—3.*   [2] *Acts xviii. 18.*

and displayed by our Blessed Lord and His Apostles, we learn the great importance of retaining those religious forms to which we are accustomed, even though they are in themselves indifferent, or not of Divine origin; and, as this is a truth which is not well understood by the world at large, it may be of use to make some observations upon it.

We sometimes meet with men, who ask *why* we observe these or those ceremonies or practices; why, for example, we use Forms of prayer so cautiously and strictly ? or why we persist in kneeling at the Sacrament of the Lord's Supper ? why in bowing at the name of Jesus ? or why in celebrating the public worship of God only in consecrated places ? why we lay such stress upon these things ? These, and many such questions may be asked, and all with this argument: "They are indifferent matters; we do not read of them in the Bible."

Now the direct answer to this objection is, that the Bible was never *intended* to enjoin us these things, but *matters of faith;* and that though it happens to mention our practical duties, and some points of form and discipline, still, that it does not set about telling us what to do, but chiefly what to believe; and that there are many duties and many crimes which are not mentioned in Scripture, and which we must find out by our own understanding, enlightened by God's Holy Spirit. For instance, there is no prohibition of suicide, duelling, gaming, in Scripture; yet we know them to be great sins ; and it would be no excuse in a man to say that he does not find them forbidden in Scripture, because he may discover God's will in this matter independently of Scripture. And in like manner, various matters of form and discipline are binding, though Scripture says nothing about them; for we learn the duty in another way. No matter how we learn God's will, whether from Scripture, or Antiquity, or what St. Paul calls "Nature," so that we can be sure it *is* His will. Matters of faith, indeed, He reveals to us by inspiration, because they are supernatural : but matters of moral duty, through our own conscience and divinely-guided reason; and matters of form, by tradition and long usage, which bind us to the observance of them, though they are not enjoined in Scripture. This, I say, is the proper answer to the question, "Why do you observe rites and forms which are not enjoined in Scripture?" though, to speak the truth, our chief ordinances *are* to be found there, as the Sacraments, Public Worship, the Observance of the Lord's-day, Ordination, Marriage, and the like. But I shall make another answer, which is suggested by the event commemorated this day, our Lord's conforming to the Jewish Law in the rite of circumcision; and my answer is this.

Scripture tells us what to believe, and what to aim at and maintain, but it does not tell us *how* to do it; and as we cannot do it at all unless we do it in this manner, or that, in fact we must add something to what Scripture tells us. For example, Scripture tells us to meet together for prayer, and has connected the grant of the Christian blessings on God's part, with the observance of *union* on ours; but since it does not tell us the times and *places of* prayer, the Church *must* complete that which Scripture has but enjoined generally. Our Lord has instituted two Sacraments, Baptism and the Lord's Supper; but has not told us, except generally, with what forms we are to administer them. Yet we *cannot* administer them without some sort of prayers; whether we use always the same, or not the same, or unpremeditated prayers. And so with many other solemn acts, such as Ordination, or Marriage, or Burial of the Dead, it is evidently pious, and becomes Christians to perform them decently and in faith; yet how is this to be done, unless the Church sanctions Forms of doing it?

The Bible then may be said to give us the *spirit* of religion; but the Church must provide the body in which that spirit is to be lodged. Religion must be realized in particular acts, in order to its continuing alive. Religionists, for example, who give up the Church rites, are forced to recall the strict Judaical Sabbath. There is no such thing as abstract religion. When persons attempt to worship in this (what they call) more spiritual manner, they end, in fact, in not worshipping at all. This frequently happens. Every one may know it from his own experience of himself. Youths, for instance (and perhaps those who should know better than they), sometimes argue with them-selves, "What is the need of praying statedly morning and evening? why use a form of words? why kneel? why cannot I pray in bed, or walking, or dressing?" they end in not praying at all. Again, what will the devotion of the country people be, if we strip religion of its external symbols, and bid them seek out and gaze *oon the Invisible?* Scripture gives the *spirit*, and the

Church the *body*, to our worship; and we may as well expect that the spirits of men might be seen by us without the intervention of their bodies, as suppose that the Object of faith can be realized in a world of sense and excitement, without the instrumentality of an outward form to arrest and fix attention, to stimulate the careless, and to encourage the desponding. But observe what follows:—who would say our bodies are not part of ourselves? We may apply the illustration; for in like manner the forms of devotion are parts of devotion. Who can in practice separate his view of body and spirit? for example, what a friend would he be to us who should treat us ill, or deny us food, or imprison us; and say, after all, that it was our body he ill-treated, and not our soul? Even so, no one can really respect religion, and insult its forms. Granting that the forms are not immediately from God, still long use has made them divine *to us;* for the spirit of religion has so penetrated and quickened them, that to destroy them is, in respect to the multitude of men, to unsettle.and dislodge the religious principle itself. In most minds usage has so identified them with the notion of religion, that the one cannot be extirpated without the other. Their faith will not bear transplanting. Till we have given some attention to the peculiarities of human nature, whether from watching our own hearts, or from experience of life, we can scarcely form a correct estimate how intimately great and little matters are connected together in all cases; how the circumstances and accidents (as they might seem) of our habits are almost conditions of those habits *themselves. How* common it is for men to have *seasons* of seriousness, how exact is their devotion during them, how suddenly they come to an end, how completely all traces of them vanish, yet how comparatively trifling is the cause of the relapse, a change of place or occupation, or a day's interruption of regularity in their religious course! Consider the sudden changes in opinion and profession, religious or secular, which occur in life, the proverbial fickleness of the multitude, the influence of watchwords and badges upon the fortunes of political parties, the surprising falls which sometimes overtake well-meaning and really respectable men, the inconsistencies of even the holiest and most perfect, and you will have some insight into the danger of practising on the externals of faith and devotion. Precious doctrines are strung, like jewels, upon slender threads.

Our Saviour and His Apostles sanction these remarks, in their treatment of those Jewish ceremonies, which have led me to make them. St. Paul calls them weak and unprofitable, weak and beggarly elements.[1] So they were in themselves, but to those who were used to them, they were an edifying and living service. Else, why did the Apostles observe them? Why did they recommend them to the Jews whom they converted? Were they merely consulting for the prejudices of a reprobate nation? The Jewish rites were to disappear; yet no one was bid forcibly to separate himself from what he had long used, lest he lost his sense of religion also. Much more will this hold good with forms such as ours, which so far from being abrogated by the Apostles, were introduced by them or their immediate successors; and which,

[1] Heb. vii. 18 ; Gal. iv. 9.

besides the influence they exert over us from long usage, are, many of them, witnesses and types of precious gospel truths; nay, much more, possess a sacramental nature, and are adapted and reasonably accounted to convey a gift, even where they are not formally sacraments by Christ's institution. Who, for instance, could be hard-hearted and perverse enough to ridicule the notion that a father's blessing may profit his children, even though Christ and His Apostles have not in so many words declared it?

Much might be said on this subject, which is a very important one. In these times especially, we should be on our guard against those who hope, by inducing us to lay aside our forms, at length to make us lay aside our Christian hope altogether. This is why the Church itself is attacked, because it is the living form, the visible body of religion; and shrewd men know that when it goes, religion will go too. This is why they rail at so many usages as superstitious; or propose alterations and changes, a measure especially calculated to shake the faith of the multitude. Recollect, then, that things indifferent in themselves become important to us when we are used to them. The services and ordinances of the Church are the outward form in which religion has been for ages represented to the world, and has ever been known to us. Places consecrated to God's honour, clergy carefully set apart for His service, the Lord's-day piously observed, the public forms of prayer, the decencies of worship, these things, viewed as a whole, are *sacred* relatively to us, even if they were not, as they are, divinely *sanctioned*. Rites which the Church has

appointed, and with reason,—for the Church's authority
is from Christ,—being long used, cannot be disused without harm to our souls. Confirmation, for instance, may be
argued against, and undervalued ; but surely no one who
in the common run of men wilfully resists the Ordinance,
but will thereby be *visibly* a worse Christian than he
otherwise would have been. He will find (or rather
others will find for him, for he will scarcely know it
himself), that he has declined in faith, humility, devo-
tional feeling, reverence, and sobriety. And so in the
case of all other forms, even the least binding in themselves, it continually happens that a speculative improvement is a practical folly, and the wise are taken in their
own craftiness.

Therefore, when profane persons scoff at our forms,
let us argue with ourselves thus—and it is an argument
which all men, learned or unlearned, can enter into:
" These forms, even were they of mere human origin
(which learned men say is *not* the case, but even if they
were), are at least of as spiritual and edifying a character
as the rites of Judaism. Yet Christ and His Apostles
did not even suffer these latter to be irreverently treated
or suddenly discarded. Much less may we suffer it in
the case of our own; lest, stripping off from us the
badges of our profession, we forget there is a faith for
us to maintain, and a world of sinners to be eschewed."

SERMON VIII.

The Glory of the Christian Church.

(THE FEAST OF THE EPIPHANY.)

"Arise, shine; for thy light is come, and the glory of the Lord is risen upon thee."—ISAIAH lx. 1.

OUR Saviour said to the woman of Samaria, "The hour cometh, when ye shall neither in this mountain, nor yet at Jerusalem, worship the Father."[1] And upon to-day's Festival I may say to you in His words on another occasion, "This day is this scripture fulfilled in your ears." This day we commemorate the opening of the door of faith to the Gentiles, the extension of the Church of God through all lands, whereas, before Christ's coming, it had been confined to one nation only. This dissemination of the Truth throughout the world had been the subject of prophecy. "Enlarge the place of thy tent, and let them stretch forth the curtains of thine habitations: spare not, lengthen thy cords, and strengthen thy stakes; for thou shalt break forth on the right hand and on the left; and thy seed shall

[1] John iv. 21.

inherit the Gentiles, and make the desolate cities to be inhabited."[1]　In these words the Church is addressed as Catholic, which is the distinguishing title of the Christian Church, as contrasted with the Jewish.　The Christian Church is so constituted as to be able to spread itself out in its separate branches into all regions of the earth; so that in every nation there may be found a representative and an offshoot of the sacred and gifted Society, set up once for all by our Lord after His resurrection.

This characteristic blessing of the Church of Christ, its Catholic nature, is a frequent subject of rejoicing with St. Paul, who was the chief instrument of its propagation. In one Epistle he speaks of Gentiles being "fellow heirs" with the Jews, "and of the same body, and partakers of His promise in Christ by the Gospel."　In another he enlarges on "the mystery now made manifest to the saints," viz. "Christ among the Gentiles, the hope of glory."[2]

The day on which we commemorate this gracious appointment of God's Providence, is called the Epiphany, or bright manifestation of Christ to the Gentiles; being the day on which the wise men came from the East under guidance of a star, to worship Him, and thus became the first-fruits of the heathen world.　The name is explained by the words of the text, which occur in one of the lessons selected for to-day's service, and in which the Church is addressed.　"Arise, shine; for thy light is come, and the glory of the Lord is risen upon thee.　For, behold, the darkness shall cover the earth,

---

[1] *Isa. liv.* 2, 3.　　[2] Eph. iii. 6.　Col. i. 26, 27.

and gross darkness the people : but the Lord shall arise upon thee, and His glory shall be seen upon thee. And the Gentiles shall come to thy light, and kings to the brightness of thy rising. . . . Thy people also shall be all righteous : they shall inherit the land for ever, the branch of My planting, the work of My hands, that I may be glorified."

That this and other similar prophecies had their measure of fulfilment when Christ came, we all know ; when His Church, built upon the Apostles and Prophets, wonderfully branched out from Jerusalem as a centre into the heathen world round about, and gathering into it men of all ranks, languages, and characters, moulded them upon one pattern, the pattern of their Saviour, in truth and righteousness. Thus the prophecies concerning the Church were fulfilled at that time in two respects, as regards its sanctity and its Catholicity.

It is often asked, have these prophecies had then and since their perfect accomplishment ? Or are we to expect a more complete Christianizing of the world than has hitherto been vouchsafed it ? And it is usual at the present day to acquiesce in the latter alternative, as if the inspired predictions certainly meant more than has yet been realized.

Now so much, I think, is plain on the face of them, that the Gospel is to be preached in all lands, before the end comes: "This gospel of the kingdom shall be preached in all the world for a witness unto all nations ; and then shall the end come."[2] Whether it has been thus preached is a question of fact, which must be

[1] *Isa. lx. 1—3, 21.* [2] *Matt. xxiv. 14.*

determined, not from the prophecy, but from history ; and there we may leave it.   But as to the other expectation, that a time of greater purity is in store for the Church, that is not easily to be granted.   The very words of Christ just quoted, so far from speaking of the Gospel as tending to the conversion of the world at large, when preached in it, describe it only as a *witness* unto all the Gentiles, as if the many would not obey it.   And this intimation runs parallel to St. Paul's account of the Jewish Church, as realizing faith and obedience only in a residue out of the whole people ; and is further illustrated by St. John's language in the Apocalypse, who speaks of the " redeemed from among men " being but a remnant, "the first-fruits unto God and to the Lamb." [1]

However, I will readily allow that at first we shall feel a reluctance in submitting to this opinion, with such passages before us as that which occurs in the eleventh chapter of Isaiah's prophecy, where it is promised, "They shall not hurt nor destroy in all My holy mountain ; for the earth shall be full of the knowledge of the Lord, as the waters cover the sea."   I say it is natural, with such texts in the memory, to look out for what is commonly called a Millennium.   It may be instructive then upon this day to make some remarks in explanation of the state and prospects of the Christian Church in this respect.

Now the system of this world depends, in a way unknown to us, both on God's Providence and on human agency.   Every event, every course of action, has two

[1] Rom. xi. 5.   Rev. xiv. 4.

faces; it is divine and perfect, and it belongs to man and is marked with his sin. I observe next, that it is a peculiarity of Holy Scripture to represent the world on its providential side; ascribing all that happens in it to Him who rules and directs it, as it moves along, tracing events to His sole agency, or viewing them only so far forth as He acts in them. Thus He is said to harden Pharaoh's heart, and to hinder the Jews from believing in Christ; wherein is signified His absolute sovereignty over all human affairs and courses. As common is it for Scripture to consider Dispensations, not in their actual state, but as His agency would mould them, and so far as it really does succeed in moulding them. For instance: "God, who is rich in mercy, for His great love wherewith He loved us, even when we were dead in sins, hath quickened us together with Christ."[1] This is said as if the Ephesians had no traces left in their hearts of Adam's sin and spiritual death. As it is said afterwards, "Ye were sometimes darkness, but now are ye light in the Lord."[2]

In other words, Scripture more commonly speaks of the Divine *design* and *substantial work*, than of the *measure* of fulfilment which it receives at this time or that; as St. Paul expresses, when he says that the Ephesians were chosen, that they "*should* be holy and unblameable before Him in love." Or it speaks of the *profession* of the Christian; as when he says, " As many of you as have been baptized in Christ, have put on Christ ;"—or of the *tendency* of the Divine gift in a long period of time, and of its *ultimate fruits*; as in the

---

[1] *Eph. ii. 4, 5.*   [2] *Eph. v. 8.*

words, " Christ loved the Church, and gave Himself for it, that He might sanctify and cleanse it with the washing of water by the word, that He might present to Himself a glorious Church, not having spot, or wrinkle, or any such thing, but that it should be holy and without blemish,"[1] in which baptism and final salvation are viewed as if indissolubly connected. This rule of Scripture interpretation admits of very extensive application, and I proceed to illustrate it.

The principle under consideration is this: that, whereas God is one, and His will one, and His purpose one, and His work one; whereas all He is and does is absolutely perfect and complete, independent of time and place, and sovereign over creation, whether inanimate or living, yet that in His actual dealings with this world that is, in all in which we see His Providence (in that man is imperfect, and has a will of his own, and lives in time, and is moved by circumstances), He seems to work by a process, by means and ends, by steps, by victories hardly gained, and failures repaired, and sacrifices ventured. Thus it is only when we view His dispensations at a distance, as the Angels do, that we see their harmony and their unity ; whereas Scripture, anticipating the end from the beginning, places at their very head and first point of origination all that belongs to them respectively in their fulness.

We find some exemplification of this principle in the call of Abraham. In every age of the world it has held good that the just shall live by faith ; yet it was determined in the deep counsels of God, that for a while this

---

[1] *Eph.* i. 4. Gal. iii. 27. Eph. v. 25—27.

truth should be partially obscured, as far as His revelations went ; that man should live by sight, miracles and worldly ordinances taking the place of silent providences and spiritual services. In the latter times of the Jewish Law the original doctrine was brought to light, and when the Divine Object of faith was born into the world, it was authoritatively set forth by His Apostles as the basis of all acceptable worship. But observe, it had been already anticipated in the instance of Abraham ; the evangelical covenant, which was not to be preached till near two thousand years afterwards, was revealed and transacted in his person. "Abraham believed God, and it was counted unto him for righteousness." "Abraham rejoiced to see My day ; and he saw it, and was glad."[1] Nay, in the commanded sacrifice of his beloved son, was shadowed out the true Lamb which God had provided for a burnt offering. Thus in the call of the Patriarch, in whose Seed all nations of the earth should be blessed, the great outlines of the Gospel were anticipated ; in that he was called in uncircumcision, that he was justified by faith, that he trusted in God's power to raise the dead, that he looked forward to the day of Christ, and that he was vouchsafed a vision of the Atoning Sacrifice on Calvary.

We call these notices *prophecy*, popularly speaking, and doubtless such they are to us, and to be received and used thankfully ; but more properly, perhaps, they are merely instances of the harmonious movement of God's word and deed, His sealing up events from the first, His introducing them once and for all, though they

[1] *Rom. iv. 8.* John viii. 56.

are but gradually unfolded to our limited faculties, and
in this transitory scene.   It would seem that at the time
when Abraham was called, both the course of the Jewish
dispensation and the coming of Christ were (so to say)
realized; so as, in one sense, to be actually done and
over.   Hence, in one passage, Christ is called " the Lamb
slain from the foundation of the world;" in another,
it is said, that " Levi paid tithes" to Melchizedek, "in
Abraham."[1]

Similar remarks might be made on the call and reign
of David, and the building of the second Temple.[2]

In like manner the Christian Church had in the day
of its nativity all that fulness of holiness and peace
named upon it, and sealed up to it, which beseemed it,
viewed as God's design,—viewed in its essence, as it is
realized at all times and under whatever circumstances,
—viewed as God's work without man's co-operation,—
viewed as God's work in its tendency, and in its ultimate

[1] Rev. xiii. 8. Heb. vii. 9.

[2] In the instance of the first [Temple] there clearly is not the same
combination of the Mystical sense with the Temporal. The prediction
joined with the building of Solomon's Temple is of a simple kind:
perhaps it relates purely and solely to the proper Temple itself. But
the second Temple rises with a different structure of prophecy upon it.
Haggai, Zechariah, and Malachi have each delivered some symbolical
prediction, connected with it, or with its priesthood and worship.
Why this difference in the two cases? I think the answer is clear; it
is a difference obviously relating to the nearer connexion. which the
second Temple has with the Gospel. When God gave them their first
Temple, it was doomed to fall, and rise again, *under* and *during* their
first economy. The elder prophecy, therefore, was directed to the
proper history of the first Temple. But when He gave them their
second Temple, Christianity was then nearer in view; through that
second edifice lay the Gospel prospect. Its restoration, therefore, was
marked by a kind of prophecy, which had its vision towards the
Gospel.—DAVISON ON PROPHECY, Discourse vi. part 4.

blessedness ; so that the titles given it upon earth are a picture of what it will be absolutely in heaven. This might also be instanced in the case of the Jewish Church, as in Jeremiah's description : " I remember thee, the kindness of thy youth, the love of thine espousals, when thou wentest after Me in the wilderness, in a land that was not sown. Israel was holiness unto the Lord, and the first-fruits of His increase."[1] As to the Christian Church, one passage descriptive of its blessedness from its first founding has already been cited ; to which I add the following by way of specimen : " The Gentiles shall see thy righteousness, and all kings thy glory ; and thou shalt be called by a new name, which the mouth of the Lord shall name. Thou shalt also be a crown of glory in the hand of the Lord, and a royal diadem in the hand of thy God. . . . As the bridegroom rejoiceth over the bride, so shall thy God rejoice over thee." " The mountains shall depart, and the hills be removed ; but My kindness shall not depart from thee, neither shall the covenant of My peace be removed, saith the Lord that hath mercy on thee. All thy children shall be taught of the Lord, and great shall be the peace of thy children." " Behold, I have graven thee upon the palms of My hands ; thy walls are continually before Me. . . . Lift up thine eyes round about, and behold ; all these gather themselves together, and come to thee. As I live, saith the Lord, thou shalt surely clothe thee with them all, as with an ornament, and bind them on thee as a bride doeth." " Violence shall no more be heard in thy land, wasting nor destruction

[1] Jer. ii. 2, 3.

within thy borders; but thou shalt call thy walls
salvation, and thy gates praise."[1] In these passages,
which in their context certainly refer to the time of
Christ's coming, an universality and a purity are promised to the Church, which have their fulfilment only
in the course of its history, from first to last, as fore-
shortened and viewed as one whole.

Consider, again, the representations given us of Christ's
Kingdom. First, it is called the "Kingdom of *Heaven*,"
though on earth. Again, in the Angels' hymn, it is
proclaimed "on earth peace," in accordance with the
prophetic description of the Messiah as "the Prince of
Peace;" though He Himself, speaking of the earthly,
not the Divine side of His dispensation, said, He came
"not to send peace on earth, but a sword."[2] Further,
consider Gabriel's announcement to the Virgin concerning her Son and Lord: "He shall be great, and shall be
called the Son of the Highest; and the Lord God shall
give unto Him the throne of His father David; and He
shall reign over the house of Jacob for ever, and of His
kingdom there shall be no end." Or, as the same
Saviour had been foretold by Ezekiel: "I will set up
one Shepherd over them, and He shall feed them. . . .
I will make with them a covenant of peace, and will
cause the evil beasts to cease out of the land: and they
shall dwell safely in the wilderness, and sleep in the
woods. And I will make them and the places round
about My hill a blessing; and I will cause the shower
to come down in his season; there shall be showers of

[1] Isa. lxii. 3, 5; liv. 10, 13; xlix. 16, 18; lx. 18.
[2] Matt. x. 34.

blessing."[1] It is observable that in the two passages last cited, the Christian Church is considered as merely the continuation of the Jewish, as if the Gospel existed in its germ even under the Law.

Now it is undeniable, and so blessed a truth that one would not wish at all to question it, that when Christ first came, His followers were in a state of spiritual purity, far above anything which we witness in the Church at this day. That glory with which her face shone, as Moses' of old time, from communion with her Saviour on the holy Mount, is the earnest of what will one day be perfected ; it is a token held out to us in our dark age, that His promise stands sure, and admits of accomplishment. They continued in "gladness and singleness of heart, praising God, and having favour with all the people." Here was a pledge of eternal blessedness, the same in kind as a child's innocence is a forerunner of a holy immortality ; and as the baptismal robe of the fine linen, clean and white, which is the righteousness of saints ;—a pledge like the typical promises made to David, Solomon, Cyrus, or Joshua the high-priest. Yet at the same time the corruptions in the early Church, Galatian misbelief, and Corinthian excess, show too clearly that her early glories were not more than a pledge, except in the case of individuals,— a pledge of God's purpose, a witness of man's depravity.

The same interpretation will apply to the Scripture account of the Elect People of God, which is but the Church of Christ under another name. On them, upon their election, are bestowed, as on a body, the gifts of

[1] *Luke i. 32, 33. Ezek.* xxxiv. 23, 25, 26.

justification, holiness, and final salvation. The perfections of Christ are shed around them; His image is reflected from them; so that they receive His name as being in Him, and beloved of God in the Beloved. Thus in their election are sealed up, to be unrolled and enjoyed in due season, the successive privileges of the heirs of light. In God's *purpose*—according to His *grace* —in the *tendency* and ultimate effects of His dispensation—to be called and chosen is to be saved. "Whom He did foreknow, He also did predestinate; whom He did predestinate, them He also called; whom He called them He also justified; whom He justified, them He also glorified."[1] Observe, the whole scheme is spoken of as of a thing past; for in His deep counsel He contemplated from everlasting the one entire work, and, having decreed it, it is but a matter of time, of sooner or later, when it will be realized. As the Lamb was slain from the foundation of the world, so also were His redeemed gathered in from the first according to His foreknowledge; and it is not more inconsistent with the solemn announcement of the text just cited, that some once elected should fall away (as we know they do), than that an event should be spoken of in it as past and perfect, which is incomplete and future. All accidents are excluded, when He speaks; the present and the to come, delays and failures, vanish before the thought of His perfect work. And hence it happens that the word " elect " in Scripture has two senses, standing both for those who are called *in order* to salvation, and for those who at the last day shall be the *actually resulting fruit*

[1] Rom. viii. 29, 30.

of that holy call. For God's Providence moves by great and comprehensive laws; and His word is the mirror of His designs, not of man's partial success in thwarting His gracious will.

The Church then, considered as one army militant, proceeding forward from the house of bondage to Canaan, gains the victory, and accomplishes what is predicted of her, though many soldiers fall in the battle. While, however, they remain within her lines, they are included in her blessedness so far as to be partakers of the gifts flowing from election. And hence it is that so much stress is to be laid upon the duty of united worship; for thus the multitude of believers coming together, claim as one man the grace which is poured out upon the one undivided body of Christ mystical. "Where two or three are gathered together in His name, He is in the midst of them;" nay rather, blessed be His name! He is so one with them, that they are not their own, lose for the time their earth-stains, are radiant in His infinite holiness, and have the promise of His eternal favour. Viewed as one, the Church is still His image as at the first, pure and spotless, His spouse all-glorious within, the Mother of Saints; according to the Scripture, "My dove, My undefiled is but one; she is the only one of her mother, she is the elect one of her that bare her. . . Thou art all fair, My love; there is no spot in thee."[1]

And what is true of the Church as a whole, is represented in Scripture as belonging also in some sense to each individual in it. I mean, that as the Christian body was set up in the image of Christ, which is

[1] *Cant. vi. 9; iv. 7.*

gradually and in due season to be realized within it, so in like manner each of us, when made a Christian, is entrusted with gifts, which centre in eternal salvation. St. Peter says, we are "saved" through baptism; St. Paul, that we are "saved" according to God's mercy by "the washing of regeneration;" our Lord joins together water and the Spirit; St. Paul connects baptism with putting on Christ; and in another place with being "sanctified and justified in the name of the Lord Jesus, and by the Spirit of our God."[1] To the same purport are our Lord's words: "He that heareth My word, and believeth on Him that sent Me, *hath* everlasting life, and shall not come into condemnation, but *is passed* from death unto life."[2]

These remarks have been made with a view of showing the true sense in which we must receive, on the one hand, the prophetic descriptions of the Christian Church; on the other, the grant of its privileges, and of those of its separate members. Nothing is more counter to the spirit of the Gospel than to hunger after signs and wonders; and the rule of Scripture interpretation now given, is especially adapted to wean us from such wanderings of heart. It is our duty, rather it is our blessedness, to walk by faith; therefore we will take the promises (with God's help) in faith; we will believe they are fulfilled, and enjoy the fruit of them before we see it. We will fully acknowledge, as being firmly persuaded, that His word cannot return unto Him void;

---

[1] 1 Pet. iii. 21. Tit. iii. 5. John iii. 5. Gal. iii. 27. 1 Cor. vi. 11.
[2] John v. 24.

that it has its mission, and must prosper so far as substantially to accomplish it. We will adore the Blessed
Spirit ·as coming and going as He listeth, and doing
wonders daily which the world knows not of. We will
consider Baptism and the other Christian Ordinances
effectual signs of grace, not forms and shadows, though
men abuse and profane them; and particularly, as
regards our immediate subject, we will unlearn, as
sober and serious men, the expectation of any public
displays of God's glory in the edification of His Church,
seeing she is all-glorious *within*, in that inward shrine,
made up of faithful hearts, and inhabited by the Spirit
of grace. We will put off, so be it, all secular, all
political views of the victories of His kingdom. While
labouring to unite its fragments, which the malice of
Satan has scattered to and fro, to recover what is cast
away, to purify what is corrupted, to strengthen what is
weak, to make it in all its parts what Christ would have
it, a Church Militant, still (please God) we will not
reckon on any visible fruit of our labour. We will be
content to believe our cause triumphant, when we see
it apparently defeated. We will silently bear the insults
of the enemies of Christ, and resign ourselves meekly to
the shame and suffering which the errors of His followers
bring upon us. We will endure offences which the early
Saints would have marvelled at, and Martyrs would have
died to redress. We will work with zeal, but as to the
Lord and not to men; recollecting that even Apostles
saw the sins of the Churches they planted; that St. Paul
predicted that "evil men and seducers would wax worse
and *worse;*" *and that* St. John seems even to consider

extraordinary unbelief as the very sign of the times of
the Gospel, as if the light increased the darkness of
those who hated it. "Little children, it is the last
time; and as ye have heard that Antichrist shall come,
even now are there many Antichrists, whereby we know
that it is the last time."[1]

Therefore we will seek within for the Epiphany of
Christ. We will look towards His holy Altar, and
approach it for the fire of love and purity which there
burns. We will find comfort in the illumination which
Baptism gives. We will rest and be satisfied in His
ordinances and in His word. We will bless and praise
His name, whenever He vouchsafes to display His
glory to us in the chance-meeting of any of His Saints,
and we will ever pray Him to manifest it in our
own souls.

[1] 2 Tim. iii. 13.   1 John ii. 18.

SERMON IX.

St. Paul's Conversion viewed in reference to his Office.

(THE FEAST OF THE CONVERSION OF ST. PAUL.)

"I am the least of the Apostles, that am not meet to be called an Apostle, because I persecuted the Church of God. But by the grace of God I am what I am: and His grace which was bestowed upon me was not in vain; but I laboured more abundantly than they all: yet not I, but the grace of God which was with me."—I COR. xv. 9, 10.

TO-DAY we commemorate, not the whole history of St. Paul, nor his Martyrdom, but his wonderful Conversion. Every season of his life is full of wonders, and admits of a separate commemoration; which indeed we do make, whenever we read the Acts of the Apostles, or his Epistles. On this his day, however, that event is selected for remembrance, which was the beginning of his wonderful course; and we may profitably pursue (please God) the train of thought thus opened for us.

We cannot well forget the manner of his conversion. He was journeying to Damascus with authority from the chief priests to seize the Christians, and bring them to Jerusalem. He had sided with the persecuting party from their first act of violence, the martyrdom of

St. Stephen ; and he continued foremost in a bad cause, with blind rage endeavouring to defeat what really was the work of Divine power and wisdom. In the midst of his fury he was struck down by a miracle, and converted to the faith he persecuted. Observe the circumstances of the case. When the blood of Stephen was shed, Saul, then a young man, was standing by, "consenting unto his death," and "kept the raiment of them that slew him."[1] Two speeches are recorded of the Martyr in his last moments ; one, in which he prayed that God would pardon his murderers,—the other his witness, that he saw the heavens opened, and Jesus on God's right hand. His prayer was wonderfully answered. Stephen saw his Saviour ; the next vision of that Saviour to mortal man was vouchsafed to that very young man, even Saul, who shared in his murder and his intercession.

Strange indeed it was; and what would have been St. Stephen's thoughts could he have known it! The prayers of righteous men avail much. The first Martyr had power with God to raise up the greatest Apostle. Such was the honour put upon the first-fruits of those sufferings upon which the Church was entering. Thus from the beginning the blood of the Martyrs was the seed of the Church. Stephen, one man, was put to death for saying that the Jewish people were to have exclusive privileges no longer ; but from his very grave rose the favoured instrument by whom the thousands and ten thousands of the Gentiles were brought to the knowledge of the Truth !

---

1 Acts xxii. 20.

1. Herein then, first, is St. Paul's conversion memorable; that it was a triumph over the enemy. When Almighty God would convert the world, opening the door of faith to the Gentiles, who was the chosen preacher of His mercy? Not one of Christ's first followers. To show His power, He put forth His hand into the very midst of the persecutors of His Son, and seized upon the most strenuous among them. The prayer of a dying man is the token and occasion of that triumph which He had reserved for Himself. His strength is made perfect in weakness. As of old, He broke the yoke of His people's burden, the staff of their shoulder, the rod of their oppressor.[1] Saul made furiously for Damascus, but the Lord Almighty "knew his abode, and his going out and coming in, and his rage against Him;" and "because his rage against Him, and his tumult, came up before Him," therefore, as in Sennacherib's case, though in a far different way, He "put His hook in his nose, and His bridle in his lips, and turned him back by the way by which he came."[2] He "spoiled principalities and powers, and made a show of them openly,"[3] triumphing over the serpent's head while his heel was wounded. Saul, the persecutor, was converted, and preached Christ in the synagogues.

2. In the next place, St. Paul's conversion may be considered as a suitable introduction to the office he was called to execute in God's providence. I have said it was a triumph over the enemies of Christ; but it was also an expressive emblem of the nature of

---

[1] Isa. ix. 4.   [2] Isa. xxxvii. 28, 29.   [3] Col. ii. 15.

God's general dealings with the race of man. What are we all but rebels against God, and enemies of the Truth? what were the Gentiles in particular at that time, but "alienated" from Him, "and enemies in their mind by wicked works?"[1] Who then could so appropriately fulfil the purpose of Him who came to call sinners to repentance, as one who esteemed himself the least of the Apostles, that was not meet to be called an Apostle, because he had persecuted the Church of God? When Almighty God in His infinite mercy purposed to form a people to Himself out of the heathen, as vessels for glory, first He chose the instrument of this His purpose as a brand from the burning, to be a type of the rest. There is a parallel to this order of Providence in the Old Testament. The Jews were bid to look unto the rock whence they were hewn.[2] Who was the especial Patriarch of their nation?—Jacob. Abraham himself, indeed, had been called and blessed by God's mere grace. Yet Abraham had remarkable faith. Jacob, however, the immediate and peculiar Patriarch of the Jewish race, is represented in the character of a sinner, pardoned and reclaimed by Divine mercy, a wanderer exalted to be the father of a great nation. Now I am not venturing to describe him as he really was, but as he is represented to us; not personally, but in that particular point of view in which the sacred history has placed him; not as an individual, but as he is typically, or in the way of doctrine. There is no mistaking the marks of his character and fortunes in the *history*, designedly

---

[1] Col. i. 21.   [2] Isa. li. 1.

(as it would seem) recorded to humble Jewish pride. He makes his own confession, as St. Paul afterwards: "I am not worthy of the least of all Thy mercies."[1] Every year, too, the Israelites were bid to bring their offering, and avow before God, that "a Syrian ready to perish was their father."[2] Such as was the father, such (it was reasonable to suppose) would be the descendants. None would be "greater than their father Jacob,"[3] for whose sake the nation was blest.

In like manner St. Paul is, in one way of viewing the Dispensation, the spiritual father of the Gentiles; and in the history of his sin and its most gracious forgiveness, he exemplifies far more than his brother Apostles his own Gospel; that we are all guilty before God, and can be saved only by His free bounty. In his own words, "for this cause obtained he mercy, that in him first Jesus Christ might show forth all *long-suffering, for a pattern* to them which should hereafter believe on Him to life everlasting."[4]

3. And, in the next place, St. Paul's previous course of life rendered him, perhaps, after his conversion, more fit an instrument of God's purposes towards the Gentiles, as well as a more striking specimen of it. Here it is necessary to speak with caution. We know that, whatever were St. Paul's successes in the propagation of the Gospel, they were in their source and nature not his, but through "the grace of God which was with him." Still, God makes use of human means, and it is allowable to inquire reverently what these were, and

---

[1] Gen. xxxii. 10.   [2] Deut. xxvi. 5.
[3] *John iv. 12.*   [4] 1 Tim. i. 16.

why St. Paul was employed to convert the Heathen world rather than St. James the Less, or St. John. Doubtless his intellectual endowments and acquirements were among the circumstances which fitted him for his office. Yet, may it not be supposed that there was something in his previous religious history which especially disciplined him to be "all things to all men?" Nothing is so difficult as to enter into the characters and feelings of men who have been brought up under a system of religion different from our own; and to discern how they may be most forcibly and profitably addressed, in order to win them over to the reception of Divine truths, of which they are at present ignorant. Now St. Paul had had experience in his own case, of a state of mind very different from that which belonged to him as an Apostle. Though he had never been polluted with Heathen immorality and profaneness, he had entertained views and sentiments very far from Christian, and had experienced a conversion to which the other Apostles (as far as we know) were strangers. I am far indeed from meaning that there is aught favourable to a man's after religion in an actual unsettlement of principle, in his lapsing into infidelity, and then returning again to religious belief. This was not St. Paul's case; *he* underwent no radical change of religious principle. Much less would I give countenance to the notion, that a previous immoral life is other than a grievous permanent hindrance and a curse to a man, after he has turned to God. Such considerations, however, are out of place, in speaking of St. Paul. *What I mean is,* that his awful rashness and blindness, his self-confident, headstrong, cruel rage against the worshippers of the true Messiah, then his strange conversion, then the length of time that elapsed before his solemn ordination, during which he was left to meditate in private on all that had happened, and to anticipate the future,—all this constituted a peculiar preparation for the office of preaching to a lost world, dead in sin. It gave him an extended insight, on the one hand, into the ways and designs of Providence, and, on the other hand, into the workings of sin in the human heart, and the various modes of thinking in which the mind is actually trained. It taught him not to despair of the worst sinners, to be sharp-sighted in detecting the sparks of faith amid corrupt habits of life, and to enter into the various temptations to which human nature is exposed. It wrought in him a profound humility, which disposed him (if we may say so) to bear meekly the abundance of the revelations given him; and it imparted to him a practical wisdom how to apply them to the conversion of others, so as to be weak with the weak, and strong with the strong, to bear their burdens, to instruct and encourage them, to "strengthen his brethren," to rejoice and weep with them; in a word, to be an earthly *Paraclete*, the comforter, help, and guide of his brethren. It gave him to know in some good measure the *hearts of men ;* an attribute (in its fulness) belonging to God alone, and possessed by Him in union with perfect purity from all sin; but which in us can scarcely exist without our own melancholy experience, in some degree, of moral evil in ourselves, since the innocent (it is their privilege) have not eaten of the tree of the knowledge of good and evil.

4. Lastly, to guard against misconception of these last remarks, I must speak distinctly on a part of the subject only touched upon hitherto, viz. on St. Paul's spiritual state before his conversion. For, in spite of what has been said by way of caution, perhaps I may still be supposed to warrant the maxim sometimes maintained, that the greater sinner makes the greater saint.

Now, observe, I do not allege that St. Paul's previous sins made him a more spiritual Christian afterwards, but rendered him *more fitted for a particular purpose* in God's providence,—more fitted, when converted, to reclaim others ; just as a knowledge of languages (whether divinely or humanly acquired) fits a man for the office of missionary, without tending in any degree to make him a better man. I merely say, that if we take two men *equally* advanced in faith and holiness, that one of the two would preach to a variety of men with the greater success who had the greater experience in his own religious history of temptation, the war of flesh and spirit, sin, and victory over sin ; though, at the same time, at first sight it is of course unlikely that he who had experienced all these changes of mind *should* be equal in faith and obedience to the other who had served God from a child.

But, in the next place, let us observe, how very far St. Paul's conversion is, in a matter of fact, from holding out any encouragement to those who live in sin, or *any self-satisfaction* to those who have lived in it; as if their present or former disobedience could be a gain to them.

Why was mercy shown to Saul the persecutor; he himself gives us the reason, which we may safely make use of. "I obtained mercy, because I did it ignorantly in unbelief."[1] And why was he "enabled" to preach the Gospel? "Because Christ counted him faithful." We have here the reason more clearly stated even than in Abraham's case, who was honoured with special Divine revelations, and promised a name on the earth, because God "knew him, that he would command his children and his household after him, to keep the way of the Lord, to do justice and judgment."[2] Saul was ever faithful, according to his notion of "the way of the Lord." Doubtless he sinned deeply and grievously in persecuting the followers of Christ. Had he known the Holy Scriptures, he never would have done so; he would have recognised Jesus to be the promised Saviour, as Simeon and Anna had, from the first. But he was bred up in a human school, and paid more attention to the writings of men than to the Word of God. Still, observe, he differed from other enemies of Christ in this, that he kept a clear conscience, and habitually obeyed God according to his knowledge. God speaks to us in two ways, in our hearts and in His Word. The latter and clearer of these informants St. Paul knew little of; the former he could not but know in his measure (for it was within him), and he obeyed it. That inward voice was but feeble, mixed up and obscured with human feelings and human traditions; so that what his conscience told him

[1] *1 Tim. i. 12. 13.*   [2] *Gen. xviii. 19.*

to do, was but partially true, and in part was wrong. Yet still, believing it to speak God's will, he deferred to it, acting as he did afterwards when he "was not disobedient to the heavenly vision," which informed him Jesus was the Christ.[1] Hear his own account of himself: —"I have lived in all good conscience before God until this day." "After the most straitest sect of our religion, I lived a Pharisee." "Touching the righteousness which is in the Law, blameless."[2] Here is no ease, no self-indulgent habits, no wilful sin against the light,—nay, I will say, no pride. That is though he was doubtless influenced by much sinful self-confidence in his violent and bigoted hatred of the Christians, and though (as well as even the best of us) he was doubtless liable to the occasional temptations and defilements of pride, yet, taking pride to mean, open rebellion against God, warring against God's authority, setting up reason against God, this he had not. He "verily thought within himself that he ought to do many things contrary to the name of Jesus of Nazareth." Turn to the case of Jews and Gentiles who remained unconverted, and you will see the difference between them and him. Think of the hypocritical Pharisees, who professed to be saints, and were sinners; "full of extortion, excess, and uncleanness;"[3] believing Jesus to be the Christ, but not confessing Him, as "loving the praise of men more than the praise of God."[4] St. Paul himself gives us an account of them in the second chapter of his Epistle to the Romans. Can it be made to apply to his own previous state? Was the

[1] Acts xxvi. 19.   [2] Acts xxiii. 1 ; xxvi. 5.   Phil. iii. 6.
[3] *Matt.* xxiii. 25, 27.   [4] John xii. 43.

name of God blasphemed among the Gentiles through
him?—On the other hand, the Gentile reasoners sought
a vain wisdom.[1]   These were they who despised religion
and practical morality as common matters, unworthy the
occupation of a refined and cultivated intellect.   " Some
mocked, others said, We will hear thee again of this
matter." [2]   They prided themselves on being above
vulgar prejudices,—on being indifferent to the traditions
afloat in the world about another life,—on regarding all
religions as equally true and equally false.   Such a hard,
vain-glorious temper our Lord solemnly condemns, when
He says to the Church at Laodicea, " I would thou wert
cold or hot."

The Pharisees, then, were breakers of the Law ; the
Gentile reasoners and statesmen were infidels.   Both
were proud, both despised the voice of conscience.   We
see, then, from this review, the kind of sin which God
pities and pardons.   All sin, indeed, when repented of,
He will put away ; but pride hardens the heart against
repentance, and sensuality debases it to a brutal nature.
The Holy Spirit is quenched by open transgressions of
conscience and by contempt of His authority.   But, when
men err in ignorance, following closely their own notions
of right and wrong, though these notions are mistaken,—
great as is their sin, if they might have possessed themselves of truer notions (and very great as was St. Paul's
sin, because he certainly might have learned from the
Old Testament far clearer and diviner doctrine than the
tradition of the Pharisees),—yet such men are not left
by the God of all grace.   God leads them on to the light,

[1] *1 Cor. i. 22.*   [2] Acts xvii. 32.

in spite of their errors in faith, if they continue strictly to obey what they believe to be His will. And, to declare this comfortable truth to us, St. Paul was thus carried on by the providence of God, and brought into the light by a miracle; that we may learn, by a memorable instance of His grace, what He ever does, though He does not in ordinary cases thus declare it openly to the world.

Who has not felt a fear lest he be wandering from the true doctrine of Christ? Let him cherish and obey the holy light of conscience within him, as Saul did; let him carefully study the Scriptures, as Saul did not; and the God who had mercy even on the persecutor of His saints, will assuredly shed His grace upon him, and bring him into the truth as it is in Jesus.

SERMON X.

Secrecy and Suddenness of Divine Visitations.

(THE FEAST OF THE PURIFICATION OF THE BLESSED VIRGIN MARY.)

" The kingdom of God cometh not with observation."—LUKE xvii. 20.

WE commemorate on this day the Presentation of
Christ in the Temple according to the injunction of
the Mosaic Law, as laid down in the thirteenth chapter
of the Book of Exodus and the twelfth of Leviticus.
When the Israelites were brought out of Egypt, the first-
born of the Egyptians (as we all know) were visited by
death, " from the first-born of Pharaoh that sat on his
throne, unto the first-born of the captive that was in the
dungeon ; and all the first-born of cattle."[1] Accordingly,
in thankful remembrance of this destruction, and their
own deliverance, every male among the Israelites who was
the first-born of his mother, was dedicated to God ; likewise, every first-born of cattle. Afterwards, the Levites
were taken, as God's peculiar possession, instead of the
first-born :[2] but still the first-born were solemnly brought

---

[1] Exod. xi. 29.　　　　　[2] Numb. iii. 12, 13.

to the Temple at a certain time from their birth, presented to God, and then redeemed or bought off at a certain price. At the same time certain sacrifices were offered for the mother, in order to her purification after child-birth; and therefore to-day's Feast, in memory of Christ's Presentation in the Temple, is commonly called the Purification of the Blessed Virgin Mary.

Our Saviour was born without sin. His Mother, the Blessed Virgin Mary, need have made no offering, as requiring no purification. On the contrary, it was that very birth of the Son of God which sanctified the whole race of woman, and turned her curse into a blessing. Nevertheless, as Christ Himself was minded to "fulfil all righteousness," to obey all ordinances of the covenant under which He was born, so in like manner His Mother Mary submitted to the Law, in order to do it reverence.

This, then, is the event in our Saviour's infancy which we this day celebrate; His Presentation in the Temple when His Virgin Mother was ceremonially purified. It was made memorable at the time by the hymns and praises of Simeon and Anna, to whom He was then revealed. And there were others, besides these, who had been "looking for redemption in Jerusalem," who were also vouchsafed a sight of the Infant Saviour. But the chief importance of this event consists in its being a fulfilment of prophecy. Malachi had announced the Lord's visitation of His Temple in these words, "The Lord whom ye seek shall suddenly come to His Temple;"[1] words which, though variously fulfilled during His ministry, had their first accomplishment in the

---

[1] Mal. iii. 1

humble ceremony commemorated on this day. And, when we consider the grandeur of the prediction, and how unostentatious this accomplishment was, we are led to muse upon God's ways, and to draw useful lessons for ourselves. This is the reflection which I propose to make upon the subject of this Festival.

I say, we are to-day reminded of the noiseless course of God's providence,—His tranquil accomplishment, in the course of nature, of great events long designed; and again, of the suddenness and stillness of His visitations. Consider what the occurrence in question consists in. A little child is brought to the Temple, as all first-born children were brought. There is nothing here uncommon or striking, so far. His parents are with him, poor people, bringing the offering of pigeons or doves, for the purification of the mother. They are met in the Temple by an old man, who takes the child in his arms, offers a thanksgiving to God, and blesses the parents; and next are joined by a woman of a great age, a widow of eighty-four years, who had exceeded the time of useful service, and seemed to be but a fit prey for death. She gives thanks also, and speaks concerning the child to other persons who are present. Then all retire.

Now, there is evidently nothing great or impressive in this; nothing to excite the feelings, or interest the imagination. We know what the world thinks of such a group as I have described. The weak and helpless, whether from age or infancy, it looks upon negligently and passes by. Yet all this that happened was really the solemn *fulfilment of* an ancient and emphatic prophecy.   The infant in arms was the Saviour of the world, the rightful heir, come in disguise of a stranger to visit His own house.   The Scripture had said, " The Lord whom ye seek shall suddenly come to His Temple: but who may abide the day of His coming, and who may stand when He appeareth?"   He had now taken possession.   And further, the old man who took the child in his arms, had upon him the gifts of the Holy Ghost, had been promised the blessed sight of his Lord before his death, came into the Temple by heavenly guidance, and now had within him thoughts unutterable, of joy, thankfulness, and hope, strangely mixed with awe, fear, painful wonder, and " bitterness of spirit." Anna too, the woman of fourscore and four years, was a prophetess ; and the bystanders, to whom she spoke, were the true Israel, who were looking out in faith for the predicted redemption of mankind, those who (in the words of the prophecy) " sought " and in prospect " delighted " in the " Messenger " of God's covenant of mercy.   " The glory of this latter House shall be greater than of the former,"[1] was the announcement made in another prophecy.   Behold the glory ; a little child and his parents, two aged persons, and a congregation without name or memorial.   " The kingdom of God cometh not with observation."

Such has ever been the manner of His visitations, in the destruction of His enemies as well as in the deliverance of His own people ;—silent, sudden, unforeseen, as regards the world, though predicted in the face of all men, and in their measure comprehended and waited

[1] Haggai ii. 9.

for by His true Church. Such a visitation was the flood; Noah a preacher of righteousness, but the multitude of sinners judicially blinded. "They did eat, they drank, they married wives, they were given in marriage, until the day that Noe entered into the ark, and the flood came and destroyed them all." Such was the overthrow of Sodom and Gomorrah. "Likewise as it was in the days of Lot; they did eat, they drank, they bought, they sold, they planted, they builded; but the same day that Lot went out of Sodom, it rained fire and brimstone from heaven, and destroyed them all."[1] Again, "The horse of Pharaoh went in with his chariots and with his horsemen into the sea, and the Lord brought again the waters of the sea upon them."[2] The overthrow of Sennacherib was also silent and sudden, when his vast army least expected it: "The Angel of the Lord went forth, and smote in the camp of the Assyrians a hundred fourscore and five thousand."[3] Belshazzar and Babylon were surprised in the midst of the king's great feast to his thousand lords. While Nebuchadnezzar boasted, his reason was suddenly taken from him. While the multitude shouted with impious flattery at Herod's speech, then "the Angel of the Lord smote him, because he gave not God the glory."[4] Whether we take the first or the final judgment upon Jerusalem, both visitations were foretold as sudden. Of the former, Isaiah had declared it should come "*suddenly*, at an instant;"[5] of the latter, Malachi, "The Lord whom ye seek shall *suddenly* come to His Temple."

[1] Luke xvii. 27—29. [2] Exod. xv. 19. [3] Isa. xxxvii. 36.
[4] *Acts xii. 23.* [5] Isa. xxx. 13.

And such, too, will be His final visitation of the whole earth: men will be at their work in the city and in the field, and it will overtake them like a thunder-cloud. "Two women shall be grinding together; the one shall be taken, and the other left. Two men shall be in the field; the one shall be taken, and the other left."[1]

And it is impossible that it should be otherwise, in spite of warnings ever so clear, considering how the world goes on in every age. Men, who are plunged in the pursuits of active life, are no judges of its course and tendency on the whole. They confuse great events with little, and measure the importance of objects, as in perspective, by the mere standard of nearness or remoteness. It is only at a distance that one can take in the outlines and features of a whole country. It is but holy Daniel, solitary among princes, or Elijah the recluse of Mount Carmel, who can withstand Baal, or forecast the time of God's providences among the nations. To the multitude all things continue to the end, as they were from the beginning of the creation. The business of state affairs, the movements of society, the course of nature, proceed as ever, till the moment of Christ's coming. "The sun was risen upon the earth," bright as usual, on that very day of wrath in which Sodom was destroyed. Men cannot believe their own time is an especially wicked time; for, with Scripture unstudied and hearts untrained in holiness, they have no standard to compare it with. They take warning from no troubles or perplexities, which rather carry them away to search out the earthly causes of

[1] Luke xvii. 35, 36.

them, and the possible remedies. They consider them as conditions of this world, necessary results of this or that state of society. When the power of Assyria became great (we might suppose), the Jews had a plain call to repentance. Far from it; they were led to set power against power: they took refuge against Assyria in Egypt, their old enemy. Probably they reasoned themselves into what they considered a temperate, enlightened, cheerful view of national affairs; perhaps they might consider the growth of Assyria as an advantage rather than otherwise, as balancing the power of Egypt, and so tending to their own security. Certain it is, we find them connecting themselves first with one kingdom, and then with the other, as men who could read (as they thought) "the signs of the times," and made some pretences to political wisdom. Thus the world proceeds till wrath comes upon it and there is no escape. "To-morrow," they say, "shall be as this day, and much more abundant."[1]

And in the midst of this their revel, whether of sensual pleasure, or of ambition, or of covetousness, or of pride and self-esteem, the decree goes forth to destroy. The decree goes forth in secret; Angels hear it, and the favoured few on earth; but no public event takes place to give the world warning. The earth was doomed to the flood one hundred and twenty years before the "decree brought forth,"[2] or men heard of it. The waters of Babylon had been turned, and the conqueror was marching into the city, when Belshazzar made his great feast. Pride infatuates man, and self-indulgence

---

[1] *Isa. lvi. 12.*   [2] *Zeph. ii. 2.*

and luxury work their way unseen,—like some smouldering fire, which for a while leaves the outward form of things unaltered. At length the decayed mass cannot hold together, and breaks by its own weight, or on some slight and accidental external violence. As the Prophet says: "This iniquity shall be to you as a breach ready to fall, swelling out (or bulging) in a high wall, whose breaking cometh *suddenly at an instant.*" The same inward corruption of a nation seems to be meant in our Lord's words, when He says of Jerusalem: "Wheresoever the carcase is, there will the eagles be gathered together."[1]

Thoughts such as the foregoing are profitable at all times; for in every age the world is profane and blind, and God hides His providence, yet carries it forward. But they are peculiarly apposite now, in proportion as the present day bears upon it more marks than usual of pride and judicial blindness. Whether Christ is at our doors or not, but a few men in England may have grace enough safely to conjecture; but that He is calling upon us all to prepare as for His coming, is most evident to those who have religious eyes and ears. Let us then turn this Festival to account, by taking it as the Memorial-day of His visitations. Let us from the events it celebrates, lay up deep in our hearts the recollection, how mysteriously little things are in this world connected with great; how single moments, improved or wasted, are the salvation or ruin of all-important interests. Let us bear the thought upon us, when we come to worship in God's House, that any

[1] Matt. xxiv. 28.

such season of service may, for what we know, be wonderfully connected with some ancient purpose of His, announced before we were born, and may have its determinate bearing on our eternal welfare; let us fear to miss the Saviour, while Simeon and Anna find Him. Let us remember that He was not manifested again in the Temple, except once, for thirty years, while a whole generation, who were alive at His first visitation, died off in the interval. Let us carry this thought into our daily conduct; considering that, for what we know, our hope of salvation may in the event materially depend on our avoiding this or that momentary sin. And further, from the occurrences of this day let us take comfort, when we despond about the state of the Church. Perhaps we see not God's tokens; we see neither prophet nor teacher remaining to His people; darkness falls over the earth, and no protesting voice is heard. Yet, granting things to be at the very worst, still, when Christ was presented in the Temple, the age knew as little of it as it knows of His providence now. Rather, the worse our condition is, the nearer to us is the Advent of our Deliverer. Even though He is silent, doubt not that His army is on the march towards us. He is coming through the sky, and has even now His camp upon the outskirts of our own world. Nay, though He still for a while keep His seat at His Father's right hand, yet surely He sees all that is going on, and waits and will not fail His hour of vengeance. Shall He not hear His own elect, when they cry day and night to Him? His Services of prayer and praise continue, and are scorned by the multitude.

Day by day, Festival by Festival, Fast after Fast, Season by Season, they continue according to His ordinance, and are scorned. But the greater His delay, the heavier will be His vengeance, and the more complete the deliverance of His people.

May the good Lord save His Church in this her hour of peril; when Satan seeks to sap and corrupt where he dare not openly assault! May He raise up instruments of His grace, "not ignorant of the devices" of the Evil One, with seeing eyes, and strong hearts, and vigorous arms to defend the treasure of the faith once committed to the Saints, and to arouse and alarm their slumbering brethren! "For Sion's sake will I not hold my peace, and for Jerusalem's sake I will not rest, until the righteousness thereof go forth as brightness, and the salvation thereof as a lamp that burneth. . . . Ye that make mention of the Lord, keep not silence, and give Him no rest, till He establish, and till He make Jerusalem a praise in the earth. . . . Go through, go through the gates: prepare ye the way of the people; cast up, cast up the highway, gather out the stones, lift up a standard for the people."[1] Thus does Almighty God address His "watchmen on the walls of Jerusalem;" and to the Church herself He says, to our great comfort: "No weapon that is formed against thee shall prosper, and every tongue that shall rise against thee in judgment thou shalt condemn. This is the heritage of the servants of the Lord, and their righteousness is of Me saith the Lord."[2]

---

[1] Isa. lxii. 1, 6, 7. 10.   [2] Isa. liv. 17.

SERMON XI.

𝔇𝔦𝔳𝔦𝔫𝔢 𝔇𝔢𝔠𝔯𝔢𝔢𝔰.

(THE FEAST OF ST. MATTHIAS THE APOSTLE.)

" Hold that fast which thou hast, that no man take thy crown."—
REV. iii. 11.

THIS is the only Saint's day which is to be celebrated
with mingled feelings of joy and pain. It records
the fall as well as the election of an Apostle. St. Matthias was chosen in place of the traitor Judas. In the
history of the latter we have the warning recorded in
very deed, which our Lord in the text gives us in
word, "Hold that fast which thou hast, that no man
take thy crown." And doubtless many were the warnings such as this, addressed by our Lord to the wretched
man who in the end betrayed Him. Not only did He
call him to reflection and repentance by the hints which
He let drop concerning him during the Last Supper, but
in the discourses previous to it He may be supposed to
have intended a reference to the circumstances of His
apostate disciple. "Watch ye, therefore," He said, "lest
coming suddenly, He find you sleeping."—I called Judas

just now *wretched;* for we must not speak of sinners, according to the falsely charitable way of some, styling them *unfortunate* instead of wicked, lest we thus learn to excuse sin in ourselves.   He was doubtless *inexcusable,* as we shall be, if we follow his pattern; and he must be viewed, not with pity, but with fear and awe.

The reflection which rises in the mind on a consideration of the election of St. Matthias, is this: how easily God may effect His purposes without us, and put others in our place, if we are disobedient to Him.   It often happens that those who have long been in His favour grow secure and presuming.   They think their salvation certain, and their service necessary to Him who has graciously accepted it.   They consider themselves as personally bound up with His purposes of mercy manifested in the Church; and so marked out that, if they could fall, His word would fail.   They come to think they have some peculiar title or interest in His promises, over and above other men (however derived, it matters not, whether from His eternal decree, or, on the other hand, from their own especial holiness and obedience), but practically such an interest that the very supposition that they can possibly fall offends them.   Now, this feeling of self-importance is repressed all through the Scriptures, and especially by the events we commemorate to-day.   Let us consider this subject.

Eliphaz the Temanite thus answers Job, who in his distress showed infirmity, and grew impatient of God's correction.   "Can a man be profitable unto God, as he that is wise may be profitable unto himself?   Is it any *pleasure* to the Almighty, that thou art righteous? or is

it gain to Him, that thou makest thy ways perfect?"[1]
And the course of His providence, as recorded in
Scripture, will show us that, in dealing with us His
rational creatures, He goes by no unconditional rule,
which makes us absolutely His from the first; but, as
He is "no respecter of persons," so on the other hand
righteousness and judgment are the basis of His
throne; and that whoso rebels, whether Archangel or
Apostle, at once forfeits His favour; and this, even for
the sake of those who do not rebel.

Not long before the fall and treachery of Judas,
Christ pronounced a blessing, as it seemed, upon all the
twelve Apostles, the traitor included. "Ye which have
followed Me, in the regeneration when the Son of Man
shall sit in the throne of His glory, ye shall also sit
upon twelve thrones, judging the twelve tribes of
Israel."[2] Who would not have thought from this
promise, taken by itself, and without reference to the
eternal Rule of God's government, which is always
understood, even when not formally enunciated, that
Judas was sure of eternal life? It is true our Saviour
added, as if with an allusion to him, "many that are
first shall be last;" yet He said nothing to undeceive
such as might refuse to consult and apply the fundamental law of His impartial providence. All His
twelve Apostles seemed, from the letter of His words, to
be predestined to life; nevertheless, in a few months,
Matthias held the throne and crown of one of them.—
And there is something remarkable in the circumstance
itself, that our Lord *should* have made up their number

---

[1] *Job xxii. 2, 3.*   [2] Matt. xix. 28.

to a full twelve, after one had fallen; and, perhaps, there may be contained in it some symbolical allusion to the scope of His decrees, which we cannot altogether enter into. Surely, had He willed it, eleven would have accomplished His purpose as well as twelve. Why, when one had fallen, should He accurately fill up the perfect number? Yet not only in the case of the Apostles, but in that of the tribes of Israel also, if He rejects one, He divides another into two.[1] Why is this, but to show us, as it would appear, that in this election of us, He does not look at us as mere *individuals*, but as a body, as a certain definite whole, of which the parts may alter in the process of disengaging them from this sinful world,—with reference to some glorious and harmonious design upon *us*, who are the immediate objects of His bounty, and shall be the fruit of His love, if we are faithful? Why, but to show us that He could even find other Apostles to suffer for Him, —and, much more, servants to fill His lower thrones, should we be wanting and transgress His strict and holy law ?

This is but one instance, out of many, in the revealed history of His moral government. He was on the point of exemplifying the same Rule in the case of the Israelites, when Moses stayed His hand. God purposed to consume them, when they rebelled, and instead to make of Moses' seed a great nation. This happened twice.[2] The second time, God declared what was His end in view, in fulfilling which the Israelites were but His instruments. "I have pardoned according to thy

[1] *Rev. vii.*   [2] Exod. xxxii. 32, 33. Numb. xiv. 20, 21

word; but as truly as I live, *all the earth shall be filled with the glory of the Lord."* Again, on the former occasion, He gave the Rule of His dealings with them. Moses wished for the sake of his people to be himself excluded from the land of promise : "If thou wilt forgive their sin :—and if not, blot me, I pray Thee, out of Thy book which Thou hast written. And the Lord said unto Moses, *Whosoever hath sinned against Me, him* will I blot out of My book." So clearly has He shown us from the beginning, that His own glory is the *End,* and justice the essential *Rule,* of His providence.

Again, Saul was chosen, and thought himself secure. His conduct evinced the self-will of an independent monarch, instead of one who felt himself to be a mere instrument of God's purposes, a minister of His glory, under the obligation of a law of right and wrong, and strong only as wielded by Him who formed him. So, when he sinned, Samuel said to him : "Thou hast done foolishly : thou hast not kept the commandment of the Lord thy God .... for *now would the Lord have established* thy kingdom upon Israel for ever. But now thy kingdom shall not continue : the Lord hath sought Him a man after His own heart."[1] And again, "The Lord hath rent the kingdom of Israel from thee this day, and hath given it to a neighbour of thine, that is better than thou."[2]

In like manner, Christ also, convicting the Jews out of their own mouth : " He will miserably destroy those wicked men, and will *let out His vineyard unto other husbandmen,* which shall render Him the fruits in their

[1] 1 Sam. xiii. *13, 14.*   [2] Ibid. xv. 28.

seasons."[1] Consider how striking an instance the Jews
formed, when the Gospel was offered them, of the general
Rule which I am pointing out. They were rejected.
How hard they thought it, St. Paul's Epistles show.
They did not shrink from declaring, that, if Jesus were
the Christ, and the Gentiles made equal with them,
God's promise was broken ; and you may imagine how
forcibly they might have pleaded the prophecies of the
Old Testament, which seemed irreversibly to assign
honour and power (not to say *temporal* honour and
power) to the Israelites *by name.* Alas ! they did not
seek out and use the one clue given them for their
religious course, amid all the mysteries both of Scripture and the world,—the one solemn *Rule* of God's
dealings with His creatures. They did not listen for
that small still voice, running under all His dispensations, most clear to those who would listen, amid all
the intricacies of His providence and His promises.
Impressed though it be upon the heart by nature, and
ever insisted on in Revelation, as the basis on which
God has established all His decrees, it was to them a
hard saying. St. Paul retorts it on their consciences,
when they complained. "God," he says "will render to
every man according to his deeds. To them who by
patient continuance in well-doing seek for glory and
honour and immortality, eternal life ; *but* unto them
that are contentious, and do not obey the Truth, but
obey unrighteousness, indignation and wrath ;—tribulation and anguish upon every soul of man that doeth
evil, of the Jew first, and also of the Gentile ; but glory,

[1] Matt. xxi. 41.

honour, and peace, to every man that worketh good, to the Jew first, and also to the Gentile : for *there is no respect of persons with God.*"[1]

Such was the unchangeable Rule of God's government, as it is propounded by St. Paul in explanation of the Jewish election, and significantly prefixed to his discourse upon the Christian. Such as was the Mosaic, such also is the Gospel Covenant, made without respect of persons; rich, indeed, in privilege and promise far above the Elder Dispensation, but bearing on its front the same original avowal of impartial retribution,— "peace to every man that worketh good," "wrath to the disobedient;" predestining to glory, characters not persons, pledging the gift of perseverance not to individuals, but to a body of which the separate members might change. This is the doctrine set before us by that Apostle to whom was revealed in an extraordinary way the nature of the Christian Covenant, its peculiar blessedness, gifts, and promises. The New Covenant was, so far, not unlike the Old, as some reasoners in these days would maintain.

We are vouchsafed a further witness to it, in the favoured Evangelist, who finally closed and perfected the volume of God's revelations, after the death of his brethren. "Behold, I come quickly, and My reward is with Me, to give every man according as his work shall be..... Blessed are they that do His commandments, *that they may have right* to the tree of life, and may enter in through the gates into the city."[2]

And a third witness that the Christian Election is, like the Jewish, conditional, is our Lord's own declaration,

[1] *Rom. ii. 6—11.* [2] *Rev. xxii. 12, 14.*

which He left behind Him with His Apostles when He was leaving the world, as recorded by the same Evangelist. " If a man *abide not in Me*," He said, " he is cast forth as a branch, and is withered; and men gather them and cast them into the fire, and they are burned." And, lest restless and reluctant minds should shelter their opposition to this solemn declaration under some supposed obscurity in the expression of " abiding in Him," and say that none abide in Him but the predestined, He adds, for the removal of all doubt, " *If ye keep my commandments*, ye shall abide in my love."[1]

Lastly, in order to complete the solemn promulgation of His Eternal Rule, He exemplified it, while He spoke it, in the instance of an Apostle. He knew whom He had chosen; that they were " not all clean," that " one of them was a devil;" yet He chose all twelve, as if to show that souls chosen for eternal life might fall away. Thus, in the case of the Apostles themselves, in the very foundation of His Church, He laid deep the serious and merciful warning, if we have wisdom to lay it to heart, " Be not high-minded, but fear;" for, if God spared not Apostles, neither will He spare thee!

What solemn overpowering thoughts must have crowded on St. Matthias, when he received the greetings of the eleven Apostles, and took his seat among them as their brother! His very election was a witness against himself if he did not fulfil it. And such surely will ours be in our degree. We take the place of others who have gone before, as Matthias did; we are " baptized for the dead," filling up the ranks of soldiers,

[1] John xv. 16.

some of whom, indeed, have fought a good fight, but many of whom in every age have made void their calling. Many are called, few are chosen. The monuments of sin and unbelief are set up around us. The casting away of the Jews was the reconciling of the Gentiles. The fall of one nation is the conversion of another. The Church loses old branches, and gains new. God works according to His own inscrutable pleasure ; He has left the East, and manifested Himself Westward. Thus the Christian of every age is but the successor of the lost and of the dead. How long we of this country shall be put in trust with the Gospel, we know not ; but while we have the privilege, assuredly we do but stand in the place of Christians who have either utterly fallen away, or are so corrupted as scarcely to let their light shine before men. We are at present witnesses of the Truth ; and our very glory is our warning. By the superstitions, the profanities, the indifference, the unbelief of the world called Christian, we are called upon to be lowly-minded while we preach aloud, and to tremble while we rejoice. Let us then, as a Church and as individuals, one and all, look to Him who alone can keep us from falling. Let us with single heart look up to Christ our Saviour, and put ourselves into His hands, from whom all our strength and wisdom is derived. Let us avoid the beginnings of temptation ; let us watch and pray lest we enter into it. Avoiding all speculations which are above us, let us follow what tends to edifying. Let us receive into our hearts the great truth, that we who have been freely accepted and sanctified *as members of* Christ, shall hereafter be judged

to our works, done in and through Him; that the
Sacraments unite us to Him, and that faith makes the
Sacraments open their hidden virtue, and flow forth in
pardon and grace. Beyond this we may not inquire.
How it is one man perseveres and another falls, what
are the exact limits and character of our natural corruption,—these are over-subtle questions; while we know
for certain, that though we can do nothing of ourselves,
yet that salvation is in our own power, for however deep
and far-spreading is the root of evil in us, God's grace
will be sufficient for our need.

SERMON XII.

The Reverence due to the Virgin Mary.

(THE FEAST OF THE ANNUNCIATION OF THE BLESSED
VIRGIN MARY.)

"From henceforth all generations shall call me blessed."—LUKE i. 48.

TO-DAY we celebrate the Annunciation of the Virgin
Mary; when the Angel Gabriel was sent to tell her
that she was to be the Mother of our Lord, and when
the Holy Ghost came upon her, and overshadowed her
with the power of the Highest. In that great event was
fulfilled her anticipation as expressed in the text. All
generations have called her blessed.[1] The Angel began
the salutation; he said, "Hail, thou that art highly
favoured; the Lord is with thee; blessed[2] art thou
among women." Again he said, "Fear not, Mary, for
thou hast found favour with God; and, behold, thou shalt
conceive in thy womb, and bring forth a Son, and shalt
call His name Jesus. He shall be great, and shall be
called the Son of the Highest." Her cousin Elizabeth
was the next to greet her with her appropriate title.
Though she was filled with the Holy Ghost at the time

[1] μακαριοῦσι.   [2] εὐλογημένη.

she spake, yet, far from thinking herself by such a gift equalled to Mary. she was thereby moved to use the lowlier and more reverent language. "She spake out with a loud voice, and said, *Blessed art thou* among women, and blessed is the fruit of thy womb. And whence is this to me, that the mother of my Lord should come to me?" .... Then she repeated, "Blessed is she that believed; for there shall be a performance of those things which were told her from the Lord." Then it was that Mary gave utterance to her feelings in the Hymn which we read in the Evening Service. How many and complicated must they have been! In her was now to be fulfilled that promise which the world had been looking out for during thousands of years. The Seed of the woman, announced to guilty Eve, after long delay, was at length appearing upon earth, and was to be born of her. In her the destinies of the world were to be reversed, and the serpent's head bruised. On her was bestowed the greatest honour ever put upon any individual of our fallen race. God was taking upon Him her flesh, and humbling Himself to be called her offspring;—such is the deep mystery! She of course would feel her own inexpressible unworthiness; and again, her humble lot, her ignorance, her weakness in the eyes of the world. And she had moreover, we may well suppose, that purity and innocence of heart, that bright vision of faith, that confiding trust in her God, which raised all these feelings to an intensity which we, ordinary mortals, cannot understand. *We* cannot understand them; we repeat her hymn day after day,—yet consider for an instant in how different a mode *we* say it from that in which she at first uttered it. *We* even hurry it over, and do not think of the meaning of those words which came from the most highly favoured, awfully gifted of the children of men. " My soul doth magnify the Lord, and my spirit hath rejoiced in God my Saviour. For He hath regarded the low estate of His hand-maiden : for, behold, from henceforth all generations shall call me blessed. For He that is mighty hath done to me great things ; and holy is His name. And His mercy is on them that fear Him from generation to generation."

Now let us consider in what respects the Virgin Mary is Blessed ; a title first given her by the Angel, and next by the Church in all ages since to this day.

1. I observe, that in her the curse pronounced on Eve was changed to a blessing. Eve was doomed to bear children in sorrow ; but now this very dispensation, in which the token of Divine anger was conveyed, was made the means by which salvation came into the world. Christ might have descended from heaven, as He went back, and as He will come again. He might have taken on Himself a body from the ground, as Adam was given ; or been formed, like Eve, in some other divinely-devised way. But, far from this, God sent forth His Son (as St. Paul says), "made of a woman." For it has been His gracious purpose to turn *all* that is ours from evil to good. Had He so pleased, He might have found, when we sinned, other beings to do Him service, casting us into hell ; but He purposed to save and to change *us*. And in like manner all that belongs to us, our reason, our affections, *our pursuits*, our relations in life, He

needs nothing put aside in His disciples, but all sanctified. Therefore, instead of sending His Son from heaven.
He sent Him forth as the Son of Mary, to show that all
our sorrow and all our corruption can be blessed and
changed by Him. The very punishment of the fall, the
very taint of birth-sin, admits of a cure by the coming
of Christ.

2. But there is another portion of the original punishment of woman, which may be considered as repealed
when Christ came. It was said to the woman, "Thy
husband shall rule over thee;" a sentence which has
been strikingly fulfilled. Man has strength to conquer
the thorns and thistles which the earth is cursed with,
but the same strength has ever proved the fulfilment of
the punishment awarded to the woman. Look abroad
through the Heathen world, and see how the weaker
half of mankind has everywhere been tyrannized over
and debased by the strong arm of force. Consider all
those Eastern nations, which have never at any time
reverenced it, but have heartlessly made it the slave of
every bad and cruel purpose. Thus the serpent has
triumphed,—making the man still degrade himself by
her who originally tempted him, and her, who then
tempted, now suffer from him who was seduced. Nay,
even under the light of revelation, the punishment on
the woman was not removed at once. Still (in the
words of the curse), her husband ruled over her. The
very practice of polygamy and divorce, which was
suffered under the patriarchal and Jewish dispensation proves it.

But when Christ came as the seed of the woman, He

vindicated the rights and honour of His mother. Not that the distinction of ranks is destroyed under the Gospel; the woman is still made inferior to man, as he to Christ; but the slavery is done away with. St. Peter bids the husband "give honour unto the wife, *because* the weaker, in that both are heirs of the grace of life."[1] And St. Paul, while enjoining subjection upon her, speaks of the especial blessedness vouchsafed her in being the appointed entrance of the Saviour into the world. "Adam was first formed, then Eve; and Adam was not deceived, but the woman being deceived was in the transgression." But "notwithstanding, she shall be saved through the Child-bearing;"[2] that is, through the birth of Christ from Mary, which was a blessing, as upon all mankind, so peculiarly upon the woman Accordingly, from that time, Marriage has not only been restored to its original dignity, but even gifted with a spiritual privilege, as the outward symbol of the heavenly union subsisting betwixt Christ and His Church.

Thus has the Blessed Virgin, in bearing our Lord, taken off or lightened the peculiar disgrace which the woman inherited for seducing Adam, sanctifying the one part of it, repealing the other.

3. But further, she is doubtless to be accounted blessed and favoured in herself, as well as in the benefits she has done us. Who can estimate the holiness and perfection of her, who was chosen to be the Mother of Christ? If to him that hath, more is given, and holiness and Divine favour go together (and this we are

---

[1] *1 Pet. iii. 7.*   [2] 1 Tim. ii. 16.

expressly told), what must have been the transcendent purity of her, whom the Creator Spirit condescended to overshadow with His miraculous presence? What must have been her gifts, who was chosen to be the only near earthly relative of the Son of God, the only one whom He was bound by nature to revere and look up to; the one appointed to train and educate Him, to instruct Him day by day, as He grew in wisdom and in stature? This contemplation runs to a higher subject, did we dare follow it; for what, think you, was the sanctified state of that human nature, of which God formed His sinless Son; knowing as we do, " that which is born of the flesh is flesh," and that "none can bring a clean thing out of an unclean?"[1]

Now, after dwelling on thoughts such as these, when we turn back again to the Gospels, I think every one must feel some surprise, that we are not told more about the Blessed Virgin than we find there. After the circumstances of Christ's birth and infancy, we hear little of her. Little is said in praise of her. She is mentioned as attending Christ to the cross, and there committed by Him to St. John's keeping; and she is mentioned as continuing with the Apostles in prayer after His ascension; and then we hear no more of her. But here again in this silence we find instruction, as much as in the mention of her.

1. It suggests to us that Scripture was written, not to exalt this or that particular Saint, but to give glory to Almighty God. There have been thousands of holy souls in the times of which the Bible history treats

---

[1] 1 John iii. 6. Job xiv. 4.

whom we know nothing of, because their lives did not
fall upon the line of God's public dealings with man.
In Scripture we read not of all the good men who
ever were, only of a few, viz. those in whom God's
name was especially honoured. Doubtless there have
been many widows in Israel, serving God in fastings
and prayers, like Anna; but she only is mentioned in
Scripture, as being in a situation to glorify the Lord
Jesus. She spoke of the Infant Saviour "to all them
that looked for redemption in Jerusalem." Nay, for
what we know, faith like Abraham's, and zeal like
David's, have burned in the breasts of thousands whose
names have no memorial; because, I say, Scripture is
written to show us the course of God's great and marvellous providence, and we hear of those Saints only
who were the instruments of His purposes, as either
introducing or preaching His Son. Christ's favoured
Apostle was St. John, His personal friend; yet how little
do we know of St. John compared with St. Paul;—and
why? because St. Paul was the more illustrious propa-
gator and dispenser of His Truth. As St. Paul himself
said, that he "knew no man after the flesh,"[1] so His
Saviour, with somewhat a similar meaning, has hid from
us the knowledge of His more sacred and familiar
feelings, His feelings towards His Mother and His friend.
These were not to be exposed, as unfit for the world to
know,—as dangerous, because not admitting of being
known, without a risk lest the honour which those
Saints received through grace should eclipse in our
minds the honour of Him who honoured them. Had

[1] 2 Cor. v. 16.

the blessed Mary been more fully disclosed to us in the heavenly beauty and sweetness of the spirit within her, true, *she* would have been honoured, *her* gifts would have been clearly seen ; but, at the same time, the Giver would have been somewhat less contemplated, because no design or work of His would have been disclosed in her history. She would have seemingly been introduced for *her* sake, not for His sake. When a Saint is seen working *towards* an end appointed by God, we *see* him to be a mere instrument, a servant though a favoured one; and though we admire him, yet, after all, we glorify God in him. We pass on *from* him to the work to which he ministers. But, when any one is introduced, full of gifts, yet without visible and immediate subserviency to God's designs, such a one seems revealed for his own sake. We should rest, perchance, in the thought of him, and think of the creature more than the Creator. Thus it is a dangerous thing, it is too high a privilege, for sinners like ourselves, to know the best and innermost thoughts of God's servants. We cannot bear to see such men in their own place, in the retirement of private life, and the calmness of hope and joy. The higher their gifts, the less fitted they are for being seen. Even St. John the Apostle was twice tempted to fall down in worship before an Angel who showed him the things to come. And, if he who had seen the Son of God was thus overcome by the creature, how is it possible we could bear to gaze upon the creature's holiness in its fulness, especially as we should be more able to enter into it, and estimate it, than to *comprehend* the infinite perfections of the Eternal

Godhead? Therefore, many truths are, like the "things which the seven thunders uttered,"[1] "sealed up" from us. In particular, it is in mercy to us that so little is revealed about the Blessed Virgin, in mercy to our weakness, though of her there are "many things to say," yet they are "hard to be uttered, seeing we are dull of hearing."[2]

2. But, further, the more we consider who St. Mary was, the more dangerous will such knowledge of her appear to be. Other saints are but influenced or inspired by Christ, and made partakers of Him mystically. But, as to St. Mary, Christ derived His manhood from her, and so had an especial unity of nature with her; and this wondrous relationship between God and man it is perhaps impossible for us to dwell much upon without some perversion of feeling. For, truly, she is raised above the condition of sinful beings, though by nature a sinner; she is brought near to God, yet is but a creature, and seems to lack her fitting place in our limited understandings, neither too high nor too low. We cannot combine, in our thought of her, all we should ascribe with all we should withhold. Hence, following the example of Scripture, we had better only think of her with and for her Son, never separating her from Him, but using her name as a memorial of His great condescension in stooping from heaven, and not "abhorring the Virgin's womb." And this is the rule of our own Church, which has set apart only such Festivals in honour of the Blessed Mary, as may also be Festivals in honour of our Lord; the Purification commemorating His presentation in the

[1] *Rev. x. 4.*   [2] Heb. v. 11.

Temple, and the Annunciation commemorating His Incarnation. And, with this caution, the thought of her may be made most profitable to our faith; for nothing is so calculated to impress on our minds that Christ is really partaker of our nature, and in all respects man, save sin only, as to associate Him with the thought of her, by whose ministration He became our brother.

To conclude. Observe the lesson which we gain for ourselves from the history of the Blessed Virgin; that the highest graces of the soul may be matured in private, and without those fierce trials to which the many are exposed in order to their sanctification. So hard are our hearts, that affliction, pain, and anxiety are sent to humble us, and dispose us towards a true faith in the heavenly word, when preached to us. Yet it is only our extreme obstinacy of unbelief which renders this chastisement necessary. The aids which God gives under the Gospel Covenant, have power to renew and purify our hearts, without uncommon providences to discipline us into receiving them. God gives His Holy Spirit to us silently; and the silent duties of every day (it may be humbly hoped) are blest to the sufficient sanctification of thousands, whom the world knows not of. The Blessed Virgin is a memorial of this; and it is consoling as well as instructive to know it. When we quench the grace of Baptism, then it is that we need severe trials to restore us. This is the case of the multitude, whose best estate is that of chastisement, repentance, supplication, and absolution, again and again. But there are those who go on in a calm and unswerving course, *learning* day by day to love Him who has redeemed them, and overcoming the sin of their nature by His heavenly grace, as the various temptations to evil successively present themselves. And, of these undefiled followers of the Lamb, the Blessed Mary is the chief. Strong in the Lord, and in the power of His might, she "staggered not at the promise of God through unbelief;" she believed when Zacharias doubted,—with a faith like Abraham's she believed and was blessed for her belief, and had the performance of those things which were told her by the Lord. And when sorrow came upon her afterwards, it was but the blessed participation of her Son's sacred sorrows, not the sorrow of those who suffer for their sins.

If we, through God's unspeakable gift, have in any measure followed Mary's innocence in our youth, so far let us bless Him who enabled us. But so far as we are conscious of having departed from Him, let us bewail our miserable guilt. Let us acknowledge from the heart that no punishment is too severe for us, no chastisement should be unwelcome (though it is a sore thing to learn to welcome pain), if it tend to burn away the corruption which has propagated itself within us. Let us count all things as gain, which God sends to cleanse away the marks of sin and shame which are upon our foreheads. The day will come at length, when our Lord and Saviour will unveil that Sacred Countenance to the whole world, which no sinner ever yet could see and live. Then will the world be forced to look upon Him, whom they pierced with their unrepented wickednesses ; "all faces will gather blackness."[1] Then they will discern, what they

---

[1] Joel ii. 6

do not now believe, the utter deformity of sin ; while the Saints of the Lord, who seemed on earth to bear but the countenance of common men, will wake up one by one after His likeness, and be fearful to look upon. And then will be fulfilled the promise pledged to the Church on the Mount of Transfiguration. It will be "good" to be with those whose tabernacles might have been a snare to us on earth, had we been allowed to build them. We shall see our Lord, and His Blessed Mother, the Apostles and Prophets, and all those righteous men whom we now read of in history, and long to know. Then we shall be taught in those Mysteries which are now above us. In the words of the Apostle, "Beloved, now are we the sons of God, and it doth not yet appear what we shall be ; but we know that, when He shall appear, we shall be like Him, for we shall see Him as He is : and every man that hath this hope in Him, purifieth himself, even as He is pure."[1]

[1] 1 John iii. 2, 3. On the subject of this Sermon, *vide* Bishop Bull's Sermon on Luke i. 48, 49.

SERMON XIII.

Christ, a Quickening Spirit.

(THE FEAST OF THE RESURRECTION OF OUR LORD.)

"Why seek ye the living among the dead? He is not here, but is risen."
—LUKE xxiv. 5, 6.

SUCH is the triumphant question with which the
Holy Angels put to flight the sadness of the women
on the morning of Christ's resurrection. "O ye of little
faith," less faith than love, more dutiful than understanding, why come ye to anoint His Body on the third
day? Why seek ye the Living Saviour in the tomb?
The time of sorrow is run out; victory has come,
according to His Word, and ye recollect it not. "He
is not here, but is risen!"

These were deeds done and words spoken eighteen
hundred years since; so long ago, that in the world's
thought they are as though they never had been; yet
they hold good to this day. Christ is to us now, just
what He was in all His glorious Attributes on the morning of the Resurrection; and we are blessed in knowing
it, even more than the women to whom the Angels spoke,
according to His own assurance, "Blessed are they that
have not seen, and yet have believed."

On this highest of Festivals, I will attempt to set before you one out of the many comfortable subjects of reflection which it suggests.

1. First, then, observe how Christ's resurrection harmonizes with the history of His birth. David had foretold that His " soul should not be left in hell " (that is, the unseen state), neither should " the Holy One of God see corruption." And with a reference to this prophecy, St. Peter says, that it " was not possible that He should be holden of death ;"[1] as if there were some hidden inherent vigour in Him, which secured His manhood from dissolution. The greatest infliction of pain and violence could only destroy its powers for a season ; but nothing could make it decay. " Thou wilt not suffer Thy *Holy* One to see corruption ;" so says the Scripture, and elsewhere calls Him the "*Holy* child Jesus."[2] These expressions carry our minds back to the Angels' announcement of His birth, in which His incorruptible and immortal nature is implied. " That *Holy* Thing " which was born of Mary, was " the Son," not of man, but " of God." Others have all been born in sin, " after Adam's own likeness, in His image,"[3] and, being born in sin, they are heirs to corruption. " By one man sin entered into the world, and death," and all its consequences, " by sin." Not one human being comes into existence without God's discerning evidences of sin attendant on his birth. But when the Word of Life was manifested in our flesh, the Holy Ghost displayed that creative hand by which, in the beginning, Eve was formed ; and the

---

[1] Ps. xvi. 10. Acts ii. 24, 27, τὸν ὅσιον.
[2] Acts iv. 27, τὸν ἅγιον. [3] Gen. v. 3.

Holy Child, thus conceived by the power of the Highest, was (as the history shows) immortal even in His mortal nature, clear from all infection of the forbidden fruit, so far as to be sinless and incorruptible. Therefore, though He was liable to death, " it was impossible He should be *holden*" of it. Death might overpower, but it could not keep possession; " it had no dominion over Him."[1] He was, in the words of the text, "*the Living* among the dead."

And hence His rising from the dead may be said to have evinced His divine original. He was "*declared* to be the Son of God with power, according to the Spirit of Holiness;" that is, His essential Godhead, "by the resurrection of the dead."[2] He had been condemned as a blasphemer by the Jewish rulers, "because He made Himself the Son of God;" and He was brought to the death of the Cross, not only as a punishment, but as a practical refutation of His claim. He was challenged by His enemies on this score: "If thou be the Son of God, come down from the cross." Thus His crucifixion was as though a trial, a new experiment on the part of Satan, who had before tempted Him, whether he was like other men, or the Son of God. Observe the event. He was obedient unto death, fulfilling the law of that disinherited nature which He had assumed; and in order, by undergoing it, to atone for our sins. So far was permitted by God's " determinate counsel and foreknowledge;" but there the triumph of His enemies, so to account it, ended,—ended with what was necessary for our redemption. He said, "It is finished;" for His

---

[1] *Rom. vi. 9*   [2] Ibid. i. 4.

humiliation was at its lowest depth when He expired.
Immediately some incipient tokens showed themselves,
that the real victory was with Him; first, the earthquake and other wonders in heaven and earth. These
even were enough to justify His claim in the judgment
of the heathen centurion; who said at once, "Truly
this *was* the Son of God." Then followed His descent
into hell, and triumph in the unseen world, whatever
that was. Lastly, that glorious deed of power on the
third morning which we now commemorate. The dead
arose. The grave could not detain Him who "had life
in Himself." He rose as a man awakes in the morning,
when sleep flies from him as a thing of course. Corruption had no power over that Sacred Body, the fruit
of a miraculous conception. The bonds of death were
broken as "green withes," witnessing by their feebleness,
that He was the Son of God.

Such is the connexion between Christ's birth and
resurrection; and more than this might be ventured
concerning His incorrupt nature, were it not better to
avoid all risk of trespassing upon that reverence with
which we are bound to regard it. Something might be
said concerning His personal appearance, which seems to
have borne the marks of one who was not tainted with
birth-sin. Men could scarce keep from worshipping
Him. When the Pharisees sent to seize Him, all the
officers, on His merely acknowledging Himself to be
Him whom they sought, fell backwards from His presence to the ground. They were scared as brutes are
said to bo by the voice of man. Thus, being created in
God's image, He was the second Adam; and much more

than Adam in His secret nature, which beamed through His tabernacle of flesh with awful purity and brightness even in the days of His humiliation. " The first man was of the earth, earthy ; the second man was the Lord from heaven."[1]

2. And if such was His visible Majesty, while He yet was subject to temptation, infirmity, and pain, much more abundant was the manifestation of His Godhead, when He was risen from the dead. Then the Divine Essence streamed forth (so to say) on every side, and environed His Manhood, as in a cloud of glory. So transfigured was His Sacred Body, that He who had deigned to be born of a woman, and to hang upon the cross, had subtle virtue in Him, like a spirit, to pass through the closed doors to His assembled followers ; while, by condescending to the trial of their senses, He showed that it was no mere spirit, but He Himself, as before, with wounded hands and pierced side, who spoke to them. He manifested Himself to them, in this His exalted state, that they might be His witnesses to the people ; witnesses of those separate truths which man's reason cannot combine, that He had a real human body, that it was partaker in the properties of His Soul, and that it was inhabited by the Eternal Word. They handled Him,—they saw Him come and go, when the doors were shut,—they felt, what they could not see, but could witness even unto death, that He was " their Lord and their God ;"—a triple evidence, first, of His Atonement; next of their own Resurrection unto glory; lastly, of His Divine Power to conduct them safely to it.

[1] *1 Cor.* xv. 47.

Thus manifested as perfect God and perfect man, in the fulness of His sovereignty, and the immortality of His holiness, He ascended up on high to take possession of His kingdom. There He remains till the last day, "Wonderful, Counsellor, The Mighty God, The Everlasting Father, The Prince of Peace."[1]

3. He ascended into heaven, that He might plead our cause with the Father; as it is said, "He ever liveth to make intercession for us."[2] Yet we must not suppose, that in leaving us He closed the gracious economy of His Incarnation, and withdrew the ministration of His incorruptible Manhood from His work of loving mercy towards us. "The Holy One of God" was ordained, not only to die for us, but also to be "the beginning" of a new "creation" unto holiness, in our sinful race; to refashion soul and body after His own likeness, that they might be "raised up together, and sit together in heavenly places in Christ Jesus." Blessed for ever be His Holy Name! before He went away, He remembered our necessity, and completed His work, bequeathing to us a special mode of approaching Him, a Holy Mystery, in which we receive (we know not how) the virtue of that Heavenly Body, which is the life of all that believe. This is the blessed Sacrament of the Eucharist, in which "Christ is evidently set forth crucified among us;" that we, feasting upon the Sacrifice, may be "partakers of the Divine Nature." Let us give heed lest we be in the number of those who "discern not the Lord's Body," and the "exceeding great and precious promises" which are

---

[1] Isa. ix. 6.　　　　[2] Heb. vii. 25.

made to those who partake it. And since there is some
danger of this, I will here make some brief remarks
concerning this great gift; and, pray God that our
words and thoughts may accord to its unspeakable
sacredness.

Christ says, "As the Father hath life in Himself, so
hath He given also to the Son to have life in Himself;"
and afterwards He says, "Because I live, ye shall live
also."[1] It would seem then, that as Adam is the author
of death to the whole race of men, so is Christ the
Origin of immortality. When Adam ate the forbidden
fruit, it was as a poison spreading through his whole
nature, soul and body; and thence through every one of
his descendants. It was said to him, when he was
placed in the garden, "In the day that thou eatest
thereof, thou shalt surely die;" and we are told expressly, "in Adam *all* die." We all are born heirs to
that infection of nature which followed upon his fall.
But we are also told, "As in Adam all die, even so in
Christ shall all be made alive;" and the same law of
God's providence is maintained in both cases. Adam
spreads poison; Christ diffuses life eternal. Christ
communicates life to us, one by one, by means of that
holy and incorrupt nature which He assumed for our
redemption; how, we know not; still, though by an
unseen, surely by a real communication of Himself.
Therefore St. Paul says, that "the last Adam was made"
not merely "a living soul," but " a *quickening*" or life-
giving "Spirit," as being "the Lord from heaven."[2]
Again, in His own gracious words, He is "the Bread of

---

[1] *John v. 26; xiv. 10.*   [2] Gen. ii. 17. 1 Cor. xv. 22, 45, 47.

life." " The Bread of God is He which cometh down
from heaven, and giveth life unto the world;" or, as He
says more plainly, " I am the Bread which came down
from heaven;" " I am that Bread of life;" " I am the
living Bread which came down from heaven; if any
man eat of this bread, he shall live for ever: and the
Bread that I will give is My flesh, which I will give for
the life of the world." And again, still more clearly,
" Whoso eateth My flesh, and drinketh My blood, hath
eternal life; and I will raise him up at the last day."[1]
Why should this communion with Him be thought incredible, mysterious and sacred as it is, when we know
from the Gospel how marvellously He wrought, in the
days of His humiliation, towards those who approached
Him? We are told on one occasion, " the whole multitude sought to touch Him; for there went *virtue* out
of Him, and healed them all." Again, when the woman
with the issue of blood touched Him, He "immediately
knew that virtue had gone out of Him."[2] Such grace
was invisible, known only by the cure it effected, as in
the case of the woman. Let us not doubt, though we
do not sensibly approach Him, that He can still give us
the virtue of His purity and incorruption, as He has
promised, and in a more heavenly and spiritual manner,
than "in the days of His flesh;" in a way which does
not remove the mere ailments of this temporal state, but
sows the seed of eternal life in body and soul. Let us
not deny Him the glory of His life-giving holiness, that

---

[1] John vi. 33—54.
[2] Luke vi. 19. Mark v. 30. *Vide* Knox on the Eucharist. Remains,
vol. ii.

diffusive grace which is the renovation of our whole
race, a spirit quick and powerful and piercing, so as to
leaven the whole mass of human corruption, and make
it live. He is the first-fruits of the Resurrection : we
follow Him each in his own order, as we are hallowed
by His inward presence. And in this sense, among
others, Christ, in the Scripture phrase, is "formed in us;"
that is, the communication is made to us of His new
nature, which sanctifies the soul, and makes the body
immortal. In like manner we pray in the Service of
the Communion that " our sinful bodies may be made
clean by His body, and our souls washed through His
most precious blood ; and that we may evermore dwell
in Him and He in us."

Such then is our risen Saviour in Himself and
towards us :—conceived by the Holy Ghost; holy from
the womb; dying, but abhorring corruption; rising
again the third day by His own inherent life ; exalted
as the Son of God and Son of man, to raise us after
Him; and filling us incomprehensibly with His immortal
nature, till we become like Him; filling us with a
spiritual life which may expel the poison of the tree of
knowledge, and restore us to God. How wonderful a
work of grace! Strange it was that Adam should be
our death, but stranger still and very gracious, that God
Himself should be our life, by means of that human
tabernacle which He has taken on Himself.

O blessed day of the Resurrection, which of old time
was called the Queen of Festivals, and raised among
Christians an anxious, nay contentious diligence duly to
honour it! Blessed day, once only passed in sorrow,

when the Lord actually rose, and the disciples believed
not; but ever since a day of joy to the faith and love of
the Church! In ancient times, Christians all over the
world began it with a morning salutation. Each man
said to his neighbour, " Christ is risen;" and his neighbour answered him, " Christ is risen indeed, and hath
appeared unto Simon." Even to Simon, the coward
disciple who denied Him thrice, Christ is risen ; even to
us, who long ago vowed to obey Him, and have yet so
often denied Him before men, so often taken part with
sin, and followed the world, when Christ called us another way. " Christ is risen indeed, and hath appeared
to Simon!" to Simon Peter the favoured Apostle, on
whom the Church is built, Christ has appeared. He
has appeared to His Holy Church first of all, and in the
Church He dispenses blessings, such as the world knows
not of. Blessed are they if they knew their blessedness,
who are allowed, as we are, week after week, and
Festival after Festival, to seek and find in that Holy
Church the Saviour of their souls! Blessed are they
beyond language or thought, to whom it is vouchsafed
to receive those tokens of His love, which cannot otherwise be gained by man, the pledges and means of His
special presence, in the Sacrament of His Supper; who
are allowed to eat and drink the food of immortality,
and receive life from the bleeding side of the Son of
God! Alas! by what strange coldness of heart, or
perverse superstition is it, that any one called Christian
keeps away from that heavenly ordinance? Is it not
very grievous that there should be any one who fears to
share in the greatest conceivable blessing which could

come upon sinful men? What in truth is that fear, but unbelief, a slavish sin-loving obstinacy, if it leads a man to go year after year without the spiritual sustenance which God has provided for him? Is it wonderful that, as time goes on, he should learn deliberately to doubt of the grace therein given? that he should no longer look upon the Lord's Supper as a heavenly feast, or the Lord's Minister who consecrates it as a chosen vessel, or that Holy Church in which he ministers as a Divine Ordinance, to be cherished as the parting legacy of Christ to a sinful world? Is it wonderful that seeing he sees not, and hearing he hears not; and that, lightly regarding all the gifts of Christ, he feels no reverence for the treasure-house wherein they are stored?

But we, who trust that so far we are doing God's will, inasmuch as we are keeping to those ordinances and rules which His Son has left us, we may humbly rejoice in this day, with a joy the world cannot take away, any more than it can understand. Truly, in this time of rebuke and blasphemy, we cannot but be sober and subdued in our rejoicing; yet our peace and joy may be deeper and fuller even for that very seriousness. For nothing can harm those who bear Christ within them. Trial or temptation, time of tribulation, time of wealth, pain, bereavement, anxiety, sorrow, the insults of the enemy, the loss of worldly goods, nothing can "separate us from the love of God, which is in Christ Jesus our Lord."[1] This the Apostle told us long since; but we, in this age of the world, over and above his word, have the experience of many centuries for our comfort. We

[1] Rom. viii. 39.

have his own history to show us how Christ within us is stronger than the world around us, and will prevail. We have the history of all his fellow-sufferers, of all the Confessors and Martyrs of early times and since, to show us that Christ's arm " is not shortened, that it cannot save ; " that faith and love have a real abiding-place on earth ; that, come what will, His grace is· sufficient for His Church, and His strength made perfect in weakness ; that, " even to old age, and to hoar hairs, He will carry and deliver " her; that, in whatever time the powers of evil give challenge, Martyrs and Saints will start forth again, and rise from the˙ dead, as plentiful as though they had never been before, even " the souls of them that were beheaded for the witness of Jesus, and for the Word of God, and which had not worshipped the beast, neither his image, neither had received his mark upon their foreheads, or in their hands."[1]

Meantime, while Satan only threatens, let us possess our hearts in patience ; try to keep quiet ; aim at obeying God, in all things, little as well as great; do the duties of our calling which lie before us, day by day; and " take no thought for the morrow, for sufficient unto the day is the evil thereof."[2]

[1] Rev. xx. 4.   [2] Matt. vi. 34.

SERMON XIV.

𝔖𝔞𝔳𝔦𝔫𝔤 𝔎𝔫𝔬𝔴𝔩𝔢𝔡𝔤𝔢.

(MONDAY IN EASTER WEEK.)

" Hereby do we know that we know Him, if we keep His commandments."—I JOHN ii. 3.

TO know God and Christ, in Scripture language, seems to mean to live under the conviction of His presence, who is to our bodily eyes unseen. It is, in fact, to have faith, according to St. Paul's account of faith, as the substance and evidence of what is invisible. It is faith, but not faith such as a Heathen might have, but Gospel faith; for only in the Gospel has God so revealed Himself, as to allow of that kind of faith which may be called, in a special manner, knowledge. The faith of Heathens was *blind;* it was more or less a moving forward in the darkness, with hand and foot;— therefore the Apostle says, "if haply they might *feel* after Him." [1] But the Gospel is a *manifestation,* and therefore addressed to the eyes of our mind. Faith is

[1] Acts xvii. 27.

the same principle as before, but with the opportunity
of acting through a more certain and satisfactory sense
We recognise objects by the eye at once; but not by
the touch.   We know them when we see them, but
scarcely till then.   Hence it is, that the New Testament
says so much on the subject of spiritual knowledge.
For instance, St. Paul prays that the Ephesians may receive " the spirit of wisdom and revelation in the knowledge of Christ, the eyes of their understanding being
enlightened;"   and he says, that the Colossians had
"put on the new man, which is renewed in knowledge,
after the image of Him that created him."   St. Peter, in
like manner, addresses his brethren with the salutation
of " Grace and peace, through the knowledge of God, and
of Jesus our Lord ; " according to the declaration of our
Lord Himself, " This is life eternal, to know Thee, the
only true God, and Jesus Christ whom Thou hast sent."[1]
Not of course as if Christian faith had not still abundant
exercise for the other senses (so to call them) of the soul;
but that the eye is its peculiar sense, by which it is
distinguished from the faith of Heathens, nay, I may
add, of Jews.

It is plain what is the object of spiritual sight which
is vouchsafed us in the Gospel,—"God manifest in the
Flesh."   He who was before unseen has shown Himself
in Christ ; not merely displayed His glory, as (for instance) in what is called a providence, or visitation, or
in miracles, or in the actions and character of inspired
men, but really He Himself has come upon earth, and
has been seen of men in human form.   In the same

[1] *Eph. i. 17, 18.   Col. iii. 10.   2 Pet. i. 2.   John xviii. 8*

kind of sense, in which we should say we saw a servant
of His, Apostle or Prophet, though we could not see his
soul, so man has seen the Invisible God; and we have
the history of His sojourn among His creatures in the
Gospels.

To know God is life eternal, and to believe in the
Gospel manifestation of Him is to know Him; but how
are we to "know that we know Him?" How are we
to be sure that we are not mistaking some dream of our
own for the true and clear Vision? How can we tell
we are not like gazers upon a distant prospect through
a misty atmosphere, who mistake one object for another?
The text answers us clearly and intelligibly; though
some Christians have recourse to other proofs of it, or
will not have patience to ask themselves the question.
They say they are quite certain that they have true
faith; for faith carries with it its own evidence, and
admits of no mistaking the true spiritual conviction
being unlike all others. On the other hand, St. John says,
"Hereby do we know that we know Him, if we keep
His commandments." Obedience is the test of Faith.

Thus the whole duty and work of a Christian is made
up of these two parts, Faith and Obedience; "looking
unto Jesus," the Divine Object as well as Author of our
faith, and acting according to His will. Not as if a certain frame of mind, certain notions, affections, feelings,
and tempers, were not a necessary condition of a saving
state; but, so it is, the Apostle does not insist upon it,
as if it were sure to follow, if our hearts do but grow
into these two chief objects, the view of God in Christ
and the *diligent aim to* obey Him in our conduct.

I conceive that we are in danger, in this day, of insisting on neither of these as we ought; regarding all true and careful consideration of the Object of faith, as barren orthodoxy, technical subtlety, and the like, and all due earnestness about good works as a mere cold and formal morality; and, instead, making religion, or rather (for this is the point) making the test of our being religious, to consist in our having what is called a spiritual state of heart, to the comparative neglect of the Object from which it must arise, and the works in which it should issue. At this season, when we are especially engaged in considering the full triumph and manifestation of our Lord and Saviour, when He was "declared to be the Son of God with power, by the resurrection from the dead," it may be appropriate to make some remarks on an error which goes far to deprive us of the benefit of His condescension.

St. John speaks of knowing Christ and of keeping His commandments, as the two great departments of religious duty and blessedness. To know Christ is (as I have said) to discern the Father of all, as manifested through His Only-begotten Son Incarnate. In the natural world we have glimpses, frequent and startling, of His glorious Attributes; of His power, wisdom, and goodness; of His holiness, His fearful judgments, His long remembrance of evil, His long-suffering towards sinners, and His strange encompassing mercy at times when we least looked for it. But to us mortals, who live for a day, and see but an arm's length, such disclosures are like reflections of a prospect in a broken mirror; they *do not enable* us in any comfortable sense to know God.

They are such as faith may use indeed, but hardly enjoy. This then was one among the benefits of Christ's coming, that the Invisible God was then revealed in the form and history of man, revealed in those respects in which sinners most required to know Him, and nature spoke least distinctly, as a Holy yet Merciful Governor of His creatures. And thus the Gospels, which contain the memorials of this wonderful grace, are our principal treasures. They may be called the text of the Revelation; and the Epistles, especially St. Paul's, are as comments upon it, unfolding and illustrating it in its various parts, raising history into doctrine, ordinances into sacraments, detached words or actions into principles, and thus everywhere dutifully preaching His Person, work, and will. St. John is both Prophet and Evangelist, recording and commenting on the Ministry of his Lord. Still, in every case, He is the chief Prophet of the Church, and His Apostles do but explain His words and actions; according to His own account of the guidance promised to them, that it should "glorify" Him. The like service is ministered to Him by the Creeds and doctrinal expositions of the early Church, which we retain in our Services. They speak of no ideal being, such as the imagination alone contemplates, but of the very Son of God, whose life is recorded in the Gospels. Thus every part of the Dispensation tends to the manifestation of Him who is its centre.

Turning from Him to ourselves, we find a short rule given us, "If ye love Me, keep My commandments." "He that saith he abideth in Him, ought himself also so to walk, even as He walked." "If ye then be risen with Christ, seek those things which are above, where Christ sitteth on the right hand of God."[1] This is all that is put upon us, difficult indeed to perform, but easy to understand; all that is put upon us,—and for this plain reason, because Christ has done everything else. He has freely chosen us, died for us, regenerated us, and now ever liveth for us; what remains? Simply that we should do as He has done to us, showing forth His glory by good works. Thus a correct (or as we commonly call it), an orthodox faith and an obedient life, is the whole duty of man. And so, most surely, it has ever been accounted. Look into the records of the early Church, or into the writings of our own revered bishops and teachers, and see whether this is not the sum total of religion, according to the symbols of it in which children are catechized, the Creed, the Lord's Prayer, and the Ten Commandments.

However, it is objected that such a view of religious duty encourages self-deception; that a man who does no more than believe aright, and keep God's commandments, is what is called a formalist; that his heart is not interested in the matter, his affections remain unrenewed; and that, till a change takes place there, all the faith and all the obedience which mind can conceive are but external, and avail nothing; that to his heart therefore we must make our appeal, that we must bid him search himself, examine his motives, look narrowly lest he rest upon himself, and be sure that his feelings and thoughts are spiritual before he takes to himself any comfort. The merits of this view of religion shall be

[1] John xiv. 15. 1 John ii. 6. Col. iii. 1.

considered hereafter; at present, let us take it merely
in the light of an objection to what has been already
stated. I ask then in reply, how is a man to know that
his motives and affections are right except by their
fruits? Can they possibly be their own evidence? Are
they like colours, which a man knows at once without
test or calculation? Is not every feeling and opinion,
of one colour or another, fair or unpleasant, in each
man's own judgment, according to the centre light which
is set up in his soul? Is not the light that is in a man
sometimes even darkness, sometimes twilight, and sometimes of this hue or that, tinging every part of himself
with its own peculiarity? How then is it possible that
a man can duly examine his feelings and affections by
the light within him? how can he accurately decide
upon their character, whether Christian or not? It is
necessary then that he go out of himself in order to
assay and ascertain the nature of the principles which
govern him; that is, he must have recourse to his
works, and compare them with Scripture, as the only
evidence to himself, whether or not his heart is perfect
with God. It seems, therefore, that the proposed
inquiry into the workings of a man's mind means nothing at all, comes to no issue, leaves us where it found
us, unless we adopt the notion (which is seldom however openly maintained), that religious faith is its own
evidence.

On the other hand, deeds of obedience are an intelligible evidence, nay, the sole evidence possible, and, on
the whole, a satisfactory evidence of the reality of our
faith. I *do not say that* this or that good work tells

anything; but a course of obedience says much. Various deeds, done in different departments of duty, support and attest each other. Did a man act merely a bold and firm part, he would have cause to say to himself, "Perhaps all this is mere pride and obstinacy." Were he merely yielding and forgiving,—he might be indulging a natural indolence of mind. Were he merely industrious,—this might consist with ill-temper, or selfishness. Did he merely fulfil the duties of his temporal calling,—he would have no proof that he had given his heart to God at all. Were he merely regular at Church and Holy Communion,—many a man is such who has a lax conscience, who is not scrupulously fair-dealing, or is censorious, or niggardly. Is he what is called a domestic character, amiable, affectionate, fond of his family? let him beware lest he put wife and children in the place of God who gave them. Is he only temperate, sober, chaste, correct in his language? it may arise from mere dulness and insensibility, or may consist with spiritual pride. Is he cheerful and obliging? it may arise from youthful spirits and ignorance of the world. Does he choose his friends by a strictly orthodox rule? he may be harsh and uncharitable; or, is he zealous and serviceable in defending the Truth? still he may be unable to condescend to men of low estate, to rejoice with those who rejoice, and to weep with those who weep. No one is without some good quality or other: Balaam had a scruple about misrepresenting God's message, Saul was brave, Joab was loyal, the Bethel Prophet reverenced God's servants, the witch of Endor was hospitable; and therefore, of

course, no one good deed or disposition is the criterion
of a spiritual mind. Still, on the other hand, there is
no one of its characteristics which has not its appropriate outward evidence; and in proportion as these
external acts are multiplied and varied, so does the
evidence of it become stronger and more consoling.
General conscientiousness is the only assurance we can
have of possessing it; and at this we must aim, determining to obey God consistently, with a jealous care-
fulness about all things, little and great. This is, in
Scripture language, to "serve God with a perfect heart;"
as you will see at once, if you compare the respective
reformations of Jehu and Josiah. As far then as a man
has reason to hope that he is *consistent,* so far may he
humbly trust that he has true faith. To be consistent,
to "walk in all the ordinances of the Lord blameless,"
is his one business; still, all along looking reverently
towards the Great Object of faith, the Father, the Son,
and the Holy Ghost, Three Persons, One God, and the
Son Incarnate for our salvation. Certainly he will
have enough to direct his course by, with God in his
eye, and his work in his hand, though he forbear curious
experiments about his sensations and emotions ; and, if
it be objected that an evidence from works is but a cold
comfort, as being at best but faint and partial, I reply,
that, after all, it is more than sinners have a right to
ask,—that if it be little at first, it grows with our
growth in grace,—and moreover, that such an evidence,
more than any other, throws us in faith upon the loving-
kindness and meritorious sufferings of our Saviour.
Surely, *even our best doings* have that taint of sinfulness

pervading them, which will remind us ever, while we regard them, where our True Hope is lodged. Men are satisfied with themselves, not when they attempt, but when they neglect the details of duty. Disobedience blinds the conscience; obedience makes it keen-sighted and sensitive. The more we *do*, the more shall we trust in Christ; and that surely is no morose doctrine, which, after giving us whatever evidence of our safety can be given, leads us to soothe our selfish restlessness, and forget our fears, in the vision of the Incarnate Son of God.

Lastly, it may be objected, that, since many deeds of obedience are themselves acts of the mind, to do them well we must necessarily examine our feelings; that we cannot pray, for instance, without reflecting on ourselves as we use the words of prayer, and keeping our thoughts upon God; that we cannot repress anger or impatience, or cherish loving and forgiving thoughts, without searching and watching ourselves. But such an argument rests on a misconception of what I have been saying. All I would maintain is, that our duty lies in acts,— acts of course of every kind, acts of the mind, as well as of the tongue, or of the hand; but anyhow, it lies mainly in acts; it does not directly lie in moods or feelings. He who aims at praying well, loving sincerely, disputing meekly, as the respective duties occur, is wise and religious; but he who aims vaguely and generally at being in a spiritual frame of mind, is entangled in a deceit of words, which gain a meaning only by being made mischievous. Let us do our duty *as it* presents itself; this is the secret of true faith and peace. We have power over our deeds, under God's grace; we have no direct power over our habits. Let us but secure our actions, as God would have them, and our habits will follow. Suppose a religious man, for instance, in the society of strangers; he takes things as they come, discourses naturally, gives his opinion soberly, and does good according to each opportunity of good. His heart is in his work, and his thoughts rest without effort on his God and Saviour. This is the way of a Christian; he leaves it to the ill-instructed to endeavour after a (so-called) spiritual frame of mind amid the bustle of life, which has no existence except in attempt and profession. True spiritual-mindedness is unseen by man, like the soul itself, of which it is a quality; and as the soul is known by its operations, so it is known by its fruits.

I will add too, that the office of self-examination lies rather in detecting what is bad in us than in ascertaining what is good. No harm can follow from contemplating our sins, so that we keep Christ before us, and attempt to overcome them; such a review of self will but lead to repentance and faith. And, while it does this, it will undoubtedly be moulding our hearts into a higher and more heavenly state;—but still indirectly; —just as the mean is attained in action or art, not by directly contemplating and aiming at it, but negatively, by avoiding extremes.

To conclude. The essence of Faith is to look out of ourselves; now, consider what manner of a believer he is who imprisons himself in his own thoughts, and rests on *the workings of* his own mind, and thinks of

II]

his Saviour as an idea of his imagination, instead of putting self aside, and living upon Him who speaks in the Gospels.

So much then, by way of suggestion, upon the view of Religious Faith, which has ever been received in the Church Catholic, and which, doubtless, is saving. To-morrow I propose to speak more particularly of that other system, to which these latter times have given birth.

SERMON XV.

Self-Contemplation.

" Looking unto Jesus, the Author and Finisher of our faith."—
HEBREWS xii. 2.

SURELY it is our duty ever to look off ourselves, and
to look unto Jesus, that is, to shun the contemplation of our own feelings, emotions, frame and state
of mind, as if that were the main business of religion,
and to leave these mainly to be secured in their fruits.
Some remarks were made yesterday upon this " more
excellent" and Scriptural way of conducting ourselves,
as it has ever been received in the Church ; now let us
consider the merits of the rule for holy living, which
the fashion of this day would substitute for it.

Instead of looking off to Jesus, and thinking little of
ourselves, it is at present thought necessary, among the
mixed multitude of religionists, to examine the heart
with a view of ascertaining whether it is in a spiritual
state or no. A spiritual frame of mind is considered to
be one in which the heinousness of sin is perceived,
our utter worthlessness, the impossibility of our saving

M 2

ourselves, the necessity of some Saviour, the sufficiency of
our Lord Jesus Christ to be that Saviour, the unbounded
riches of His love, the excellence and glory of His work
of Atonement, the freeness and fulness of His grace, the
high privilege of communion with Him in prayer, and
the desirableness of walking with Him in all holy and
loving obedience; all of them solemn truths, too solemn
to be lightly mentioned, but our hearty reception of
which is scarcely ascertainable by a direct inspection of
our feelings.   Moreover, if one doctrine must be selected
above the rest as containing the essence of the truths,
which (according to this system) are thus vividly understood by the spiritual Christian, it is that of the necessity
of renouncing our own righteousness for the righteousness provided by our Lord and Saviour; which is considered, not as an elementary and simple principle (as
it really is), but as rarely and hardly acknowledged by
any man, especially repugnant to a certain (so-called)
pride of heart, which is supposed to run through the
whole race of Adam, and to lead every man instinctively
to insist even before God on the proper merit of his
good deeds; so that, to trust in Christ, is not merely
the work of the Holy Spirit (as all good in our souls
is), but is the especial and critical event which marks a
man, as issuing from darkness, and sealed unto the
privileges and inheritance of the sons of God.   In other
words, the doctrine of Justification by Faith is accounted
to be the one cardinal point of the Gospel; and it is
in vain to admit it readily as a clear Scripture truth
(which it is), and to attempt to go on unto perfection:
the very wish to pass forward is interpreted into a

wish to pass over it, and the test of believing it at all, is in fact to insist upon no doctrine but it. And this peculiar mode of inculcating that great doctrine of the Gospel is a proof (if proof were wanting) that the persons who adopt it are not solicitous even about *it* on its own score merely, considered as (what is called) a dogma, but as ascertaining and securing (as they hope) a certain state of heart. For, not content with the simple admission of it on the part of another, they proceed to divide faith into its kinds, living and dead, and to urge against him, that the Truth may be held in a carnal and unrenewed mind, and that men may speak without real feelings and convictions. Thus it is clear they do not contend for the doctrine of Justification as a truth external to the mind, or article of faith, any more than for the doctrine of the Trinity. On the other hand, since they use the same language about dead and living faith, however exemplary the life and conduct be of the individual under their review, they as plainly show that neither are the fruits of righteousness in their system an evidence of spiritual-mindedness, but that a something is to be sought for in the frame of mind itself. All this is not stated at present by way of objection, but in order to settle accurately what they mean to maintain. So now we have the two views of doctrine clearly before us :— the ancient and universal teaching of the Church, which insists on the Objects and fruits of faith, and considers the spiritual character of that faith itself sufficiently secured, if these are as they should be ; and the method, *now in* esteem, of attempting instead to secure directly and primarily that "mind of the Spirit," which may savingly receive the truths, and fulfil the obedience of the Gospel. That such a spiritual temper is indispensable, is agreed on all hands. The simple question is, whether it is formed by the Holy Spirit immediately acting upon our minds, or, on the other hand, by our own particular acts (whether of faith or obedience), prompted, guided, and prospered by Him; whether it is ascertainable otherwise than by its fruits; whether such frames of mind as *are* directly ascertainable and profess to be spiritual, are not rather a delusion, a mere excitement, capricious feeling, fanatic fancy, and the like.—So much then by way of explanation.

1. Now, in the first place, this modern system certainly does disparage the revealed doctrines of the Gospel, however its more moderate advocates may shrink from admitting it. Considering a certain state of heart to be the main thing to be aimed at, they avowedly make the "truth as it is in Jesus," the definite Creed of the Church, secondary in their teaching and profession. They will defend themselves indeed from the appearance of undervaluing it, by maintaining that the existence of right religious affections is a security for sound views of doctrine. And this is abstractedly true;—but not true in the use they make of it: for they unhappily conceive that they can ascertain in each other the presence of these affections; and when they find men possessed of them (as they conceive), yet not altogether orthodox in their belief, then they relax a little, and argue that an admission of *(what they* call) the strict and technical niceties of

doctrine, whether about the Consubstantiality of the Son or the Hypostatic Union, is scarcely part of the definition of a spiritual believer. In order to support this position, they lay it down as self-evident, that the main purpose of revealed doctrine is to affect the heart, —that that which does not seem to affect it does not affect it,—that what does not affect it, is unnecessary, —and that the circumstance that this or that person's heart seems rightly affected, is a sufficient warrant that such Articles as he may happen to reject, may safely be universally rejected, or at least are only accidentally important. Such principles, when once become familiar to the mind, induce a certain disproportionate attention to the doctrines connected with the work of Christ, in comparison of those which relate to His Person, from their more immediately interesting and exciting cha- racter ; and carry on the more speculative and philoso- phical class to view the doctrines of Atonement and Sanctification as the essence of the Gospel, and to advocate them in the place of those " Heavenly Things " altogether, which, as theologically expressed, they have already assailed ; and of which they now openly com- plain as mysteries for bondsmen, not Gospel consola- tions. The last and most miserable stage of this false wisdom is, to deny that in matters of doctrine there is any one. sense of Scripture such, that it is true and all others false ; to make the Gospel of Truth (so far) a revelation of words and a dead letter ; to consider that inspiration speaks merely of divine operations, not of Persons ; and that that is truth to each, which each man thinks to be true, so that one man may say that

Christ is God, another deny His pre-existence, yet each have received the Truth according to the peculiar constitution of his own mind, the Scripture doctrine having no real independent substantive meaning. Thus the system under consideration tends legitimately to obliterate the great Objects brought to light in the Gospel, and to darken what I called yesterday the eye of faith,— to throw us back into the vagueness of Heathenism, when men only felt after the Divine Presence, and thus to frustrate the design of Christ's Incarnation, so far as it is a manifestation of the Unseen Creator.

2. On the other hand, the necessity of obedience in order to salvation does not suffer less from the upholders of this modern system than the articles of the Creed. They argue, and truly, that if faith is living, works must follow; but mistaking a following *in order of conception* for a following *in order of time*, they conclude that faith ever comes first, and works afterwards; and therefore, that faith must first be secured, and that, by some means in which works have no share. Thus, instead of viewing works as the concomitant development and evidence, and instrumental cause, as well as the subsequent result of faith, they lay all the stress upon the direct creation, in their minds, of faith and spiritual mindedness, which they consider to consist in certain emotions and desires, because they can form abstractedly no better or truer notion of those qualities. Then, instead of being " careful to maintain good works," they proceed to take it for granted, that since they have attained faith (as they consider), works will follow without their trouble as a matter of course. Thus the

wise are taken in their own craftiness; they attempt to reason, and are overcome by sophisms. Had they kept to the Inspired Record, instead of reasoning, their way would have been clear; and, considering the serious exhortations to keeping God's commandments, with which all Scripture abounds, from Genesis to the Apocalypse, is it not a very grave question, which the most charitable among Churchmen must put to himself, whether these random expounders of the Blessed Gospel are not risking a participation in the woe denounced against those who preach any other doctrine besides that delivered unto us, or who "take away" from the words of the Book" of revealed Truth?

3. But still more evidently do they fall into this last imputation, when we consider how they are obliged to treat the Sacred Volume altogether, in order to support the system they have adopted. Is it too much to say that, instead of attempting to harmonize Scripture with Scripture, much less referring to Antiquity to enable them to do so, they either drop altogether, or explain away, whole portions of the Bible, and those most sacred ones? How does the authority of the Psalms stand with their opinions, except at best by a forced figurative interpretation? And our Lord's discourses in the Gospels, especially the Sermon on the Mount, are they not virtually considered as chiefly important to the persons immediately addressed, and of inferior instructiveness to us how that the Spirit (as it is profanely said) is come? In short, is not the rich and varied Revelation of our merciful Lord practically reduced to a few chapters of St. Paul's Epistles, whether rightly

(as they maintain' or (as we should say) perversely understood : I: then the Romanists have added to the Word of God is it not undeniable that there is a school of religionists among us who have taken from it?

= I would remark, that the immediate tendency of these opinions is to undervalue ordinances as well as doctrines. The same argument evidently applies; for if the renewed state of heart is (as it is supposed) attained, what matter whether Sacraments have or have not been administered? The notion of invisible grace and invisible privileges is, on this supposition, altogether superseded : that of communion with Christ is limited to the mere exercise of the affections in prayer and meditation,—to sensible effects; and he who considers he has already gained this one essential gift of grace (as he calls it), may plausibly inquire, after the fashion of the day, why he need wait upon ordinances which he has anticipated in his religious attainments, - which are but means to an end which *he* has not to seek, even if they be not outward forms altogether, —and whether Christ will not accept at the last day all who believe, without inquiring if they were members of the Church, or were confirmed, or were baptized, or received the blessing of mere men who are " earthen vessels."

6. The foregoing remarks go to show the utterly unevangelical character of the system in question; unevangelic in the full sense of the word, whether by the Gospel be meant the inspired document of it, or the doctrines brought to light through it, or the Sacra- *mental* Institutions which are the gift of it, or the

theology which interprets it, or the Covenant which
is the basis of it. A few words shall now be added,
to show the inherent mischief of the system as such;
which I conceive to lie in its necessarily involving a
continual self-contemplation and reference to self, in
all departments of conduct. He who aims at attaining
sound doctrine or right practice, more or less looks
out of himself; whereas, in labouring after a certain
frame of mind, there is an habitual reflex action of
the mind upon itself. That this is really involved in
the modern system, is evident from the very doctrine
principally insisted on by it; for, as if it were not
enough for a man to look up simply to Christ for
salvation, it is declared to be necessary that he should
be able to recognise this in himself, that he should
define his own state of mind, confess he is justified by
faith alone, and explain what is meant by that confession. Now, the truest obedience is indisputably
that which is done from love of God, without narrowly
measuring the magnitude or nature of the sacrifice
involved in it. He who has learned to give names to
his thoughts and deeds, to appraise them as if for the
market, to attach to each its due measure of commendation or usefulness, will soon involuntarily corrupt his
motives by pride or selfishness. A sort of self-approbation will insinuate itself into his mind: so subtle
as not at once to be recognised by himself,—an
habitual quiet self-esteem, leading him to prefer his
own views to those of others, and a secret, if not avowed
persuasion, that he is in a different state from the
generality of those around him. This is an incidental,

though of course not a necessary evil of religious journals; nay, of such compositions as Ministerial duties involve. They lead those who write them, in some respect or other, to a contemplation of self. Moreover, as to religious journals, useful as they often are, at the same time I believe persons find great difficulty, while recording their feelings, in banishing the thought that one day these good feelings will be known to the world, and are thus insensibly led to modify and prepare their language as if for a representation. Seldom indeed is any one in the *practice* of contemplating his better thoughts or doings without proceeding to display them to others; and hence it is that it is so easy to discover a conceited man. When this is encouraged in the sacred province of religion, it produces a certain unnatural solemnity of manner, arising from a wish to be, nay, to appear spiritual, which is at once very painful to beholders, and surely quite at variance with our Saviour's rule of anointing our head and washing our face, even when we are most self-abased in heart. Another mischief arising from this self-contemplation is the peculiar kind of selfishness (if I may use so harsh a term) which it will be found to foster. They who make self instead of their Maker the great object of their contemplation will naturally exalt themselves. Without denying that the glory of God is the great end to which all things are to be referred, they will be led to connect indissolubly His glory with their own certainty of salvation; and this partly accounts for its being so common to ━━ -igid predestinarian views, and the exclusive maintenance of justification by Faith in the same persons. And for the same reason, the Scripture doctrines relative to the Church and its offices will be unpalatable to such persons; no one thing being so irreconcileable with another, as the system which makes a man's thoughts centre in himself, with that which directs them to a fountain of grace and truth, on which God has made him dependent.

And as self-confidence and spiritual pride are the legitimate results of these opinions in one set of persons, so in another they lead to a feverish anxiety about their religious state and prospects, and fears lest they are under the reprobation of their All-merciful Saviour. It need scarcely be said that a contemplation of self is a frequent attendant, and a frequent precursor of a deranged state of the mental powers.

To conclude. It must not be supposed from the foregoing remarks that I am imputing all the consequences enumerated to every one who holds the main doctrine from which they legitimately follow. Many men zealously maintain principles which they never follow out in their own minds, or after a time silently discard, except as far as words go, but which are sure to receive a full development in the history of any school or party of men which adopts them. Considered thus, as the characteristics of a school, the principles in question are doubtless antichristian; for they destroy all positive doctrine, all ordinances, all good works; they foster pride, invite hypocrisy, discourage the weak, and deceive most fatally, while they profess to be the especial antidotes to self-deception. We have seen these effects of them two centuries since in the history of the English Branch of the Church; for what we know, a more fearful triumph is still in store for them. But, however that may be, let not the watchmen of Jerusalem fail to give timely warning of the approaching enemy, or to acquit themselves of all cowardice or compliance as regards it. Let them prefer the Old Commandment, as it has been from the beginning, to any novelties of man, recollecting Christ's words, " Blessed is he that watcheth, and keepeth his garments, lest he walk naked, and they see his shame."[1]

[1] Rev. xvi. 15.

SERMON XVI.

Religious Cowardice.

(THE FEAST OF ST. MARK THE EVANGELIST.)

" Lift up the hands which hang down, and the feeble knees."—HEBREWS
xii. 12.

THE chief points of St. Mark's history are these :—
first, that he was sister's-son to Barnabas, and
taken with him and St. Paul on their first apostolical
journey; next, that after a short time he deserted
them and returned to Jerusalem; then, that after an
interval, he was St. Peter's assistant at Rome, and com-
posed his Gospel there principally from the accounts
which he received from that Apostle ; lastly, that he
was sent by him to Alexandria, in Egypt, where he
founded one of the strictest and most powerful churches
of the primitive times.

The points of *contrast* in his history are as follows :—
that first he abandoned the cause of the Gospel as soon
as danger appeared ; afterwards, he proved himself, not
merely an ordinary Christian, but a most resolute and
exact servant of God, founding and ruling that strictest
Church of *Alexandria.*

And the *instrument* of this change was, as it appears the influence of St. Peter, a fit restorer of a timid and backsliding disciple.

The *encouragement* which we derive from these circumstances in St. Mark's history, is, that the feeblest among us may through God's grace become strong. And the *warning* to be drawn from it is, to distrust ourselves; and again, not to despise weak brethren, or to despair of them, but to bear their burdens and help them forward, if so be we may restore them. Now, let us attentively consider the subject thus brought before us.

Some men are naturally impetuous and active; others love quiet and readily yield. The over-earnest must be sobered, and the indolent must be roused. The history of Moses supplies us with an instance of a proud and rash spirit, tamed down to an extreme gentleness of deportment. In the greatness of the change wrought in him, when from a fierce, though honest, avenger of his brethren, he became the meekest of men on the earth, he evidences the power of faith, the influence of the Spirit on the heart. St. Mark's history affords a specimen of the other, and still rarer change, from timidity to boldness. Difficult as it is to subdue the more violent passions, yet I believe it to be still more difficult to overcome a tendency to sloth, cowardice, and despondency. These evil dispositions cling about a man, and weigh him down. They are minute chains, binding him on every side to the earth, so that he cannot even turn himself or make an effort *to rise.* It would seem as if right principles had yet to be planted in the indolent mind; whereas violent and obstinate tempers had already something of the nature of firmness and zeal in them, or rather what will become so with care, exercise, and God's blessing. Besides, the events of life have a powerful influence in sobering the ardent or self-confident temper. Disappointments, pain, anxiety, advancing years, bring with them some natural wisdom as a matter of course; and, though such tardy improvement bespeaks but a weak faith, yet we may believe that the Holy Ghost often blesses these means, however slowly and imperceptibly. On the other hand, these same circumstances do but increase the defects of the timid and irresolute, who are made more indolent, selfish, and faint-hearted by advancing years, and find a sort of sanction of their unworthy caution in their experience of the vicissitudes of life.

St. Mark's change, therefore, may be considered even more astonishing in its nature than that of the Jewish Lawgiver. " By faith," he was " out of weakness made strong," and becomes a memorial of the more glorious and marvellous gifts of the last and spiritual Dispensation.

Observe in what St. Mark's weakness lay. There is a sudden defection, which arises from self-confidence. Such was St. Peter's. He had trusted too much to his mere good feelings; he was honest and sincere, and he thought that he could do what he wished to do. How far apart from each other are to wish and to do! yet we are apt to confuse them. Sometimes indeed earnest desire of an object will by a sudden impulse

[The upper portion of the page is illegible.]

In St. Mark's history, however, we have no evidence of self-confidence; rather, we may discern in it the state of multitudes at the present day, who proceed through life with a certain sense of religion on their minds, who have been brought up well and know the Truth, who acquit themselves respectably while danger is at a distance, but disgrace their profession when brought into any unexpected trial. His mother was a woman of influence among the Christians at Jerusalem; his mother's brother, Barnabas, was an eminent Apostle. Doubtless he had received a religious education; and, as being the friend of Apostles and in the bosom of the pure Church of Christ, he had the best models of sanctity before his eyes, the clearest teaching, the fullest influences of grace. He was shielded from temptation. The time came when his real proficiency in faith and obedience was to be tried. Paul and Barnabas were sent forth to preach to the Heathen; and they took Mark with them as an attendant. First they sailed to Cyprus, the native place of Barnabas: they travelled about it, and then crossed over to the main land. This seems to have been their first entrance upon an unknown country. Mark was discouraged at the prospect of danger, and returned to Jerusalem.

Now, who does not see that such a character as this, such a trial, and such a fall, belong to other days, besides those of the Apostles? Or rather, to put the question to us more closely, who will deny that there are multitudes in the Church at present, who have no evidence to themselves of more than that passive faith and virtue, which in Mark's case proved so unequal even to a slight trial? Who has not some misgivings of heart, lest, in times such as these, when Christian firmness is so little tried, his own loyalty to his Saviour's cause be perchance no truer or firmer than that of the sister's-son of a great Apostle? When the Church is at peace, as it has long been in this country, when public order is preserved in the community, and the rights of person and property secured, there is extreme danger lest we judge ourselves by what is without us, not by what is within. We take for granted we are Christians, *because we have* been taught aright, and are regular in our attendance upon the Christian ordinances. But, great privilege and duty as it is to use the means of grace, reading and prayer are not enough; nor, by themselves will they ever make us real Christians. They will give us right knowledge and good feelings, but not firm faith and resolute obedience. Christians, such as Mark, will abound in a prosperous Church; and, should trouble come, they will be unprepared for it. They have so long been accustomed to external peace that they do not like to be persuaded that danger is at hand. They settle it in their imagination that they are to live and die undisturbed. They look at the world's events, as they express it, *cheerfully*, and argue themselves into self-deception. Next, they make concessions, to fulfil their own predictions and wishes; and surrender the Christian cause, that unbelievers may not commit themselves to an open attack upon it. Some of them are men of cultivated and refined taste; and these shrink from the rough life of pilgrims, to which they are called, as something strange and extravagant. They consider those who take a simpler view of the duties and prospects of the Church to be enthusiastic, rash, and intemperate, or perverse-minded. To speak plainly, a state of persecution is not (what is familiarly called) their *element;* they cannot breathe in it. Alas! how different from the Apostle, who had learned in whatsoever state he was, therewith to be content, and who was all things to all men. If then there be times when we have grown thus torpid from long security, and are tempted to prefer the treasures of Egypt to the reproach *of Christ,* what can we do, what ought we to do, but to

pray God in some way or other to try the very heart of
the Church, and to afflict us here rather than hereafter?
Dreadful as is the prospect of Satan's temporary
triumph, fierce as are the horsehoofs of his riders, and
detestable as is the cause for which they battle, yet
better such anguish should come upon us, than that the
recesses of our heritage should be the hiding-places of a
self-indulgent spirit and the schools of lukewarmness.
May God arise and shake terribly the earth (though it
be an awful prayer), *rather* than the double-minded
should lie hid among us, and souls be lost by present
ease! Let Him arise, if there be no alternative, and
chasten us with His sweet discipline, as our hearts may
best bear it; bringing our sins out in this world, that
we be not condemned in the day of the Lord ; shaming
us here, reproving us by the mouth of His servants, then
restoring us, and leading us on by a better way to a
truer and holier hope! Let Him winnow us, till the
chaff be clean removed! though, in thus invoking Him,
we know not what we ask, and, feeling the end itself to
be good, yet cannot worthily estimate the fearfulness of
that chastisement which we so freely speak about.
Doubtless we do not, cannot measure the terrors of the
Lord's judgments ; we use words cheaply.   Still, it cannot be wrong to use them, seeing they are the best
offering we can make to God; and, so that we beg Him
the while to lead us on, and give us strength to bear the
trial according as it opens upon us.   So may we issue
Evangelists for timid deserters of the cause of truth;
speaking the words of Christ, and showing forth His
life *and death; rising* strong from our sufferings, and

.... and zeal of
.... to another.

.... envy and a vain
.... the advan-
.... No men to have the troubles of
.... Even in the
...., if we im-
.... when we forget
........——. .... and it fit us to enjoy
... .

SERMON XVII.

The Gospel Witnesses.

(THE FEAST OF ST. PHILIP AND ST. JAMES, THE APOSTLES.)

" In the mouth of two or three witnesses shall every word be established."—2 COR. xiii. 1.

IT has pleased Almighty God, in His great mercy, to give us accumulated evidence of the truth of the Gospel; to send out His Witnesses again and again, Prophet after Prophet, Apostle after Apostle, miracle after miracle, that reason might be brought into captivity, as well as faith rewarded, by the fulness of His revelations. The double Festival which we are now celebrating, reminds us of this. Our Service is this day distinguished by the commemoration of two Apostles, who are associated together in our minds in nothing except in their being Apostles, in both of them being Witnesses, separate Witnesses of the life, death, and resurrection of Christ. Thus this union, however originating, of the Feast Days of Apostles, who are not especially connected in Scripture, will serve to remind us of the diversity and number of the Witnesses by whom one and the same Sacred Truth has been delivered to us.

But, further than this. Even the twelve Apostles, many as they were, form not the whole company of the Witnesses vouchsafed to us. In order more especially to confirm to us, that the Word has really become incarnate, and has sojourned among men, another distinct Witness is vouchsafed to us in the person of St. Paul. What could be needed beyond the preaching of the Twelve? they all were attendants upon Christ, they had heard His words, they had imbibed His Spirit; and, as agreeing one and all in the matter of their testimony, they afforded full evidence to those who required it, that, though their Master wrote not His Gospel for us with His own finger, nevertheless we have it whole and entire. Yet He did more than this. When the time came for publishing it to the world at large, while He gradually initiated their minds into the full graciousness of the New Covenant, as reaching to Gentile as well as Jew, He raised up to Himself, by direct miracle and inspiration, a fresh and independent Witness of it from among His persecutors; so that from that time the Dispensation had (as it were) a second beginning, and went forward upon a twofold foundation, the teaching, on the one hand, of the Apostles of the Circumcision, and of St. Paul on the other. Two schools of Christian doctrine forthwith existed,—if I may use the word "school," to denote a difference, not of doctrine itself, but of history, between the Apostles. Of the Gentile school, were St. Luke, St. Clement, and others, followers of St. Paul. Of the School of the Circumcision,

St. Peter, and still more, St. John; St. James, and we may add, St. Philip. St. James is known to belong to the latter, in his history as Bishop of Jerusalem; and, though little is known of St. Philip, yet what is known of him indicates that he too is to be ranked with St. John, whom he followed (as history informs us), in observing the Jewish rule of celebrating the Easter Feast, and not the tradition of St. Peter and St. Paul. I propose upon this Festival to set before you some considerations which arise out of this view of the Scripture history.

Christianity was, and was not, a new religion, when first preached to the world; it seemed to supersede. but it was merely the fulfilment, the due development and maturity, of the Jewish Law, which, in one sense, vanished away, in another, was perpetuated for ever. This need not be proved here; I will but refer you, by way of illustration, to the language of Prophecy, as (for instance) to the forty-ninth chapter of the Book of Isaiah, in which the Jewish Church is comforted in her afflictions by the promise of her propagation and triumphs (that is, in her Christian form) among the Gentiles. "Zion said, The Lord hath forsaken me, and my Lord hath forgotten me. Can a woman forget her sucking child, that she should not have compassion on the son of her womb? Yea, they may forget, yet will I not forget thee . . . . Lift up thine eyes round about, and behold; all these gather themselves together, and come to thee. As I live, saith the Lord, thou shalt surely clothe thee with them all, as with an ornament, and *bind them on thee* as a bride doth . . . . The children which thou shalt have, after thou hast lost the other, shall say again in thine ears, The place is too strait for me, give place to me that I may dwell. Then shalt thou say in thine heart, Who hath begotten me these, seeing I have lost my children, and am desolate, a captive, and removing to and fro? . . . . Behold, I will lift up Mine hand to the Gentiles, and set up My standard to the people; . . . and kings shall be thy nursing-fathers, and their queens thy nursing-mothers." The Jewish Church, then, was not superseded, though the Nation was; it merely changed into the Christian, and thus was at once the same, and not the same, as it had been before.

Such being the double aspect of God's dealings towards His Church, when the time came for His exhibiting it in its new form as a Catholic, not a local Institution, he was pleased to make a corresponding change in the internal ministry of the Dispensation; imposing upon St. Paul the particular duty of formally delivering and adapting to the world at large that Old Essential Truth, the guardianship of which He had already committed to St. James and St. John. In consequence of this accidental difference of office, superficial readers of Scripture have sometimes spoken as if there were some real difference between the respective doctrines of those favoured Instruments of Providence. Unbelievers have objected that St. Paul introduced a new religion, such as Jesus never taught; and, on the other hand, there are Christians who maintain that St. Paul's doctrine is peculiarly the teaching of the Holy *Ghost,* and intended to supersede both our Lord's recorded words, and those of His original followers. Now a very remarkable circumstance it certainly is, that Almighty God has thus made two beginnings to His Gospel; and, when we have advanced far enough in sacred knowledge to see how they harmonize together, and concur in that wonderful system, which Primitive Christianity presents, and which was built on them both, we shall find abundant matter of praise in this Providential arrangement. But at first there doubtless is something which needs explanation : for we see, in matter of fact, that different classes of religionists do build their respective doctrines upon the one foundation and on the other, upon the Gospels and upon St. Paul's Epistles ; the more enthusiastic upon the latter, the cold, proud, and heretical, upon the former; and though we may be quite sure that no part of Scripture favours either coldness or fanaticism, and, in particular, may zealously repel the impiety, as well as the daring perverseness, which would find countenance for an imperfect Creed in the heavenly words of the Evangelists, yet the very fact that hostile parties do agree in dividing the New Testament into about the same two portions, is just enough at first sight to show that there *is* some difference or other, whether in tone or doctrine, which needs accounting for.

This state of the case, whether a difficulty or not, may, I conceive, any how be turned into an evidence in behalf of the truth of Christianity. Some few remarks shall here be made to explain my meaning ; nor is it superfluous to direct attention to the subject; for, though points *of evidence* seldom avail to the conversion of unbelievers, they are always edifying and instructive to Christians, as confirming their faith, and filling them with admiration and praise of God's marvellous works, which have more and more the stamp of Truth upon them, the deeper we examine them. This was the effect produced on the Apostles' minds by their own miracles, and on the Saints in the Apocalypse by the sight of God's judgments; prompting them to cry out in awe and thankfulness, " Lord, Thou art God, which hast made Heaven and earth !"   " Great and marvellous are Thy works, Lord God Almighty ; just and true are Thy ways, Thou King of Saints " [1]

My remark then is simply this ;—that supposing an essential unanimity of teaching can be shown to exist between the respective writings of St. Paul and his brethren, then the existing difference, whatever it is, whether of phraseology, of subject, or of historical origin, in a word, the difference of school, only makes that agreement the more remarkable, and after all, only guarantees them as two independent Witnesses to the same Truth.   Now to illustrate this argument.

I suppose the points of difference between St. Paul and the Twelve will be considered to be as follows :— that St. Paul, on his conversion, " conferred not with flesh and blood,[2] neither went up to Jerusalem to them which were Apostles before him ;—that, on the face of Scripture, there appears some sort of difference in view-ing the Dispensation between St. Paul and the original Apostles; that St. Paul on one occasion "withstood Peter to the face," and says that "those who. seemed to be

[1] *Acts* iv. 24.   Rev. xv. 3.　　　[2] Gal. i. 16, 17.

somewhat," referring apparently to James and John, "in conference added nothing to him;"[1] and St. Peter, on the other hand, observes, that in St. Paul's Epistles there "are some things hard to be understood;" while St. James would even seem to qualify St. Paul's doctrine concerning the pre-eminence of faith;[2]—that St. James, not to mention St. John, was stationary, having taken on himself a local episcopate, while St. Paul was subjected to what are now called missionary labours, and laid the foundation of churches without undertaking the government of any of them;—that St. Paul speaks with especial earnestness concerning the abolition of the Jewish Law, and the admission of the Gentiles into the Church, subjects not prominently put forward by the other Apostles;—that St. Paul declares distinctly and energetically, that we are elected to salvation by God's free grace, and justified by faith,[3] and traces out, in the way of system, all Christian holiness and spiritual-mindedness from this beginning; whereas, St. James says we are justified by works,[4] St. John that we shall be "judged according to our works," and St. Peter that "the Father judgeth according to every man's work, without respect of persons,"[5] phrases which are but symbols of the general character of their own and of our Lord's teaching;—lastly, that there is more expression of kindled and active affections towards God and towards man in St. Paul's writings than in those of his brethren. This is not the place to explain what needs explaining in this list of contrasts; nor indeed is there

[1] Gal. ii. 6, 11.   [2] 2 Peter iii. 16.   James ii. 14—26.   [3] Rom. v 1.
     [4] James ii. 24.   [5] Rev. xx. 13.   1 Pet. i. 17.

any real difficulty at all (I may say) in reconciling the one side with the other, where the heart is right and the judgment fairly clear and steady. It has often been done most satisfactorily. But let us take them as they stand, prior to all explanation; let a disputer make the most of them. So much at least is proved, that St. Paul and St. James were two independent witnesses (whether concordant or not) of the Gospel doctrines, which is abundantly confirmed by all those circumstances which objectors sometimes enlarge upon, St. Paul's peculiar education, connexions and history. Take these differences at the worst, and then on the other hand take account of the wonderful agreement after all in opinion, manner of thought, feeling, and conduct, nay, in religious vocabulary, between the two Schools (as I have called them),—most wonderful, considering that the very idea of the Christian system in all its parts was virtually a new thing in the particular generation in which it was promulgated,—and if it does not impress us with the conviction that an Unseen Hand, a Divine Presence, was in the midst of it, controlling the human instruments of His work, and ruling it that they should and must agree in speaking His Word, in spite of whatever differences of natural disposition and education, surely we may as well deny the agency of the Creator, His power, wisdom, and goodness, in the appointments of the material world.—The following are some instances of the kind of agreement I speak of.

1. Take the New Testament, as we have received it. It deserves notice, that in spite of what partisans *would* desire, after all we cannot divide its contents

between the two Schools under consideration. Admitting there were two principles at work in the development of the Christian Church, they are inextricably united as regards the documents of faith; so that the modern parties in question, whether their particular view be right or wrong, are at least attempting a return to a state prior to the existence of the New Testament. Consider the Epistle to the Hebrews,—which would be sufficient evidence, were there no other, of the identity of St. Paul's doctrine with St. James's. Be as disputatious as you will about its author, still it comes at least from the School of St. Paul, if not from that Apostle himself. The parallelisms between it and his acknowledged writings forbid any other supposition. Now look through it from beginning to end, observe well its exhortations to obedience, its warnings against apostasy, its solemn announcement of the terrors of the Gospel, and further, its honourable treatment of the Jewish Law, which it sets forth as fulfilled (following our Saviour's doctrine), not disrespectfully superseded by the Gospel, and then say whether this Epistle alone be not a wonderful monument of the essential unity of the Gospel creed among all its original disseminators. Again, consider the Epistles to Timothy and Titus, which are confessedly St. Paul's, and try to discriminate, if you can, between the ethical character which they display, and that of St. James's Epistle. Next observe the position of St. Luke's writings in the Inspired Volume, an Evangelist following the language of St. Matthew, yet the associate of St. Paul. Examine the speeches of St. Paul in the Book of Acts, and consider whether he is not at once the Apostle of the Gentiles, and the fellow-disciple of those who had attended our Lord's Ministry.[1] Consider, too, the history of St. Peter, and see whether the revelations made to him in order to the conversion of Cornelius, do not form a link between "St. Paul's Gospel" and that of his earlier brethren. Lastly, count up the particular parts of St. Paul's writings, in which that Apostle may be supposed to speak a different doctrine from the rest, and determine their extent and number. Are there much more than nine chapters of his Epistle to the Romans, four of that to the Galatians, three in the Ephesians, a passage in the Colossians, and a few verses in the Philippians? Are there not in other chapters of these very Epistles clear and explicit statements, running counter to these supposed peculiarities, agreeing with St. James, and so protesting (as it were) against those who would put asunder Apostles whom God has joined together? These shall be presently instanced; but for the moment concede the whole of the Epistles just mentioned,—yet you cannot make more than five out of fourteen, which is the whole number of his Epistles; and these, however sacred and authoritative, are not after all of greater prominence and dignity than some of the remaining nine. It would appear then, from the very face of the New Testament, that the differences between St. Paul's doctrine and that of his brethren, (whatever they were), admitted of an amalgamation, as far as Christian Teaching went, from the moment when that office was first exercised in the Church.

1 *Vide, e.g.* Acts xx. 25 ; xxviii. 31.

2. In the case of the original Apostles, the intention of delivering and explaining their Divine Master's teaching cannot be mistaken. Now, of course, St. Paul, vrofessing to preach Christ's Gospel, could not but avow such an intention also ; but it should be noticed, considering that he was not with our Lord on earth, how he devotes himself to the sole thought of Him ; that is, it *would* be remarkable, were not St. Paul divinely chosen and called, as we believe him to have been. Simon Magus professed to be a Christian, yet his aim was that of exalting himself. It was quite possible for St. Paul to have acknowledged Christ generally as his Master, and still not practically to have preached Christ. Yet how full he is of his Saviour! He could not be more so, if he had attended Him all through His ministry. The thought of Christ is the one thought in which he *lives ;* it is the fervent love, the devoted attachment, the zeal and reverence of one who had " heard and seen, and looked upon and handled, the Word of life."[1] What a remarkable attestation is here to the Sovereignty of the Unseen Saviour! What was Paul, and what was James, " but ministers," by whom the world believed on Him? They clearly were nothing beyond this. This is a striking fulfilment of our Lord's declaration concerning the ministration of the Spirit ; " He shall glorify Me."[2] St. John records it ; St. Paul exemplifies it.

It is remarkable too, how St. Paul concurs with the other Apostles in referring to our Lord's words and actions, though much opportunity for this does not occur

[1] *1 John i. 1.*   [2] *John xvi. 14.*

in his writings: that is, it is plain, that he was not exalting a mere name or idea, any more than the rest, but a Person, a really existing Master. For instance, St. John says, "That which we have seen and heard, declare we unto you;" and St. Peter, "This voice which came from heaven we heard, when we were with Him in the Holy Mount;" again, "We are witnesses of all things which He did."[1] In like manner St. Paul enumerates, as his "Gospel," not mere principles of religion, but the facts of Christ's life, recurring to that very part of the Dispensation, in which he was inferior to his brethren. "I delivered unto you first of all, that which I also received, how that Christ died for our sins according to the Scriptures, . . . was buried, . . . rose again the third day, and that He was seen of Cephas, then of the Twelve, after that . . . of about five hundred brethren at once . . . after that . . . of James, then of all the Apostles;" he adds, with expressions of self-abasement, "And last of all, He was seen of me."[2] Again in his directions for administering the Lord's Supper, he refers carefully to our Lord's manner of ordaining it, as recorded in the Gospels; again, in the seventh chapter of the same Epistle, there would seem a repeated reference to our Lord's words in the Gospel; "unto the married I command, yet not I, but the Lord." In the same chapter the verse beginning, "This I speak for your own profit," has been supposed with reason to refer to St. Luke's account of Martha's complaint of Mary, and our Lord's speech thereupon. In his first Epistle to Timothy, he alludes to our Lord's appearance before

[1] 1 John i. 8. 2 Pet. i. 18. Acts x. 39. [2] 1 Cor. xv. 3—8.

Pilate. In his farewell address to the elders of Ephesus he has preserved one of His sayings which the Gospels do not contain; "It is more blessed to give than to receive."[1] And in the Epistle to the Hebrews reference is made to Christ's agony in the garden.

3. The doctrine of the Incarnation, or the Gospel Economy, as embracing the two great truths of the Divinity of Christ and the Atonement, was not (as far as we know) clearly revealed, during our Lord's ministry. Yet, observe how close is St. Paul's agreement with St. John. "The Word was with God, and the Word was God, and the Word was made flesh."—"Christ Jesus, being in the form of God, thought it not robbery to be equal with God; yet humbled Himself, being made in the likeness of men." St. John calls Christ "the Only-begotten Son in the bosom of the Father;" and St. Paul, "the First-begotten." St. John says, that He hath "declared the Father," and, in His own sacred words, that "he that hath seen Him, hath seen the Father;" St. Paul declares that He is "the Image of the Invisible God,"—"the brightness of His glory, and the express Image of His Person." St. John says, "All things were made by Him;" St. Paul, that "By Him God made the worlds." Further, St. John says, "The blood of Jesus Christ cleanseth us from all sin;"—St. Paul, that "in Him we have redemption through His blood, even the forgiveness of sins;"—St. John, that "if any man sin, we have an Advocate with the Father, Jesus Christ the righteous;"—St. Paul, that He "is even at the right hand of God, and also maketh intercession for us;"—

[1] Acts xx. 35.

St. John, that " He is the propitiation not for our sins only, but also for those of the whole world ;"—St. Paul, that He has " reconciled" Jew and Gentile " in one body by the cross."[1]

Now, considering the mysteriousness of these doctrines, the probability that there would be some diversity of teaching, in the case of two different minds, and the actual differences existing among various sects at the time, I must consider this exact accordance between St. John and St. Paul (men to all appearance as unlike each other by nature as men could be) to be little short of a demonstration of the reality of the divine doctrines to which they witness. " The testimony of two men is true ;" and still more clearly so in this case, supposing (what unbelievers may maintain, but they alone) that any rivalry of schools existed between these holy Apostles.

4. To continue our review. St. John and St. Paul both put forward the doctrine of Regeneration, both connect it with Baptism, both denounce the world as sinful and lost. They both teach the peculiar privilege of Christians, as God's adopted children, and make the grant of this and all other privileges, depend on faith.[2] Now the ideas and the terms employed are peculiar; and, after all allowance for what might have been anticipated by former dispensations and existing schools

---

[1] John i. 1, 14.   Philip. ii. 5—8.   John i. 18.   Heb. i. 6. John i. 18 ; xiv. 9.   Col. i. 15.   Heb. i. 3.   John i. 3.   Heb. i. 2. 1 John i. 7.   Col. i. 14.   1 John ii. 1.   Rom. viii. 34.   1 John ii. 2. Ephes. ii. 16.

[2] John iii. 3—5, 16, 19.   1 John iii. 1 ; v. 19.   Rom. iii. 19 ; v. 1, 2; viii. 14, 15.   Tit. iii. 5, &c.

of religion, yet, could it be shown, that ever so much of this doctrine was already familiar to the Jewish Church, this does not account for the unanimity with which they respectively adopt and modify it. I add some parallel texts on this part of the subject. St. John delivers our Saviour's prediction : " If I depart, I will send the Comforter unto you ; He will guide you into all truth ;"—St. Paul, " God hath revealed (the mysteries of the Gospel) unto us by His Spirit ;"—" All these (gifts) worketh that one and the self-same Spirit, dividing to every man severally as He will." St. Paul says, " He which stablisheth us with you in Christ, and hath anointed us, is God ;"—St. John, " Ye have an unction from the Holy One." St. John, in accordance with the teaching of his Lord, declares, " There is a sin unto death ; I do not say that a man shall pray for it ;" and St. Paul, that " it is impossible for those who were once enlightened, if they shall fall away, to renew them again unto repentance."[1]

5. We all recollect St. Paul's praise of charity as the fulfilling of the Law, and the characteristic precept of the Gospel. Yet is not the pre-eminent importance of it as clearly set forth by St. John, when he says, " We know that we have passed from death unto life, because we love the brethren," and the nature of it by St. James in his description of " the wisdom that is from above ?" Again, it is observable, that our Lord's precept, adopted from the Law, of loving our neighbour as ourselves, is handed down at once by St. Paul and St. James.[2]

[1] John xvi. 7, 13. 1 Cor. ii. 10 ; xii. 11. 2 Cor. i. 21. 1 John ii. 21 ; v. 16. Heb. vi. 4—6.

[2] *1 John iii. 14. James iii.* 17. Rom. xiii. 9. James ii. 8.

5. We know that an especial stress is laid by our Lord on the duty of Almsgiving. St. John and St. James follow Him in so doing;[1] and St. Paul likewise. That Apostle's words, in the Galatians, are especially in point here, as expressly acknowledging this agreement between himself and his brethren. "When James, Cephas, and John, who seemed to be pillars, perceived the grace that was given unto me, they gave to me and Barnabas the right hand of fellowship, that we should go unto the heathen, and they unto the circumcision; *only they would that we should remember the poor; the same which I also was forward to do*."[2]

7. Self-denial, mortification of life, bearing our cross, are especially insisted on by Christ. St. Paul delivers clearly and strongly the same doctrine, declaring that he himself was "crucified with Christ," and "died daily."[3] The duty of Fasting may here be mentioned, as one in which St. Paul unhesitatingly enters into and enforces our Lord's religious system.

8. I need not observe how urgent and constant is St. Paul in his exhortations to Intercession; yet, St. James equals him in his short Epistle, which contains a passage longer and more emphatic than any which can be found in St. Paul.[4] Again, both Apostles insist on the practice of sacred Psalmody as a duty. St. James, "Is any afflicted? let him pray. Is any merry? let him sing psalms." St. Paul, "Speaking

[1] 1 John iii. 17   James ii. 15, 16.   [2] Gal. ii. 9, 10.
[3] Gal. ii. 20.   1 Cor. xv. 31.
[4] *Ephes.* vi. 18.   1 Thess. v. 17.   James v. 14—18.

to each other in psalms, and hymns, and spiritual songs."[1]

9. St. Paul makes much of the Holy Eucharist; nay, to him the Church is indebted for the direct and clear proof we possess of the sacramental virtue of that Ordinance. Far different is the conduct of innovators; who are impatient of nothing more than of ordinances which they find established. He also recognises the obligation of the Lord's day,[2] he being the Apostle who denounces, as other Jewish rites, so also the Sabbath.

10. St. Jude bids us "contend earnestly for the faith once delivered to the Saints." In like manner, St. Paul enjoins Timothy to "hold fast the form of sound words, which he had heard of him;" and Titus, to "hold fast the faithful word as he had been taught, that he might be able by sound doctrine both to exhort and to convince the gainsayers."[3] St. Paul bids us "speak the Truth in love;" St. John says, he "loves Gaius in the Truth."[4]

11. It is observable that our Lord speaks of His Gospel being preached, not chiefly as a means of converting, but as a witness against the world. This is confessedly a remarkable ground to be taken by the Founder of a new religion. "The Gospel of the kingdom shall be preached in all the world, for a witness unto all nations."[5] Accordingly, He Himself witnessed even before the heathen Pilate, "To this end was I born, and for this cause came I into the world, that I

[1] James v. 13.   Ephes. v. 19.   [2] Acts xx. 7.   1 Cor. xvi. 2.
[3] Jude 3.   2 Tim. i. 13.   Titus i. 9.
[4] Ephes. *iv. 15.*   *3 John 1.*   [5] Matt. xxiv. 14; xviii. 81.

should bear witness unto the Truth."[1] Yet, surely, it is still more remarkable, that the Apostle of the Gentiles should take up precisely the same view, even referring to our Lord's Confession before Pilate, when giving Timothy his charge to preach the Truth, declaring, that the Gospel is "a savour of death unto death," as well as "of life unto life," and foretelling the growth of "evil men and seducers" after his departure.[2]

12. Observe the agreement of sentiment in the following texts : St. James, taught by his Lord and Master says, "Be ye doers of the word, and not hearers only, deceiving your own selves." St. Paul nearly in the same words, "Not the hearers of the law are just before God, but the doers of the law shall be justified."[3] Again, did we not know whence the following passages come, should we not assign them to St. James ? "God will render to every man according to his deeds; to them, who by patient continuance in well-doing, seek for glory, and honour, and immortality, eternal life ; but unto them that are contentious, and do not obey the truth, but obey unrighteousness, indignation, and wrath . . . . for there is no respect of persons with God." This, as well as the text just cited, is to be found in the opening of that Epistle, in which St. Paul appears most to differ from St. James ; now observe how he closes it. "Why dost thou judge thy brother ? And why dost thou set at nought thy brother ? For we shall all stand before the judgment-seat of Christ . . . . Every one of us shall give account of himself to God." Again, in

----

[1] John xviii. 37.　　[2] 1 Tim. vi. 13.　2 Cor. ii. 16.　2 Tim. iii. 13.
[3] James i. 22.　Rom. ii. 13.

another Epistle: "We must all be made manifest before the judgment-seat of Christ; that every one may receive the things done in his body, according to that he hath done, whether it be good or bad. Knowing therefore the terror of the Lord, we persuade men."[1]

13. St. John, after our Lord's example, implies especial praise upon those who follow an unmarried life, involving the letter in the spirit, as is frequent in Scripture.[2] "These are they which were not defiled with women, for they are virgins; these are they which follow the Lamb whithersoever He goeth." St. Paul gives more direct praise to the same state, and gives the same reason for its especial blessedness; "He that is

---

[1] Rom. ii. 6—8, 11; xiv. 10—12. 2 Cor. v. 10, 11.

[2] *Vide* Hos. xiii. 14. John xi. 23, 40; xiii. 8; xviii. 9. And especially, as being a parallel case, Matt. xviii. 3—6, and so again, Matt. x. 38. Rev. vii. 14.—The parallel is instructively brought out in separate passages in the "Christian Year:"

> " Yet in that throng of selfish hearts untrue,
> Thy sad eye rests upon Thy faithful few,
> Children *and* childlike souls are there," &c.—*Advent.*

. . . " There hangs a radiant coronet,
> All gemm'd with pure and living light,
> Too dazzling for a sinner's sight,
> Prepared for virgin souls, and them
> Who seek the martyr's diadem.
> *Nor deem*, who, to that bliss aspire,
> Must win their way through blood and fire," &c.
> *Wednesday before Easter.*

In other words, Childhood, Virginity, Martyrdom, are made in Scripture at once the Types and Standards of religious Perfection, as they are represented in the three Saints' Days following Christmas-Day,— St. Stephen's, St. John's, and Holy Innocents'. So again, Poverty, Luke vi. 20; xii. 33; Matt. xi. 5, with Matt. v. 3. But this rule of interpretation, and the light it throws upon Gospel duties and the Christian character, cannot be more than alluded to in a note.

unmarried careth for the things that belong to the Lord, how he may please the Lord . . . . I speak this for your own profit . . . . that ye may attend upon the Lord without distraction."[1]

14. St. Paul says, "Be careful for nothing, but in every thing by prayer and supplication with thanksgiving, let your requests be made known unto God;" St. Peter in like manner, "Casting all your care upon Him, for He careth for you." Both after our Lord's exhortation, "Be not careful for the morrow, for the morrow shall take care for the things of itself."[2]

15. Lastly, as Christ foretells the approaching visitations of the Jewish Church, and the necessity of looking out for them, so St. Peter declares, "The end of all things is at hand; be ye therefore sober, and watch unto prayer." St. James, "Be ye also patient, stablish your hearts, for the coming of the Lord draweth nigh."[3]   And St. Paul in like manner, "Let your moderation be known unto all men ; the Lord is at hand."

These instances may suffice by way of pointing out the argument for the truth of Christianity, which, as I conceive, lies in the *historical* difference existing between the respective schools of St. Paul and St. James.   Such a difference there is, as every one must grant: I mean that St. Paul did, as a matter of fact, begin his preaching upon his own independent revelations.   And thus, however we may be able (as assuredly every Christian

---

[1] Rev. xiv. 4.   1 Cor. vii. 32, 35.
[2] Phil. iv. 6.   1 Pet. v. 7.   Matt. vi. 34.
[3] 1 Pet. iv. 7.   Phil. iv. 5.   James v. 8.

s gradually able, in proportion to his diligence and prayer) to reconcile and satisfy himself as regards St. Paul's apparent discordances in doctrine from the rest of the Apostles, so much after all must remain, just enough, that is, to build the foregoing argument upon. At the same time, as if to ensure even the historical harmony of the whole Dispensation, we are allowed to set against our information concerning this separate origin of the two Apostolical Schools, the following facts; first, that St. Paul ever considered himself ecclesiastically subordinate to the Church at Jerusalem, and to St. James, as the Book of Acts shows us; next, that St. John, the beloved disciple, who "was in Christ before him," was appointed to outlive him, and, as a faithful Steward, to seal up, avouch, and deliver over inviolate to the Church after him, the pure and veritable teaching of his Lord.

As to the point of *doctrinal* agreement and difference which I have been employed in ascertaining, it is scarcely necessary to observe, that beyond controversy the agreement is in essentials—the nature and office of the Mediator, the gifts which He vouchsafes to us, and the temper of mind and the duties required of a Christian; whereas the difference of doctrine between them, even admitting there is a difference, relates only at the utmost to the Divine counsels, the sense in which the Jewish law is abolished, and the condition of justification, whether faith or good works. I would not (God forbid!) undervalue these or any other questions on which inspiration has spoken; it is our duty to search *diligently* after every jot and tittle of the Truth graciously revealed to us, and to maintain it: but I am here speaking as to an unbeliever, and he must confess, that viewing the Gospel Creed in what may be called its historical proportions, a difference of opinion as to these latter subjects cannot detract from that real and substantial agreement of System, visible in the course of doctrine which the Two Witnesses respectively deliver.

Next, speaking as a Christian, who will admit neither inconsistency to exist between the inspired documents of faith, nor points of trivial importance in the revelation, I observe notwithstanding, that the foregoing argument affords us additional certainty respecting the characteristic doctrines as well as the truth of Christianity. An agreement between St. Paul and St. John in behalf of a certain doctrine is an agreement not of mere texts, but of separate Witnesses, an evidence of the prominence of the doctrine delivered in the Gospel system. In this way, if in no other, we learn the momentous character of some particular tenets of revelation which heretics have denied, as the Eternity, or, again, the Personality of the Divine Word.

Further, we are thus permitted more clearly to ascertain the main outlines of the Christian *character;* for instance, that love is its essence,—its chief characteristics, resignation, and composure of mind, neither anxious for the morrow, nor hoping from this world —and its duties, almsgiving, self-denial, prayer and praise.

Lastly, the very circumstance that Almighty God has chosen this mode of introducing the Gospel into the world, I mean, this employment of a double agency, opens a wide field of thought, had we light to trace out the parallel providences which seem to lie amid the intricacies of His dealings with mankind. As it is, we can but gaze with the Apostle in wonder and adoration upon the mystery of His counsels. "O the depth of the riches both of the wisdom and knowledge of God! how unsearchable are His judgments, and His ways past finding out! For who hath known the mind of the Lord? Or who hath been His counsellor? Or who hath first given to Him, and it shall be recompensed unto him again? For of Him, and through Him, and to Him, are all things: to whom be glory for ever. Amen."[1]

[1] Rom. xi. 33—36.

SERMON XVIII.

Mysteries in Religion.

(THE FEAST OF THE ASCENSION OF OUR LORD.)

"It is Christ that died, yea rather, that is risen again, Who is even at the right hand of God, Who also maketh intercession for us."—
ROM. viii. 34.

THE Ascension of our Lord and Saviour is an event
ever to be commemorated with joy and thanksgiving,
for St. Paul tells us in the text that He ascended to the
right hand of God, and there makes intercession for us.
Hence it is our comfort to know, that "if any man sin,
we have an Advocate with the Father, Jesus Christ the
righteous, and He is the propitiation for our sins."[1]   As
the Jewish High Priest, after the solemn sacrifice for
the people on the great day of Atonement, went into
the Holy of Holies with the blood of the victim, and
sprinkled it upon the Mercy-Seat, so Christ has entered
into Heaven itself, to present (as it were) before the
Throne that sacred Tabernacle which was the instrument of His passion,—His pierced hands and wounded

---

[1] 1 John ii. 1, 2.

side,—in token of the atonement which He has effected
for the sins of the world.

Wonder and awe must always mingle with the thankfulness which the revealed dispensation of mercy raises
in our minds. And this, indeed, is an additional cause
of thankfulness, that Almighty God has disclosed to us
enough of His high Providence to raise such sacred and
reverent feelings. Had He merely told us that He had
pardoned us, we should have had overabundant cause
for blessing and praising Him; but in showing us somewhat of the means, in vouchsafing to tell what cannot
wholly be told, in condescending to abase heavenly
things to the weak and stammering tongues of earth,
He has enlarged our gratitude, yet sobered it with fear.
We are allowed with the Angels to obtain a glimpse of
the mysteries of Heaven, "to rejoice with trembling."
Therefore, so far from considering the Truths of the
Gospel as a burden, because they are beyond our understanding, we shall rather welcome them and exult in
them, nay, and feel an antecedent stirring of heart
towards them, for the very reason that they are above
us. Under these feelings I will attempt to suggest to
you on the present Festival some of the incentives to
wonder and awe, humility, implicit faith, and adoration,
supplied by the Ascension of Christ.

1. First, Christ's Ascension to the right hand of God
is marvellous, because it is a sure token that heaven is
a certain fixed place, and not a mere state. That bodily
presence of the Saviour which the Apostles handled is
not here; it is elsewhere,—it is in heaven. This con-
tradicts *the notions of* cultivated and speculative minds,

For once we are led on to consider how different are the character and effect of the Scripture notices of the [phenomena] of the physical world from those which philosophers [give us]. I am not deciding whether or not the one and the other are reconcilable; I merely say their respective effect is different. And when we have deduced what we deduce by our reason from the study of visible nature, and then read what we read in His Inspired word, and find the two apparently discordant, [this] — In this feeling I think we ought to have on our minds;—not an impatience to do what is beyond our powers, to weigh evidence, sum up, balance, decide, and reconcile, to arbitrate between the two voices of God,— but a sense of the utter nothingness of worms such as we are; of our plain and absolute incapacity to contemplate things *as they really are;* a perception of our emptiness, before the great Vision of God; of our " comeliness being turned into corruption, and our retaining no strength ;" a conviction, that what is put before us, in nature or in grace, though true in such a full sense that we dare not tamper with it, yet is but an intimation useful for particular purposes, useful for practice, useful in its department, " until the day-break and the shadows flee away," useful in such a way that both the one and the other represèntation may àt once be used, as two languages, as two separate approximations towards the Awful Unknown Truth, such as will not mislead us in their respective provinces. And thus while we use the language of science, without jealousy, for scientific purposes, we may confine it to these; and repel and reprove its upholders, should they attempt to exalt it and to "stretch it beyond its measure." In its own limited round it has its use, nay, may be made to fill a higher ministry, and stand as a proselyte under the shadow of the temple ; but it must not dare profane the inner courts, in which the ladder of Angels is fixed for ever, reaching even to the Throne of God, and " Jesus standing on the right hand of God."

I will but remind you on this part of the subject, that our Lord is to come from heaven " in like manner" as He *went; that He is* to come " in clouds," that

a]   P

" every eye shall see Him," and " all tribes of the earth wail because of Him." Attempt to solve this prediction, according to the received theories of science, and you will discover their shallowness. They are unequal to the depth of the problem.

2. I have made the foregoing remark in order to impress upon you the mystery with which we are encompassed all about, such as not merely to attach to one or two truths of religion, but extending to almost every sacred fact, and to every action of our lives. With the same view, let me observe upon the doctrine which accompanies the fact of the Ascension. Christ, we are told, has gone up on high " to present Himself before the face of God for us." He has " entered by His own blood once for all into the Holy Place, having effected eternal redemption." " He ever liveth to make intercession for those who come unto God by Him; He hath a priesthood which will not pass from Him." " We have such an High Priest, who is set on the right hand of the throne of the Majesty in the heavens; a Minister of the Sanctuary, and of the true Tabernacle, which the Lord pitched, and not man." [1]

These and similar passages refer us to the rites of the Jewish law. They contain notice of the type, but what is the Antitype? We can give no precise account of it. For consider; *why* was it that Christ ascended on high? With what object? What is His work? What is the meaning of His interceding for us in heaven? We know that, whatever He does, it is the gracious reality of the Mosaic figure. The High Priest

1 Heb. ix. 12, 24, 25; vii. 24, 25; viii. 1, 2.

entering with the atoning blood into the Holiest, was a representation of Christ's gracious deed in our behalf. But what is that deed? We know what the shadow is; what is the substance? The death of Christ answers to the Jewish rite of Atonement; how does He vouchsafe to fulfil the rite of Intercession? Instead of explaining, Scripture does but continue to answer us in the language of the type; even to the last it veils His deed under the ancient figure.[1] Shall we therefore explain away its language as merely figurative, which (as the word is now commonly understood) is next to saying it has no meaning at all? Far from it. Clouds and darkness are round about Him. We are not given to see into the secret shrine in which God dwells. Before Him stand the Seraphim, veiling their faces. Christ is within the veil. We must not search curiously what is His present office, what is meant by His pleading His sacrifice, and by His perpetual intercession for us. And, since we do not know, we will studiously keep to the figure given us in Scripture: we will not attempt to interpret it, or change the wording of it, being wise above what is written. We will not neglect it, because we do not understand it. We will hold it as a Mystery, or (what was anciently called) a Truth Sacramental; that is, a high invisible grace lodged in an outward form, a precious possession to be piously and thankfully guarded for the sake of the heavenly reality contained in it. Thus much we see in it, the pledge of a doctrine which reason cannot understand, viz. of the influence

[1] Rev. viii. 3, 4.

of the prayer of faith upon the Divine counsels. The Intercessor directs or stays the hand of the Unchangeable and Sovereign Governor of the World; being at once the meritorious cause and the earnest of the intercessory power of His brethren. "Christ rose again for our justification," "The effectual fervent prayer of a righteous man availeth much," are both infinite mercies, and deep mysteries.

3. Further still, consider our Saviour's words:—"It is expedient for you that I go away: for if I go not away, the Comforter will not come unto you." He does not tell us, why it was that His absence was the condition of the Holy Spirit's presence. "If I depart," He says, "I will send Him unto you." "I will pray the Father, and He shall give you another Comforter, that He may abide with you for ever."[1] To the same purpose are the following texts: "He that believeth on Me, the works that I do shall he do also; and greater works than these shall he do, *because* I go unto My Father." "If ye loved Me, ye would rejoice, because I said, I go unto the Father; for My Father is greater than I." "Touch Me not; for I am not yet ascended to My Father; but go to My brethren, and say unto them, I ascend unto My Father and your Father, and to My God and your God."[2] Now, proud and curious reason might seek to know why He could not "pray the Father," without going to Him; why He must depart in order to send the Spirit. But faith, without asking for one ray of light more than is given, muses over the wonderful system of Providence, as seen

[1] John xvi. 7; xiv. 16.   [2] Ib. xiv. 12, 28; xx. 17.

in this world, which is ever connecting events, between which man sees no necessary bond. The whole system of what is called cause and effect, is one of mystery; and this instance, if it may be called one, supplies abundant matter of praise and adoration to a pious mind. It suggests to us, equally with the topics which have already come before us, how very much our knowledge of God's ways is but on the surface. What are those deep hidden reasons why Christ went and the Spirit came? Marvellous and glorious, beyond our understanding! Let us worship in silence; meanwhile, let us jealously maintain this, and every other portion of our Creed, lest, by dropping jot or tittle, we suffer the truths concealed therein to escape from us.

Moreover, this departure of Christ, and coming of the Holy Ghost, leads our minds with great comfort to the thought of many lower dispensations of Providence towards us. He, who, according to His inscrutable will, sent first His Co-equal Son, and then His Eternal Spirit, acts with deep counsel, which we may surely trust, when He sends from place to place those earthly instruments which carry on His purposes. This is a thought which is particularly soothing as regards the loss of friends; or of especially gifted men, who seem in their day the earthly support of the Church. For what we know, their removal hence is as necessary for the furtherance of the very objects we have at heart, as was the departure of our Saviour.

Doubtless, "it is expedient" they should be taken away; otherwise some great mercy will not come to us. They are *taken* away perchance to other duties in

God's service, equally ministrative to the salvation of
the elect, as earthly service. Christ went to intercede
with the Father: we do not know, we may not
boldly speculate,—yet, it may be, that Saints departed
intercede, unknown to us, for the victory of the Truth
upon earth; and their prayers above may be as really
indispensable conditions of that victory, as the labours
of those who remain among us. They are taken away
for some purpose surely: their gifts are not lost to us;
their soaring minds, the fire of their contemplations,
the sanctity of their desires, the vigour of their faith,
the sweetness and gentleness of their affections, were
not given without an object. Yea, doubtless, they are
keeping up the perpetual chant in the shrine above,
praying and praising God day and night in His Temple,
like Moses upon the Mount, while Joshua and his host
fight with Amalek. Can they be allotted greater
blessedness, than to have a station after the pattern
of that Saviour who has departed hence? Has *He* no
power in the world's movements because He is away?
And though He is the Living and exalted Lord of all,
and the government is on His shoulder, and they are
but His servants, without strength of themselves, laid
up moreover apart from the conflict of good and
evil in the paradise of God, yet so much light as this
is given us by the inspired pages of the Apocalypse,
that they are interested in the fortunes of the Church.
We read therein of the Martyrs crying with a loud
voice, "How long, O Lord, holy and true, dost Thou
not judge and avenge our blood on them that dwell
on the earth?" At another time, of the Elders

worshipping God, saying, "We give Thee thanks, O Lord God Almighty, which art, and wast, and art to come, because Thou hast taken to Thee Thy great power and hast reigned; and the nations were wrathful, but Thy wrath is come." And again of the Saints, saying, "Great and marvellous are Thy works, Lord God Almighty; just and true are Thy ways, Thou King of Saints. Who shall not fear Thee, O Lord, and glorify Thy name? for Thou only art holy; for all nations shall come and worship before Thee, for Thy judgments are made manifest."[1] Let us not forget that, though the prophecies of this sacred book may be still sealed from us, yet the doctrines and precepts are not; and that we lose much both in the way of comfort and instruction, if we do not use it for the purposes of faith and obedience.

What has been now said about the Ascension of our Lord comes to this; that we are in a world of mystery, with one bright Light before us, sufficient for our proceeding forward through all difficulties. Take away this Light, and we are utterly wretched,— we know not where we are, how we are sustained, what will become of us, and of all that is dear to us, what we are to believe, and why we are in being. But with it we have all and abound. Not to mention the duty and wisdom of implicit faith in the love of Him who made and redeemed us, what is nobler, what is more elevating and transporting, than the generosity of heart which risks everything on God's word, dares the powers of evil to their worst efforts, and repels the

[1] *Rev. vi. 10; xi. 17, 18; xv. 3, 4.*

... we will enjoy our privilege; we will remain where we are ... go forward, ... not knowing whither we go, knowing that "this is the victory that overcometh the world, even our faith." It is enough that ... Redeemer liveth; that He has been on earth and will come again. On Him we venture our all, we can but ... to put ourselves into His hands, our interests present and eternal, and the interests of all we love. Christ has died, "yea rather is risen again, who is even at the right hand of God, who also maketh intercession for us. Who shall separate us from His love? Shall tribulation, or distress, or persecution, or famine, or nakedness, or peril, or sword? Nay, in all these things we are more than conquerors, through Him that loved us."[3]

[1] 1 Chron. xxix. 14.   [2] 1 John v. 4.   [3] Rom. viii. 34—37.

SERMON XIX.

The Indwelling Spirit.

(THE FEAST OF PENTECOST.)

" Ye are not in the flesh, but in the Spirit, if so be that the Spirit of God dwell in you."—ROMANS viii. 9.

GOD the Son has graciously vouchsafed to reveal the Father to His creatures from without; God the Holy Ghost, by inward communications. Who can compare these separate works of condescension, either of them being beyond our understanding? We can but silently adore the Infinite Love which encompasses us on every side. The Son of God is called the Word, as declaring His glory throughout created nature, and impressing the evidence of it on every part of it. He has given us to read it in His works of goodness, holiness, and wisdom. He is the Living and Eternal Law of Truth and Perfection, that Image of God's unapproachable Attributes, which men have ever seen by glimpses on the face of the world, felt that it was sovereign, but knew not whether to say it was a fundamental Rule and self-existing Destiny, or the Offspring and Mirror of the Divine Will. Such has He been from the beginning, graciously sent forth from the Father to reflect His glory upon all things, distinct from Him, while mysteriously one with Him; and in due time visiting us with an infinitely deeper mercy, when for our redemption He humbled Himself to take upon Him that fallen nature which He had originally created after His own image.

The condescension of the Blessed Spirit is as incomprehensible as that of the Son. He has ever been the secret Presence of God within the Creation: a source of life amid the chaos, bringing out into form and order what was at first shapeless and void, and the voice of Truth in the hearts of all rational beings, tuning them into harmony with the intimations of God's Law, which were externally made to them. Hence He is especially called the "life-giving" Spirit; being (as it were) the Soul of universal nature, the Strength of man and beast, the Guide of faith, the Witness against sin, the inward Light of patriarchs and prophets, the Grace abiding in the Christian soul, and the Lord and Ruler of the Church. Therefore let us ever praise the Father Almighty, who is the first Source of all perfection, in and together with His Co-equal Son and Spirit, through whose gracious ministrations we have been given to see "what manner of love" it is wherewith the Father has loved us.

On this Festival I propose, as is suitable, to describe as scripturally as I can, the merciful office of God the Holy Ghost, towards us Christians; and I trust I may do so, with the sobriety and reverence which the ·ject demands.

The Holy Spirit has from the beginning pleaded with man. We read in the Book of Genesis, that, when evil began to prevail all over the earth before the flood, the Lord said, " My Spirit shall not always strive with man; "[1] implying that He had hitherto striven with his corruption. Again, when God took to Him a peculiar people, the Holy Spirit was pleased to be especially present with them. Nehemiah says, " Thou gavest also Thy Good Spirit to instruct them,"[2] and Isaiah, " They rebelled and vexed His Holy Spirit."[3] Further, He manifested Himself as the source of various gifts, intellectual and extraordinary, in the Prophets, and others. Thus at the time the Tabernacle was constructed, the Lord filled Bezaleel " with the Spirit of God, in wisdom, and in understanding, and in knowledge, and in all manner of workmanship, to devise cunning works "[4] in metal, stone, and timber. At another time, when Moses was oppressed with his labours, Almighty God vouchsafed to " take of the Spirit " which was upon him, and to put it on seventy of the elders of Israel, that they might share the burden with him. " And it came to pass, that, when the Spirit rested upon them, they prophesied, and did not cease."[5] These texts will be sufficient to remind you of many others, in which the gifts of the Holy Ghost are spoken of under the Jewish covenant. These were great mercies ; yet, great as they were, they are as nothing compared with that surpassing grace with which we Christians are honoured; that great privilege of

[1] Gen. vi. 3. [2] Neh. ix. 20. [3] Isa. lxiii. 10.
[4] Exod. xxxi. 3, 4. [5] Numb. xi. 17, 25.

receiving into our hearts, not the mere gifts of the Spirit, but His very presence, Himself, by a real not a figurative indwelling.

When our Lord entered upon His Ministry, He acted as though He were a mere man, needing grace, and received the consecration of the Holy Spirit for our sakes. He became the Christ, or Anointed, that the Spirit might be seen to come from God, and to pass from Him to us. And, therefore, the heavenly Gift is not simply called the Holy Ghost, or the Spirit of God, but the Spirit of Christ, that we might clearly understand, that He comes to us from and instead of Christ. Thus St. Paul says, " God hath sent forth the Spirit of His Son into your hearts ;" and our Lord breathed on His Apostles, saying, " Receive ye the Holy Ghost ;" and He says elsewhere to them, " If I depart, I will send Him unto you."[1]   Accordingly this " Holy Spirit of promise " is called " the earnest of our inheritance," " the seal and earnest of an Unseen Saviour ;"[2] being the present pledge of Him who is absent,—or rather more than a pledge, for an earnest is not a mere token which will be taken from us when it is fulfilled, as a pledge might be, but a something in advance of what is one day to be given in full.

This must be clearly understood ; for it would seem to follow, that if so, the Comforter who has come instead of Christ, must have vouchsafed to come in the same sense in which Christ came ; I mean, that He has come, not merely in the way of gifts, or of

---

[1] Gal. iv. 6.   John xx. 22 ; xvi. 7.
[2] Eph. i. 14.   2 Cor. i. 22 ; v. 5.

influences, or of operations, as He came to the Prophets, for then Christ's going away would be a loss, and not a gain, and the Spirit's presence would be a mere pledge, not an earnest; but He comes to us as Christ came, by a real and personal visitation. I do not say we could have inferred this thus clearly by the mere force of the above cited texts; but it being actually so revealed to us in other texts of Scripture, we are able to see that it may be legitimately deduced from these. We are able to see that the Saviour, when once He entered into this world, never so departed as to suffer things to be as before He came; for He still is with us, not in mere gifts, but by the substitution of His Spirit for Himself, and that, both in the Church and in the souls of individual Christians.

For instance, St. Paul says in the text, "Ye are not in the flesh, but in the Spirit, if so be that the Spirit of God *dwell in you.*" Again, "He shall quicken even your mortal bodies by His Spirit that *dwelleth* in you." "Know ye not that your body is the Temple of the Holy Ghost which is in you?" "Ye are the Temple of the Living God, as God hath said, I will dwell in them, and walk in them." The same Apostle clearly distinguishes between the indwelling of the Spirit, and His actual operations within us, when he says, "The love of God is shed abroad in our hearts by the Holy Ghost which is given unto us;" and again, "The Spirit Himself beareth witness with our spirit that we are the children of God."[1]

Here let us observe, before proceeding, what indirect

[1] Rom. viii. 9, 11. 1 Cor. vi. 19. 2 Cor. vi. 16. Rom. v. 5; viii. 16.

evidence is afforded us in these texts of the Divinity of the Holy Spirit. Who can be personally present at once with every Christian, but God Himself? Who but He, not merely ruling in the midst of the Church invisibly, as Michael might keep watch over Israel, or another Angel might be "the Prince of Persia,"—but really taking up His abode as one and the same in many separate hearts, so as to fulfil our Lord's words, that it was expedient that He should depart; Christ's bodily presence, which was limited to place, being exchanged for the manifold spiritual indwelling of the Comforter within us? This consideration suggests both the dignity of our Sanctifier, and the infinite preciousness of His Office towards us.

To proceed: The Holy Ghost, I have said, dwells in body and soul, as in a temple. Evil spirits indeed have power to possess sinners, but His indwelling is far more perfect; for He is all-knowing and omnipresent, He is able to search into all our thoughts, and penetrate into every motive of the heart. Therefore, He pervades us (if it may be so said) as light pervades a building, or as a sweet perfume the folds of some honourable robe; so that, in Scripture language, we are said to be in Him, and He in us. It is plain that such an inhabitation brings the Christian into a state altogether new and marvellous, far above the possession of mere gifts, exalts him inconceivably in the scale of beings, and gives him a place and an office which he had not before. In St. Peter's forcible language, he becomes "partaker of the Divine Nature," and has "power" or authority, as St. John says, "to become the son of God." Or, to use the

words of St. Paul, "he is a new creation; old things
are passed away, behold all things are become new."
His rank is new; his parentage and service new. He
is "of God," and "is not his own," "a vessel unto
honour, sanctified and meet for the Master's use, and
prepared unto every good work."[1]

This wonderful change from darkness to light, through
the entrance of the Spirit into the soul, is called Regeneration, or the New Birth; a blessing which, before
Christ's coming, not even Prophets and righteous men
possessed, but which is now conveyed to all men freely
through the Sacrament of Baptism. By nature we are
children of wrath; the heart is sold under sin, possessed
by evil spirits; and inherits death as its eternal portion.
But by the coming of the Holy Ghost, all guilt and pol-
lution are burned away as by fire, the devil is driven
forth, sin, original and actual, is forgiven, and the whole
man is consecrated to God. And this is the reason why
He is called "the earnest" of that Saviour who died for
us, and will one day give us the fulness of His own
presence in heaven. Hence, too, He is our "seal unto
the day of redemption;" for as the potter moulds the
clay, so He impresses the Divine image on us members
of the household of God. And His work may truly be
called Regeneration; for though the original nature of
the soul is not destroyed, yet its past transgressions are
pardoned once and for ever, and its source of evil
staunched and gradually dried up by the pervading
health and purity which has set up its abode in it.

[1] 2 Pet. i. 4. John i. 12. 2 Cor. v. 17. 1 John iv. 4. 1 Cor. vi.
19, 20. 2 Tim. ii. 21.

Instead of its own bitter waters, a spring of health and salvation is brought within it; not the mere streams of that fountain, "clear as crystal," which is before the Throne of God,[1] but, as our Lord says, "a well of water *in him*," in a man's heart, "springing up into everlasting life." Hence He elsewhere describes the heart as giving forth, not receiving, the streams of grace: "Out of his belly shall flow rivers of Living Water." St. John adds, "this spake He of the Spirit."[2]

Such is the inhabitation of the Holy Ghost within us, applying to us individually the precious cleansing of Christ's blood in all its manifold benefits. Such is the great doctrine, which we hold as a matter of faith, and without actual experience to verify it to us. Next I must speak briefly concerning the manner in which the Gift of grace manifests itself in the regenerate soul; a subject which I do not willingly take up, and which no Christian perhaps is ever able to consider without some effort, feeling that he thereby endangers either his reverence towards God, or his humility, but which the errors of this day, and the confident tone of their advocates, oblige us to dwell upon, lest truth should suffer by our silence.

1. The heavenly gift of the Spirit fixes the eyes of our mind upon the Divine Author of our salvation. By nature we are blind and carnal; but the Holy Ghost by whom we are new-born, reveals to us the God of mercies, and bids us recognise and adore Him as our Father with a true heart. He impresses on us our Heavenly Father's image, which we lost when Adam

---

[1] *Rev. iv. 6. Ps. xlvi. 4.*   [2] *John iv. 14; vii. 38, 39.*

fell, and disposes us to seek His presence by the very instinct of our new nature. He gives us back a portion of that freedom in willing and doing; of that uprightness and innocence, in which Adam was created. He unites us to all holy beings, as before we had relationship with evil. He restores for us that broken bond, which, proceeding from above, connects together into one blessed family all that is anywhere holy and eternal, and separates it off from the rebel world which comes to nought. Being then the sons of God, and one with Him, our souls mount up and cry to Him continually. This special characteristic of the regenerate soul is spoken of by St. Paul soon after the text. "Ye have received the Spirit of adoption, whereby we cry, Abba, Father." Nor are we left to utter these cries to Him, in any vague uncertain way of our own; but He who sent the Spirit to dwell in us habitually, gave us also a form of words to sanctify the separate acts of our minds. Christ left His sacred Prayer to be the peculiar possession of His people, and the voice of the Spirit. If we examine it, we shall find in it the substance of that doctrine, to which St. Paul has given a name in the passage just quoted. We begin it by using our privilege of calling on Almighty God in express words as " Our Father." We proceed, according to this beginning, in that waiting, trusting, adoring, resigned temper, which children ought to feel; looking towards Him, rather than thinking of ourselves; zealous for His honour rather than fearful about our safety; resting in His present help, not with eyes timorously glancing towards the future. *His* name, *His* kingdom, *His* will, are the great objects for the Christian to contemplate and make his portion, being stable and serene, and "complete in Him," as beseems one who has the gracious presence of His Spirit within him. And, when he goes on to think of himself, he prays, that he may be enabled to have towards others what God has shown towards himself, a spirit of forgiveness and loving-kindness. Thus he pours himself out on all sides, first looking up to catch the heavenly gift, but, when he gains it, not keeping it to himself, but diffusing "rivers of living water" to the whole race of man, thinking of self as little as may be, and desiring ill and destruction to nothing but that principle of temptation and evil, which is rebellion against God;—lastly, ending, as he began, with the contemplation of His kingdom, power, and glory ever-lasting. This is the true "Abba, Father," which the Spirit of adoption utters within the Christian's heart, the infallible voice of Him who "maketh intercession for the Saints in God's way." And if he has at times, for instance, amid trial or affliction, special visitations and comfortings from the Spirit, "plaints unutterable" within him, yearnings after the life to come, or bright and passing gleams of God's eternal election, and deep stirrings of wonder and thankfulness thence following, he thinks too reverently of "the secret of the Lord," to betray (as it were) His confidence, and, by vaunting it to the world, to exaggerate it perchance into more than it was meant to convey : but he is silent, and ponders it as choice encouragement to his soul, meaning something, but he knows not how much.

2. *The indwelling of the Holy Ghost raises the soul,*

not only to the thought of God, but of Christ also. St. John says, "Truly our fellowship is with the Father, and with His Son Jesus Christ." And our Lord Himself, " If a man love Me, he will keep My words; and My Father will love him, and We will come unto him, and make our abode with him." [1] Now, not to speak of other and higher ways in which these texts are fulfilled, one surely consists in that exercise of faith and love in the thought of the Father and Son, which the Gospel, and the Spirit revealing it, furnish to the Christian. The Spirit came especially to " glorify " Christ; and vouchsafes to be a shining light within the Church and the individual Christian, reflecting the Saviour of the world in all His perfections, all His offices, all His works. He came for the purpose of unfolding what was yet hidden, whilst Christ was on earth; and speaks on the house-tops what was delivered in closets, disclosing Him in the glories of His transfiguration, who once had no comeliness in His outward form, and was but a man of sorrows and acquainted with grief. First, He inspired the Holy Evangelists to record the life of Christ, and directed them which of His words and works to select, which to omit; next, He commented (as it were) upon these, and unfolded their meaning in the Apostolic Epistles. The birth, the life, the death and resurrection of Christ, has been the text which He has illuminated. He has made history to be doctrine; telling us plainly, whether by St. John or St. Paul, that Christ's conception and birth was the real Incarnation of the Eternal Word,— His life, "God manifest in the Flesh,"—His death and

[1] *1 John i. 3. John xiv. 23.*

Q 2

resurrection, the Atonement for sin, and the Justification of all believers.   Nor was this all: he continued
His sacred comment in the formation of the Church,
superintending and overruling its human instruments,
and bringing out our Saviour's words and works, and
the Apostles' illustrations of them, into acts of obedience
and permanent Ordinances, by the ministry of Saints
and Martyrs.   Lastly, He completes His gracious work
by conveying this system of Truth, thus varied and
expanded, to the heart of each individual Christian in
whom He dwells.   Thus He vouchsafes to edify the
whole man in faith and holiness : " casting down imaginations and every high thing that exalteth itself against
the knowledge of God, and bringing into captivity every
thought to the obedience of Christ."[1]   By His wonder
working grace all things tend to perfection.   Every
faculty of the mind, every design, pursuit, subject of
thought, is hallowed in its degree by the abiding vision
of Christ, as Lord, Saviour, and Judge.   All solemn,
reverent, thankful, and devoted feelings, all that is noble,
all that is choice in the regenerate soul, all that is self-
denying in conduct, and zealous in action, is drawn forth
and offered up by the Spirit as a living sacrifice to the
Son of God.   And, though the Christian is taught not
to think of himself above his measure, and dare not
boast, yet he is also taught that the consciousness of
the sin which remains in him, and infects his best
services, should not separate him from God, but lead
him to Him who can save.   He reasons with St. Peter,
" To whom should he go ?" and, without daring to decide,

[1] 2 Cor. x. 5.

or being impatient to be told how far he is able to consider as his own every Gospel privilege in its fulness, he gazes on them all with deep thought as the Church's possession, joins her triumphant hymns in honour of Christ, and listens wistfully to her voice in inspired Scripture, the voice of the Bride calling upon and blest in the Beloved.

3. St. John adds, after speaking of "our fellowship with the Father and His Son:" "These things write we unto you, that your joy may be full." What is fulness of joy but *peace?* Joy is tumultuous only when it is not full; but peace is the privilege of those who are "filled with the knowledge of the glory of the Lord, as the waters cover the sea." "Thou wilt keep him in perfect peace, whose mind is stayed on Thee, because he trusteth in Thee."[1] It is peace, springing from trust and innocence, and then overflowing in love towards all around him. What is the effect of mere animal ease and enjoyment, but to make a man pleased with everything which happens? "A merry heart is a perpetual feast;" and such is peculiarly the blessing of a soul rejoicing in the faith and fear of God. He who is anxious, thinks of himself, is suspicious of danger, speaks hurriedly, and has no time for the interests of others; he who lives in peace is at leisure, wherever his lot is cast. Such is the work of the Holy Spirit in the heart, whether in Jew or Greek, bond or free. He Himself perchance in His mysterious nature, is the Eternal Love whereby the Father and the Son have dwelt in each other, as ancient writers have believed; and what He is in heaven, that

[1] Isa. xxvi. 3.

He is abundantly on earth. He lives in the Christian's heart, as the never-failing fount of charity, which is the very sweetness of the living waters. For where He is, "there is liberty" from the tyranny of sin, from the dread, which the natural man feels, of an offended, unreconciled Creator. Doubt, gloom, impatience have been expelled; joy in the Gospel has taken their place, the hope of heaven and the harmony of a pure heart, the triumph of self-mastery, sober thoughts, and a contented mind. How can charity towards all men fail to follow, being the mere affectionateness of innocence and peace? Thus the Spirit of God creates in us the simplicity and warmth of heart which children have, nay, rather the perfections of His heavenly hosts, high and low being joined together in His mysterious work; for what are implicit trust, ardent love, abiding purity, but the mind both of little children and of the adoring Seraphim!

Thoughts, such as these, will affect us rightly, if they make us fear and be watchful, while we rejoice. They cannot surely do otherwise; for the mind of a Christian, as I have been attempting to describe it, is not so much what we have, as what we ought to have. To look, indeed, after dwelling on it, upon the multitude of men who have been baptized in Christ's name, is too serious a matter, and we need not force ourselves to do so. We need not do so, further than to pray for them, and to protest and strive against what is evil among them; for as to the higher and more solemn thought, how persons, set apart individually and collectively, as Temples of Truth and Holiness, should become what they seem to be, and what their state is in consequence in God's sight, is a question which it is a great blessing to be allowed to put from us as not our concern. It is our concern only to look to ourselves, and to see that, as we have received the gift, we "grieve not the Holy Spirit of God, whereby we are sealed unto the day of redemption;" remembering that "if any man destroy the temple of God, him shall God destroy." This reflection and the recollection of our many backslidings, will ever keep us, please God, from judging others, or from priding ourselves on our privileges. Let us but consider how we have fallen from the light and grace of our Baptism. Were we now what that Holy Sacrament made us, we might ever "go on our way rejoicing;" but having sullied our heavenly garments, in one way or other, in a greater or less degree (God knoweth! and our own consciences too in a measure), alas! the Spirit of adoption has in part receded from us, and the sense of guilt, remorse, sorrow, and penitence must take His place. We must renew our confession, and seek afresh our absolution day by day, before we dare call upon God as "our Father," or offer up Psalms and Intercessions to Him. And, whatever pain and affliction meets us through life, we must take it as a merciful penance imposed by a Father upon erring children, to be borne meekly and thankfully, and as intended to remind us of the weight of that infinitely greater punishment, which was our desert by nature, and which Christ bore for us on the Cross.

SERMON XX.

The Kingdom of the Saints.

MONDAY IN WHITSUN WEEK.)

"The stone that smote the Image became a great Mountain, and filled the whole earth."—DANIEL ii. 35.

DOUBTLESS, could we see the course of God's dispensations in this world, as the Angels see them, we should not be able to deny that it was His unseen hand that ordered them. Even the most presumptuous sinner would find it hopeless to withstand the marks of Divine Agency in them; and would "believe and tremble." This is what moves the Saints in the Apocalypse, to praise and adore Almighty God,—the view of His wonderful works seen as a whole from first to last. "Great and marvellous are Thy works, Lord God Almighty; just and true are Thy ways, Thou King of Saints! Who shall not fear Thee, O Lord, and glorify Thy name?"[1] And perchance such a contemplation of the providences of God, whether in their own personal history, or in the affairs of their own country, or of the

---

[1] Rev. xv. 3, 4.

Church, or of the world at large, may be one of the blessed occupations of God's elect in the Intermediate State. However, even to us sinners, who have neither secured our crown like the Saints departed, much less are to be compared to the Angels who "excel in strength, that do His commandments, hearkening unto the voice of His Word,"[1] even to us is vouchsafed some insight into God's providence, by means of the records of it. History and Prophecy are given us as informants, and reflect various lights upon His Attributes and Will, whether separately or in combination. The text suggests to us an especial instance of this privilege, in the view which is allowed us of the introduction and propagation of the Gospel; and it will be fitting at a Season when we are especially commemorating its first public manifestation in the Holy Ghost's descent upon the Apostles, to make some remarks upon the wonderful providence of God as seen in it.

The words of Daniel in the text form part of the disclosure he was inspired to make to Nebuchadnezzar, of the dream that "troubled" him. After describing the great Image, with a head of fine gold, arms of silver, belly and thighs of brass, legs of iron, and feet of iron and clay, by which were signified the four Empires which preceded the coming of Christ, he goes on to foretell the rise of Christianity in these words: "Thou sawest till that a stone was cut out without hands, which smote the Image upon his feet which were of iron and clay, and brake them to pieces. Then was

[1] Ps. ciii. 20.

the iron, the clay, the brass, the silver, and the gold, broken-in pieces together, and became like the chaff;" heavy and costly as the metals were, they became as light as chaff "of the summer threshing-floors, and the wind carried them away . . . . And the stone that smote the Image became a great Mountain, and filled the whole earth."

Afterwards, he adds this interpretation: "In the days of these kings, shall the God of Heaven set up a Kingdom which shall never be destroyed; and the Kingdom shall not be left to other people, but it shall break in pieces, and consume all these kingdoms, and it shall stand for ever."

This prophecy of Daniel is fulfilled among us, at this day. We know it is so. Those four idol kingdoms are gone, and the Kingdom of Christ, made without human hands, remains, and is our own blessed portion. But to speak thus summarily, is scarcely to pay due honour to God's work, or to reap the full benefit of our knowledge of it. Let us then look into the details of this great Providence, the history of the Gospel Dispensation.

1. Observe what it was that took place. There have been many kingdoms before and since Christ came, which have been set up and extended by the sword. This, indeed, is the only way in which earthly power grows. Wisdom and skill direct its movements, but the arm of force is the instrument of its aggrandizement. And an unscrupulous conscience, a hard heart, and guilty deeds, are the usual attendants upon its growth : which is, in one form or other, but usurpation, *invasion*, conquest, and tyranny. It rises against its

neighbours, and increases by external collisions and a visible extension. But the propagation of the Gospel was the internal development of one and the same principle in various countries at once, and therefore may be suitably called invisible, and not of this world. The Jewish nation did not " push westward, and north-ward, and southward;" but a spirit went out from its Church into all lands, and wherever it came, there a new Order of things forthwith arose in the bosom of strangers; arose simultaneously, independently in each place, and recognising, but in no sense causing, the repetitions of itself which arose all around it. We know indeed that the Apostles were the instruments, the secret emissaries (as they might be called) of this work; but I am speaking of the appearance of things as a heathen might regard them. Who among the wise men or the disputers of this world will take account of a few helpless men wandering about from place to place, and preaching a new doctrine? It never can be believed, it is impossible that they should be the real agents of the revolution which followed. So we main-tain, and the world's philosophy must be consistent enough to agree with us. It looked down upon the Apostles in their day; it said they could effect nothing; let it say the same thing now in common fairness. Surely to the philosophy of this world it must appear as absurd to ascribe great changes to such weak vessels, as to attribute them to some imaginary unseen agents, to the heavenly hosts whose existence it disbelieves. As it would account the hypothesis of *Angelic interference* gratuitous, so did it then, and must still pronounce the hypothesis of the Apostolic efforts insufficient. Its own witness in the beginning becomes our evidence now.

Dismissing then the thought of the feeble and despised preachers, who went to and fro, let us see what really happened. In the midst of a great Empire, such as the world had never seen, powerful and crafty beyond all former empires, more extensive, and better organized, suddenly a new Kingdom arose. Suddenly in every part of this well-cemented Empire, in the East and West, North and South, as if by some general understanding, yet without any sufficient system of correspondence or centre of influence, ten thousand orderly societies, professing one and the same doctrine, and disciplined upon the same polity, sprang up as from the earth. It seemed as though the fountains of the great deep were broken up, and some new forms of creation were thrown forward from below, the manifold ridges of some " great Mountain," crossing, splitting, disarranging the existing system of things, levelling the hills, filling up the valleys,—irresistible as being sudden, unforeseen, and unprovided for,—till it " filled the whole earth."[1] This was indeed a " new thing;" and independent of all reference to prophecy, is unprecedented in the history of the world before or since, and calculated to excite the deepest interest and amazement in any really philosophical mind. Throughout the kingdoms and provinces of Rome, while all things looked as usual, the sun rising and setting, the seasons continuing, men's passions swaying them as from the beginning,

[1] Isa. xli. 15, 16.

heir thoughts set on their worldly business, on their gain or their pleasures, on their ambitious prospects and quarrels, warrior measuring his strength with warrior, politicians plotting, and kings banqueting, suddenly this portent came as a snare upon the whole earth. Suddenly, men found themselves encompassed with foes, as a camp surprised by night. And the nature of this hostile host was still more strange (if possible) than the coming of it. It was not a foreigner who invaded them, not a barbarian from the north, nor a rising of slaves, nor an armament of pirates, but the enemy rose up from among themselves. The first-born in every house, " from the first-born of Pharaoh on the throne, to the first-born of the captive in the dungeon," unaccountably found himself enlisted in the ranks of this new power, and estranged from his natural friends. Their brother, the son of their mother, the wife of their bosom, the friend that was as their own soul, these were the sworn soldiers of the " mighty army," that " covered the face of the whole earth."

Next, when they began to interrogate this enemy of Roman greatness, they found no vague profession among them, no varying account of themselves, no irregular and uncertain plan of action or conduct. They were all members of strictly and similarly organized societies. Every one in his own district was the subject of a new state, of which there was one visible head, and officers under him. These small kingdoms were indefinitely multiplied, each of them the fellow of the other. Wherever the Roman Emperor travelled, there he found these seeming rivals of his power, the Bishops of the

Church. Further, they one and all refused to obey his orders, and the prescriptive laws of Rome, so far as religion was concerned. The authority of the Pagan Religion, which in the minds of Romans was identified with the history of their greatness, was plainly set at nought by these upstart monarchies. At the same time they professed and observed a singular patience and subjection to the civil powers. They did not stir hand or foot in self-defence; they submitted to die, nay, accounted death the greatest privilege that could be inflicted on them. And further, they avowed one and all the same doctrine clearly and boldly; and they professed to receive it from one and the same source. They traced it up through the continuous line of their Bishops to certain twelve or fourteen Jews, who professed to have received it from Heaven. Moreover, they were bound one to another by the closest ties of fellowship; the society of each place to its ruler, and their rulers one with another by an intimate alliance all over the earth. And lastly, in spite of persecution from without, and occasional dissensions from within, they so prospered, that within three centuries from their first appearance in the Empire, they forced its sovereigns to become members of their confederation; nay, nor ended there, but as the civil power declined in strength, they became its patrons instead of its victims, mediated between it and its barbarian enemies, and after burying it in peace when its hour came, took its place, won over the invaders, subdued their kings, and at length ruled as supreme; ruled, united under one head, in the very scenes of their former suffering, in

the territory of the Empire, with Rome itself, the seat
of the Imperial government, as a centre. I am not
entering into the question of doctrine, any more than
of prophecy. I am not inquiring how far this vic-
torious Kingdom was by this time perverted from its
original character; but only directing attention to the
historical phenomenon. How strange then is the course
of the Dispensation! Five centuries compass the rise
and fall of other kingdoms; but ten were not enough
for the full aggrandizement of this. Its sovereignty
was but commencing, when other powers have run their
course and are exhausted. And now to this day, that
original Dynasty, begun by the Apostles, endures.
Through all changes of civil affairs, of race, of language,
of opinion, the succession of Rulers then begun, has
lasted on, and still represents in every country its
original founders. " Instead of its fathers, it has had
children, who have been princes in all lands." Truly,
this is the vision of a " stone *cut out without hands*,"
" smiting" the idols of the world, " breaking them in
pieces," scattering them " like chaff," and, in their place,
" filling the whole earth." If there be a Moral Governor
over the world, is there not something unearthly in all
this, something which we are forced to refer to Him
from its marvellousness, something which from its
dignity and greatness bespeaks His hand?

2. Now, with this wonderful phenomenon before us,
let us consider well the language of Christ and His
Apostles. In the very infancy of their Kingdom, while
travelling through the cities of Israel, or tossed to
and fro as *outcasts* among the heathen, they speak

confidently, solemnly, calmly, of its destined growth and triumph. Observe our Lord's language: "Jesus came into Galilee, preaching the Gospel of the Kingdom of God, and saying, The time is fulfilled, and the Kingdom of God is at hand; repent ye, and believe the Gospel." Again, "Thou art Peter, and upon this rock I will build My Church; and the gates of hell shall not prevail against it." "I appoint unto you a Kingdom, as My Father hath appointed unto Me; that ye may eat and drink at My table in My kingdom, and sit on thrones, judging the Twelve Tribes of Israel." "The Kingdom of Heaven is like to a grain of mustard seed, which a man took and sowed in his field; which indeed is the least of all seeds, but when it is grown, *it is the greatest among herbs,* and becometh a tree, *so that the birds of the air come and lodge in the branches thereof.*" Is it possible to doubt that Christ contemplated in these words the overshadowing sovereignty of His Kingdom? Let it be observed that the figure used is the same applied by Daniel to the Assyrian Empire. "The tree that thou sawest," he says to Nebuchadnezzar, "which grew and was strong . . . . . upon whose branches the fowls of the heaven had their habitation, it is thou, O King." How wondrously was the parallel prophecy fulfilled, when the mighty men of the earth fled for refuge to the Holy Church! Again, "Go ye into all the world, and preach the Gospel to every creature. He that believeth and is baptized shall be saved; but he that believeth not shall be damned."[1]

[1] Mark i. 14, 15. Matt. xvi. 18. Luke xxii. 29, 30. Matt. xiii. 31, 32. Dan. iv. 20, 22. Mark vi. 15, 16.

With what "authority" He speaks! What majestic simplicity, what unhesitating resolve, what commanding superiority is in His words! Reflect upon them in connexion with the event.

On the other hand, consider in what language He speaks of that disorganization · of society which was to attend the establishment of His kingdom. "I am come to send fire on the earth ; and what will I, if it be already kindled? But I have a baptism to be baptized with, and how am I straitened till it be accomplished!" "Think not that I am come to send peace on earth; I came not to send peace, but a sword. For I am come to set a man at variance against his father, and the daughter against her mother, and the daughter-in-law against the mother-in-law : and a man's foes shall be they of his own household." "The brother shall betray the brother to death, and the father the son; and children shall rise up against their parents, and shall cause them to be put to death; and ye shall be hated of all men for My name's sake. . . . . In those days, after that tribulation, the sun shall be darkened, and the moon shall not give her light, and the stars of heaven shall fall, and the powers of heaven shall be shaken."[1] In the last words, whatever difficulty there may be in the chronological arrangement, is contained a clear announcement under the recognised prophetical symbols, of the destruction, sooner or later, of existing political institutions. In like manner, observe how St. Paul takes for granted the troubles which were coming on the earth, and the rise of the Christian

[1] Luke xii. 49, 50. Matt. x. 34—36. Mark xiii. 12, 13, 24, 25.

n]   R

Church amidst them, and reasons on all this as if already realized. "Now hath He promised, saying, Yet once more I shake not the earth only, but also heaven. And this word, yet once more, signifieth the removing of those things that are shaken, as of things that are made, that those things which cannot be shaken may remain. Wherefore we receiving a Kingdom which cannot be moved, let us have grace, whereby we may serve God acceptably with reverence and godly fear." [1]

The language, of which the above is but a specimen, is the more remarkable, because neither Christ nor His Apostles looked forward to these wonderful changes with exultation, but with a deep feeling of mingled joy and sadness, as foreboding those miserable corruptions in the Church, which all Christians allow to have since taken place, though they may differ in their account of them. " Because iniquity shall abound, the love of many shall wax cold. . . . . There shall arise false Christs and false prophets, and shall show great signs and wonders ; insomuch that, if it were possible, they shall deceive the very elect. Behold, I have told you before." " In the last days, perilous times shall come. For men shall be lovers of their own selves, covetous, boasters, ... traitors, heady, high-minded . . . . having a form of godliness, but denying the power thereof. . . . . Evil men and seducers shall wax worse and worse, deceiving and being deceived." [2]

Now, if we had nothing more to bring forward than the two considerations which have been here insisted

[1] Heb. xii. 26—28.
[2] Matt. xxiv. 12, 24, 25. 2 Tim. iii. 1—5, 13.

the singular history of Christianity, and the clear
l confident anticipation of it by its first preachers,
should have enough of evidence, one would think,
;ubdue the most difficult inquirer to a belief of its
inity. But, to-morrow we will see, please God,
ether something may not be added to the above
w of it.

SERMON XXI.

The Kingdom of the Saints.

(TUESDAY IN WHITSUN WEEK.)

" The stone that smote the Image became a great Mountain, and filled the whole earth."—DANIEL ii. 35.

YESTERDAY I drew your notice to the outlines of the history of the Church, and the clear and precise anticipation of it, by our Lord and His Apostles. The Gospel Dispensation is confessedly a *singular* phenomenon in human affairs; singular, whether we consider the extent it occupies in history, the harmony of its system, the consistency of its design, its contrariety to the existing course of things, and success in spite of that contrariety, and lastly, the avowed intention of its first preachers to effect those objects, which it really has attained. They professed to be founding a Kingdom; a new Kingdom, different from any that had been before, as disclaiming the use of force,—in this world, yet not of this world,—while it was to be, notwithstanding, of an aggressive and *encroaching* character, an empire of conquest and aggrandizement, destroying all former powers, and itself standing for ever. Infidels often object to us, that our interpretation of the Scripture prophecies concerning Christ's Kingdom is after all but allegorical, and therefore evasive. Not so; we are on the whole willing to take our stand on their literal fulfilment. Christ preached that "the kingdom of God was at hand." He founded it and made Peter and the other Apostles His Vicegerents in it after His departure, and He announced its indefinite extension, and its unlimited duration. And, in matter of fact, it exists to this day, with its government vested in the very dynasty which His Apostles began, and its territory spread over more than the world then known to the Jews; with varying success indeed in times and places, and varying consistency and unanimity within; yet, after making every allowance for such partial failures, strictly a visible power, with a political influence founded on invisible pretensions. Thus the anticipations of its founders are unparalleled in their novelty, their boldness, and their correctness. To continue our review.

3. If the Christian Church has spread its branches high and wide over the earth, its roots are fixed as deep below the surface. The intention of Christ and His Apostles, on which I have dwelt, is itself but the accomplishment of ancient prophecy.

First, let it be observed that there was an existing belief among the heathen, at the time of its rise, that out of the East a new Empire of the world was destined to issue.[1] This rumour, however originating,

---

[1] *Vide Horsley's Dissertation* on the Prophecies among the Heathen.

was known at Rome, the then seat of dominion, and
is recorded by a Roman historian. Next, it became
matter (as it would seem) for heathen poetry. The
most celebrated of Roman poets has foretold the coming
of a new Kingdom of peace and righteousness under
the rule of a divine and divinely-favoured King, who
was to be born into the world. Could it be maintained
that he wrote from his own imagination, not from
existing traditions, this would not at all diminish the
marvel, as not in any measure tending to account for
it. In that case, the poet would but take his place
among the Prophets. Further, if we admit St. Matthew's
testimony, which we have no excuse for doubting, we
must believe, that, just at the time of Christ's birth,
certain Eastern Sages came to Jerusalem in search of
a child, of whom they expected great things, and whom
they desired to worship in His cradle. And lastly,
another Eastern Sage, fourteen hundred years before,
had declared, heathen though he was, and uninterested
in the event, that "a Star should come out of Jacob,
and a Sceptre should rise out of Israel, . . . that out
of Jacob should come He that should have dominion."[1]
Now, whether we may assume that this last prophecy is
faithfully recorded by Moses or not, so far is clear, and
not a little remarkable, that the Jewish traditions concerning the expected Empire profess to take their rise
in heathen sources.[2] It is a clear coincidence with the

[1] Numb. xxiv. 17, 19.
[2] Gen. xlix. 10, does not speak of conquest or empire, so clearly as
to constitute an exception; much less Gen. xii. 2, 3, and xxviii. 14,
*which could scarcely be so interpreted, except after other and clearer
prophecies.*

fact, already adverted to, of the prevalence of such predictions among the heathen at the time of Christ's coming.

While such was the testimony of enemies and strangers to this destined rise of a prosperous Empire from Judæa, much more full and varied are the predictions of it delivered by the natives of that country themselves. These, as contained in our holy books, have been again and again illustrated by Christian writers, and neither need nor admit of enumeration here. I will but cite one or two passages, by way of reminding you of them. "Ask of Me, and I shall give Thee the heathen for Thine inheritance, and the uttermost parts of the earth for Thy possession. Thou shalt break them with a rod of iron; Thou shalt dash them in pieces like a potter's vessel." "Gird Thy sword upon Thy thigh, O most Mighty, with Thy glory and Thy majesty. And in Thy majesty ride prosperously, because of truth, and meekness, and righteousness : and Thy right hand shall teach Thee terrible things. Thine arrows are sharp in the heart of the King's enemies, whereby the people fall under Thee..... Instead of Thy fathers shall be Thy children, whom Thou mayest make princes in all the earth." "The Lord shall send the rod of Thy strength out of Zion; rule Thou in the midst of Thine enemies..... The Lord at Thy right hand shall strike through kings in the day of His wrath." "It shall come to pass in the last days, that the Mountain of the Lord's House shall be established in the top of the mountains, and shall be exalted above the hills; and all nations shall flow unto it..... Out of Zion shall go forth the *Law,* and *the* Word of the Lord from Jeru-

salem. And He shall judge among the nations, and
shall rebuke many people; and they shall beat their
swords into plowshares, and their spears into pruning
hooks; nation shall not lift up sword against nation
neither shall they learn war any more." "It is a light
thing that Thou shouldest be My servant to raise up the
tribes of Jacob, and to restore the preserved of Israel.
I will also give Thee for a light to the Gentiles, that
Thou shouldest be My salvation unto the end of the
earth." And almost in the same words, the aged Simeon
recognises in the infant Jesus the Lord's promised
"salvation, a light to lighten the Gentiles, and the glory
of His people Israel."[1] In these passages the prediction
of bloody revolution and of peace are as strangely com-
bined, as in our Lord's account of His Kingdom, as
being at once a refuge and consolation, and a sword.
Maintain, if you will, that they have not hitherto been
so fully accomplished in its history as is conceivable;
yet, in matter of fact, has not this twofold character of
the Dispensation been in such measure realized, as
substantially answers to the words of the prediction?
Consider only the wars and tumults of the Middle Ages,
of which the Church was the occasion, and, at the same
time, its salutary influence upon the fierce and lawless
soldiers who then filled the thrones of Europe. Take
the Prophecy, take the History; and say fairly, whether,
in accordance with the Scripture prospect, we do not
actually find in the centuries I speak of, a political
power, making vassals of the kings of the earth,

---

[1] *Ps. ii. 8, 9; xlv. 3—5, 16; cx. 2, 5. Isa. ii. 2—4; xlix. 6.
Luke ii. 30—32*

humbling them beneath its feet, affording matter of endless strife, yet acting as the very bond of peace, as far as peace was really attained. How truly have "the sons of them that afflicted" the Church, "come bending unto her; and they that despised her, bowed themselves at the soles of her feet,"[1] and "the enemies of Christ been made His footstool!"

It may help us in entering into the state of the case, to consider what our surprise would be, did we, in the course of our researches into history, find any resemblance to this prophetic forecast in the annals of other kingdoms. Even one poor coincidence in the history of Rome, viz. of the anticipated and the actual duration of its greatness, does not fail to arrest our attention. We know that even before the Christian era, it was the opinion of the Roman Augurs, that the twelve vultures which Romulus had seen previous to the foundation of the city, represented the twelve centuries, assigned as the limit of its power; an anticipation which was singularly fulfilled by the event.[2] Yet what is this solitary fact to the series of varied and circumstantial prophecies which ushered in, and were fulfilled in Christianity? Extend the twelve centuries of Roman dominion to an additional half of that period, preserve its monarchical form inviolate, whether from aristocratic or popular innovation, from first to last, and trace back the pre-

---

[1] Isa. lx. 14.

[2] *Vide* Gibbon, ch. xxxv. *fin.* The ancient prediction concerning the fortunes of Russia is a more remarkable instance. A brazen equestrian statue, which had been originally in Antioch, is said, by historians of the beginning of the twelfth century, to be "inscribed with a prophecy, how the Russians in the last days should become masters of Constantinople."—*Vide Gibbon*, ch. lv.

dictions concerning it, through an antecedent period, nearly of the same duration, and then you will have assimilated its history—not altogether, but in one or two of its features—to the characteristics of the Gospel Dispensation. As it is, this Roman wonder only serves to assist the imagination in embracing the marvellousness of those systematic prophecies concerning Christ's kingdom, which, from their number, variety, succession, and contemporary influence, may almost be accounted in themselves, and without reference to their fulfilment, a complete and independent dispensation.

4. Lastly, the course of Providence co-operated with this scheme of prophecy; God's word and hand went together. The state of the Jews for the last four hundred years before Christ was a preparation deliberately carried on for that which was to follow; just as the wanderings of Abraham and his heirs, the descent into Egypt, and the captivity there, for the same period, constituted a process introductory to the establishment of the Jewish Church. Consider the nature of this preparation :—the overthrow of the nation by the Chaldeans, issued in the dispersion of its members all over the civilized world, so that in all the principal cities Jewish communities existed, which gradually attracted to their faith Gentile converts, and were in one way or other the nucleus of the Christian Church when the Gospel was at length published. Now, here, I would first direct your attention to this strange connexion, which is visible at first sight between the dispersion of the Jews and the propagation of Christianity. Does *not such a* manifest appearance of cause and effect look

very much like an indication of design? Next, I remark that this dispersion was later than the predictions
concerning the Christian Church contained in the Jewish
Scriptures: which in consequence cannot be charged
with borrowing the idea of it from any actual disposition
of things. And further, let it be observed that the disposition arose from the apparent frustration of all their
hopes; a signal instance, as it would seem, of an overruling Providence, which would not be defeated as
regards its object, in spite of the failure of those instruments, in which alone a human eye could see the means
of accomplishing it.

Before concluding, I must explain myself on one
point which has been incidentally mentioned more than
once in the foregoing remarks, viz. as to the connexion
between the temporal fortunes of the Church in the
Middle Ages, and the inspired predictions concerning it.
It may seem, before due attention has been given to the
subject, as if none but members of the Roman Communion could regard them as parts of the Divine
Dispensation; I therefore observe as follows:—

There is a considerable analogy between the history
of what are called the Middle Ages and that of the
Israelitish monarchy. That monarchy was perversely
demanded and presumptuously realized by the nation
when God had not led the way; it terminated in the
dissolution of the federal union of the Tribes, the corruption of the people, and the ruin of their temporal power.
Nevertheless, it cannot be denied, that in one sense that
kingdom was the scope of the Mosaic Institutions,[1] and

[1] Deut. xvii. 14—20.

a fulfilment of prophecy. Its kings were many of them highly favoured in themselves, and types of the promised Saviour; and their government and subjects were singularly blessed. Consider the circumstances attendant upon the building of the Temple. This may be accounted as the most glorious event in their history, the fruit of Moses' anxieties and David's labours, the completion and resting-place of the whole Dispensation, and the pledge of the more spiritual blessedness which was to come. Connect it with Solomon's reign, its peace and prosperity,—on the other hand, with its voluptuousness, its departure from the simplicity of the Mosaic Law,—with Solomon's personal character, degenerating from faith and purity into sins which we are not given to fathom. Are we able rightly to adjust the relation between the blessings destined for Israel, and the actual prosperity and greatness of this kingdom set up in rebellion against God, so as to be able to say how far it was recognised in His counsels, how far not? Can we draw the line between God's work and man's work?

I am not maintaining that the case of the Papacy is parallel to that of the Jewish Monarchy; nay, I do not introduce the latter for the sake of the analogy at all, be it stronger or fainter; but merely in order to show that it is possible for certain events to be in some sort a fulfilment of prophecy, without considering every part of them, the manner of their accomplishment, the circumstances, the instruments, and the like, to be approved by God. The Latin ecclesiastical system of the Middle Ages may anyhow be the fulfilment of that gracious design, which would have been even more exactly accomplished, had Christians possessed faith enough to keep closely to God's revealed will. For what we know, it was intended that all the kingdoms of the earth should have been made subject to the spiritual rule of the Church. The infirmity of man defeated this purpose; but it could not so far defeat it, but some sort of fulfilment took place. The mustard-plant, stopped in its natural growth, shot out irregular branches. Satan could not hinder, he could but weaken the Kingdom promised to the Saints. He could but seduce them to trust in an arm of flesh. He could but sow the seeds of decay among them, by alluring them to bow down to "Ashtoreth the goddess of the Zidonians, and Milcom the abomination of the Ammonites." Had it not been for this falling away in divers times and places, surely Christendom would not be in its present miserable state of disunion and feebleness; nor the prophecies respecting it have issued in any degree in defeat and disappointment. Still partial as is their fulfilment, there is more than enough, even in what is and has been, to attest in the Church the presence of that Almighty Hand, whose very failures (so to say) and losses are deeds of victory and triumph.

As for ourselves, what was the exact measure of the offences of our forefathers in the faith, when they tired of the Christian Theocracy, and clothed the Church with "the purple robe" of Cæsar, it avails not to determine. Not denying their sin, still after contemplating the glories of the Temple which were contemporaneous with it, we may well bewail our present fallen state,—the Priests and Levites, and chief of the Fathers, all of us "weeping with a loud voice," though the many shout for joy,—"praising" indeed, "and giving thanks unto the Lord, because He is good, for His mercy endureth for ever toward Israel," [1]—not undervaluing the blessings we have, yet humbling ourselves as the sinful offspring of sinful parents, who from the first have resisted and frustrated the grace of God, and seeing in the present feebleness and blindness of the Church, the tokens of His righteous judgments upon us; yet withal, from His continued mercies towards us, drawing the comfortable hope, that for His Son's sake He will not forsake us in time to come, and cherishing a sure trust, that, if we "give Him no rest" by our services of prayer and good works, He will at length, even yet, though doubtless in a way which we cannot understand, "establish and make Jerusalem a praise in the earth."

[1] Ezra iii. 11, 12.

SERMON XXII.

The Gospel, a Trust committed to us.

(THE FEAST OF THE HOLY TRINITY.)

" O Timothy, keep that which is committed to thy trust, avoiding profane and vain babblings, and oppositions of science, falsely so called; which some professing, have erred concerning the Faith."—1 TIM. vi. 20, 21.

THESE words are addressed in the first place to the Ministers of the Gospel, in the person of Timothy; yet they contain a serious command and warning for all Christians. For all of us, high and low, in our measure are responsible for the safe-keeping of the Faith. We have all an equal interest in it, no one less than another, though an Order of men has been especially set apart for the duty of guarding it. If we Ministers of Christ guard it not, it is *our* sin but it is *your* loss, my brethren; and as any private person would feel that his duty and his safety lay in giving alarm of a fire or of a robbery in the city where he dwelt, though there were ever so many special officers appointed for the purpose, so, doubtless, every one of us is bound in his place to contend for *the Faith*, and to have an eye to its safe custody. If indeed the Faith of Christ were vague, indeterminate, a matter of opinion or deduction, then, indeed, we may well conceive that the Ministers of the Gospel would be the only due expounders and guardians of it; then it might be fitting for private Christians to wait till they were informed concerning the best mode of expressing it, or the relative importance of this or that part of it. But this has been all settled long ago; the Gospel Faith is a definite deposit,—a treasure, common to all, one and the same in every age, conceived in set words, and such as admits of being received, preserved, transmitted. We may safely leave the custody of it even in the hands of individuals; for in so doing, we are leaving nothing at all to private rashness and fancy, to pride, debate, and strife. We are but allowing men to "contend earnestly for the Faith once delivered to the Saints;" the Faith which was put into their hands one by one at their baptism, in a form of words called the Creed, and which has come down to them in that very same form from the first ages. This Faith is what even the humblest member of the Church may and must contend for; and in proportion to his education, will the circle of his knowledge enlarge. The Creed delivered to him in Baptism will then unfold, first, into the Nicene Creed (as it is called), then into the Athanasian; and, according as his power of grasping the sense of its articles increases, so will it become his duty to contend for them in their fuller and more accurate form. All these unfoldings of the Gospel Doctrine will become to him precious as the original articles, *because* they are in fact nothing more or less than the one true explanation of them delivered down to us from the first ages, together with the original baptismal or Apostles' Creed itself. As all nations confess to the existence of a God, so all branches of the Church confess to the Gospel doctrine; as the tradition of men witnesses to a Moral Governor and Judge, so the tradition of Saints witnesses to the Father Almighty, and His only Son, and the Holy Ghost. And as neither the superstitions of polytheism, nor the atheistic extravagances of particular countries at particular times, practically interfere with our reception of the one message which the sons of Adam deliver; so, much less, do the local heresies and temporary errors of the early Church, and its superadded corruptions, its schismatic offshoots, or its partial defections in later ages, impair the evidence and the claim of its teaching, in the judgment of those who sincerely wish to know the Truth once delivered to it. Blessed be God! we have not to find the Truth, it is put into our hands; we have but to commit it to our hearts, to preserve it inviolate, and to deliver it over to our posterity.

This then is the meaning of St. Paul's injunction in the text, given at the time when the Truth was first published. "Keep that which is committed to thy trust," or rather, "keep the deposit;" turn away from those "profane emptinesses" which pretenders to philosophy and science bring forward against it. Do not be moved by them; do not alter your Creed for them; for the end of such men is error. They go on disputing and refining, giving new meanings, modifying received ones, still with *the idea* of the True Faith in their minds

n7

s

as the scope of their inquiries; but at length they "miss"
it. They shoot on one side of it, and embrace a deceit
of their own instead of it.

By the Faith is evidently meant, as St. Paul's words
show, some definite doctrine; not a mere temper of
mind or principle of action, much less, vaguely, the
Christian cause; and accordingly, in his Second Epistle
to Timothy, the Apostle mentions as his comfort in the
view of death, that he had "kept the Faith." In the
same Epistles he describes it more particularly as "the
Form" or outline "of sound words," "the excellent deposit;" phrases which show that the deposit certainly
was a series of truths and rules of some sort (whether
only doctrinal, or preceptive also, and ecclesiastical),
and which are accurately descriptive of the formulary
since called the Apostles' Creed.[1] And these same
sacred truths which Timothy had received in trust, he
was bid "commit" in turn "to faithful men," who
should be "able to teach others also." By God's grace,
he was enabled so to commit them; and they being
thus transmitted from generation to generation, have,
through God's continued mercy, reached even unto us
"upon whom the ends of the world are come."

I propose in what follows, to set before you the
account given us in Scripture of this Apostolic Faith;
being led to do so on the one hand by the Day, on
which we commemorate its fundamental doctrine, and

---

[1] *Vide* also, among other passages, 1 John ii. 21—27, which refers
to nothing short of a definite doctrine; *e. g.* "Let that therefore abide
in you, *which ye have heard* from the beginning." Again, 2 Tim. ii.
18, "Who *concerning the Truth* have erred, *saying that the Resurrec-
on is past already*, and overthrow the *faith* of some."

on the other, by the mistaken views entertained of it by many persons in this day, which seem to require notice.

Perhaps it may be right first to state what these erroneous opinions are; which I will do briefly. They are not novel, as scarcely any religious error can be, and assuredly what has once or twice died away in former times will come to its end in like manner once more. I do not speak as if I feared it could overcome the Ancient Truth once delivered to the Saints; but still our watchfulness and care are the means appointed for its overthrow, and are not superseded, but rather encouraged, and roused, by the anticipation of ultimate success.

It is a fashion of the day, then, to suppose that all insisting upon precise Articles of Faith is injurious to the cause of spiritual religion, and inconsistent with an enlightened view of it; that it is all one to maintain, that the Gospel requires the reception of definite and positive Articles, and to acknowledge it to be technical and formal; that such a notion is superstitious, and interferes with the "liberty wherewith Christ has made us free;" that it argues a deficient insight into the principles and ends, a narrow comprehension of the spirit of His Revelation. Accordingly, instead of accepting reverently the doctrinal Truths which have come down to us, an attempt is made by the reasoners of this age to compare them together, to weigh and measure them, to analyse, simplify, refashion them; to reduce them to system, to arrange them into primary and secondary, to harmonize *them into* an intelligible dependence upon

each other. The teacher of Christianity, instead of delivering its Mysteries, and (as far as may be) unfolding
them, is taught to scrutinise them, with a view of separating the inward holy sense from the form of words, in
which the Spirit has indissolubly lodged them. He
asks himself, what is the *use* of the message which has
come down to him? what the comparative value of this
or that part of it? He proceeds to assume that there is
some one end of his ministerial labours, such as to be
ascertainable by him, some one revealed object of God's
dealings with man in the Gospel. Then, perhaps, he arbi-
trarily assigns this end to be the salvation of the world,
or the conversion of sinners. Next he measures all the
Scripture doctrines by their respective sensible tendency
to effect this end. He goes on to discard or degrade
this or that sacred truth as superfluous in consequence,
or of inferior importance; and throws the stress of his
teaching upon one or other, which he pronounces to
contain in it the essence of the Gospel, and on which he
rests all others which he retains. Lastly, he recon-
structs the language of theology to suit his (so-called)
improved views of Scripture doctrine.

For instance, you will meet with writers who consider
that all the Attributes and Providences of God are virtually expressed in the one proposition, "God is Love;"
the other notices of His Unapproachable Glory contained in Scripture being but modifications of this. In
consequence, they are led on to deny, first, the doctrine
of eternal punishment, as being inconsistent with this
notion of Infinite Love; next, resolving such expressions as the "wrath of God" into a figure of speech,

they deny the Atonement, viewed as a real reconciliation of an offended God to His creatures. Or again, they say that the object of the Gospel Revelation is merely practical, and therefore, that theological doctrines are altogether unnecessary, mere speculations, and hindrances to the extension of religion; or, if not purely injurious, at least requiring modification. Hence you may hear them ask, "What is the *harm* of being a Sabellian, or Arian? how does it affect the moral character?" Or, again, they say that the great end of the Gospel is the union of hearts in the love of Christ and of each other, and that, in consequence, Creeds are but fetters on souls which have received the Spirit of Adoption; that Faith is a mere temper and a principle, not the acceptance for Christ's sake of a certain collection of Articles. Others, again, have rested the whole Gospel upon the doctrines of the Atonement and Sanctification. And others have seemed to make the doctrine of Justification by Faith the one cardinal point, upon which the gates of life open and shut. Let so much suffice in explanation of the drift of the following remarks.

St. Paul, I repeat, bids us hold fast the faith which is entrusted to our custody; and that Faith is a "Form of sound words," an "Outline," which it is our duty, according to our opportunities, to fill up and complete in all its parts. Now, let us see how much the very text of Scripture will yield us of these elementary lines of Truth, of the unchangeable Apostolic Rule of Faith, of which we are bound to be so jealous.

Its essential *doctrine* of course is what St. John terms

generally "the doctrine of Christ," and which, in the case of every one calling himself Christian, is the profession necessary (as he tells us) for our receiving him into our houses. St. Paul speaks in much the same compendious way concerning the Gospel Faith, when he says, "Other foundation can no man lay than that is laid, which is Jesus, the Christ." However, in an earlier passage of the same Epistle, he speaks more explicitly: "I determined not to know anything among you save Jesus Christ, and Him crucified." Thus the Crucifixion of Christ was one essential part of the outline of sound words, preached and delivered by the Apostle. In his Epistle to the Romans, he adds another article of faith: "If thou shalt confess with thy mouth the Lord Jesus, and shalt believe in thine heart that God hath raised Him from the dead, thou shalt be saved." Here then the doctrine of the Resurrection is added to that of the Crucifixion. Elsewhere he says: "There is One God, and one Mediator between God and man, the Man Christ Jesus, who gave Himself a ransom for all to be testified in due time; even whereunto I am ordained a preacher." Here Christ's Mediation and Atonement are added as doctrines of Apostolical preaching. Further, towards the end of an Epistle already quoted, he speaks still more distinctly of the Gospel which he had preached, and had delivered over to his converts; and which, he adds, all the other Apostles preached also. "I put into your hands, first of all, what had before been put into mine, how that Christ died for our sins according to the Scriptures, and *tha'* He was buried, and that He rose again the third day according to the Scriptures." [1] Here we find an approximation to the Articles of the Creed, as the Church has ever worded them.

But the letter of Scripture gives us still further insight into the subjects of the Sacred Deposit, of which St. Paul speaks in the text. In the course of the very Epistle in which it occurs, he delivers to Timothy a more explicit "Form of sound words" than any I have cited from his writings. He writes to tell him " how to conduct himself in the Church of the Living God," which he had to govern, and how to preserve it as "the pillar and ground of the Truth;" and proceeds to remind him what that Truth is. "God was manifested in the flesh, justified in the Spirit, seen of Angels, preached unto the Gentiles, believed on in the world, received up into glory." Here is mention, among other doctrines, of the Incarnation and the Ascension. It seems then to have been an article of the original Apostles' Creed, that Christ was not a mere man, but God Incarnate. In like manner, when the Ethiopian asked to be baptized, and Philip said he might if he "believed with all his heart," this was his confession: "I believe that Jesus Christ is the Son of God." This, it should be observed, · is his confession, *after* Philip had "*preached unto him Jesus.*" [2]

Now, let us pass on to the very words in which that Baptism itself was administered; words which the Eunuch might not understand indeed at the time, but

[1] 2 John 9—11. 1 Cor. iii. 11 ; ii. 2. Rom. x. 9. 1 Tim. ii. 5—7. 1 Cor. xv. 3, 4.
[2] 1 Tim. iii. 15, 16. Acts viii. 35—37.

which were then committed to him to feed upon in his
heart by faith, and by the influence of the grace at the
same time given, gradually to enter into. Those words
were first ordained by Christ Himself, as some mysterious key by which the fountains of grace might be
opened upon the baptismal water,—"In the Name of
the Father and of the Son, and of the Holy Ghost;"
and they shew that not only the doctrine of Christ, but
that of the Trinity also, formed an essential portion of
the Sacred Treasure, of which the Church was ordained
to be the Preacher. Lastly, in the Epistle to the
Hebrews we are presented with an enumeration of
some other of the fundamental Articles of Faith which
the Apostles delivered. St. Paul therein speaks of
"the foundation of repentance from dead works, and of
Faith towards God, of the doctrine of Baptisms, and of
Laying on of hands, and of Resurrection of the dead,
and of Eternal Judgment."[1]

Observe then, how many Articles of that Faith, which
the Church has ever confessed, are incidentally brought
before us as such, and delivered as such in very form, in
the course of Scripture narrative and precept;—the
· doctrine of the Trinity; of the Incarnation of the Son
of God, His Mediatorship, His Atonement for our sins
on the Cross, His Death, Burial, Resurrection on the
third day, and Ascension; of Pardon on Repentance,
Baptism as the instrument of it, Imposition of hands,
the General Resurrection and the Judgment once for all.
I might also appeal to such passages as that in the First

---

[1] Matt. xxviii. 19. Heb. vi. 1, 2. *Vide* also 2 Tim. ii. 16—18,
above referred to.

Epistle to the Corinthians, where St. Paul says, " To us there is one God the Father, ... and one Lord Jesus Christ;"[1] but I wished to confine myself to texts in which the doctrines specified are expressly introduced as portions of a Formulary or Confession, committed or accepted, whether on the part of Ministers of the Church at Ordination, or of each member of it when he was baptized.

It may be proper to add, that the history of the Primitive Church altogether concurs in this view of the nature of Gospel Faith which Scripture sets before us. I mean we have sufficient evidence that, in matter of fact, such Creeds as St. Paul's did exist in its various branches, not differing from each other, except (for instance) as the Lord's Prayer in St. Matthew's Gospel differs from St. Luke's version of it; that this one and the same Faith was committed to every Christian everywhere on his baptism; and that it was considered as the especial trust of the Church of each place and of its Bishop, as having been received by continual transmission from its original Founder, whether Apostle or Evangelist.

Enough has been already said by way of proving from Scripture how precise, positive, manifold, are the Articles of our Faith, and how St. Paul insists on this their definiteness and minuteness; enough to show that we may not slur them over, nor heap them together confusedly, nor tamper with them, with the profaneness either of carelessness or of curious disputing,—in a word, that they are *sacred*. But this sacred character of our trust may

---

[1] 1 Cor. viii. 6.

be shown by several distinct considerations, which shall now be set before you.

1. First, from the very circumstance that it *is* a trust. The plain and simple reason for our preaching and preserving the Faith, is because we have been told to do so. It is an act of mere obedience to Him who has "put us in trust with the Gospel." Our one great concern as regards it, is to deliver it over safe. This is the end in view, which all men have before them, who are anyhow trusted in worldly matters. "It is required in stewards, that a man be found faithful."[1] Our Lord had said, that "this Gospel of the Kingdom shall be preached in all the world *as a witness* unto all nations." Accordingly, His Apostle declares, speaking of his persecutions, "None of these things move me, . . . so that I might finish . . . the Ministry which I have received of the Lord Jesus, fully to *witness* the Gospel of the grace of God." And again, when his departure is at hand, he comforts himself with the reflection, that he has "kept the Faith."[2] To keep the Faith in the world till the end, may, for what we know, be a sufficient object of our preaching and confessing, though nothing more come of it. Hence then the force of the words addressed to Timothy: "Hold fast," "keep;" "This charge I commit unto thee;" "continue thou in the things entrusted thee;" "put the brethren in remembrance;" "commit thou the same to faithful men;" "refuse profane and old wives' fables;" "shun profane vain talking;" "avoid foolish and unlearned questions." Were there no other reason for the Articles of the

[1] 1 Cor. iv. 2.   [2] Matt. xxiv. 14.   Acts xx. 24.   2 Tim. iv. 7.

Creed being held sacred, their being a trust would be sufficient. Till we feel that we *have* a trust, a treasure to transmit, for the safety of which we are answerable, we have missed one chief peculiarity in our actual position. Yet did men feel this adequately, they would have little heart to indulge in the random speculations which at present are so familiar to their minds.

2. This sense of the seriousness of our charge is increased by considering, that after all we do not know, and cannot form a notion, what is the real final object of the Gospel Revelation. Men are accustomed to say, that it is the salvation of the world, which it certainly is not. If, instead of this, we say that Christ came "to purify unto Himself a peculiar people," then, indeed, we speak a great Truth; but this, though a main end of our preaching, is not its simple and ultimate object. Rather, as far as we are told at all, that object is the glory of God; but we cannot understand what is meant by this, or how the Dispensation of the Gospel promotes it. It is enough for us that we must act with the simple thought of God before us, make all ends subordinate to this, and leave the event to Him. We know, indeed, to our great comfort, that we cannot preach in vain. His heavenly word "shall not return unto Him void, but shall prosper in the thing whereto He sent it." Still it is surely our duty to preach, "whether men will hear, or whether they will forbear." We must preach, as our Lord enjoins in a text already quoted, "as a witness." Accordingly He Himself, before the heathen Pilate, "bore witness unto the truth;" and St. Paul conjures us to keep our sacred charge as in the presence of Him,

who "before Pontius Pilate witnessed a good confession." Doubtless, His glory is set forth in some mysterious way in the rejection, as well as in the reception of the Gospel; and we must co-operate with Him. We must co-operate so far, as to be content to wound as well as to heal, to condemn as well as to absolve. We must not shrink from being " a savour from death unto death," as well as of "life unto life." We must stedfastly believe, however painful may be the duty, that we are in either case offering up a " sweet savour of Christ unto God both in them that are saved, and in them that perish." We must learn to acquiesce and concur in the order of God's providence, and bear to rejoice over great Babylon and her inhabitants, when the wrath of God has fallen upon her.

This consideration is an answer to those who would limit our message to what is influential and convincing in it, and measure its divinity by its success. But I have introduced it rather to show generally, how utterly we are in the dark about the whole subject ; and there-fore, as being in the dark, how necessary it is to gird our garments about us, and hold fast our treasure, and hasten forward, lest we betray our trust. We have no means of knowing how far a small mistake in the Faith may carry us astray. If we do not know why it is to be proclaimed to all, though all will not hear, much less do we know why this or that doctrine is revealed, or what is the importance of it. The grant of grace in Baptism follows upon the accurate enunciation of one or two words ; and if so much depends on one sacred observance, *even down* to the letter in which it is committed to us,

why should not at least the substantial sense of other
truths, nay, even the primitive wording of them, have
some especial claim upon the Church's safe guardianship
of them ?   St. Paul's Articles of Belief are precise and
individual; why should we not take them as we find
them ?   Why should we be wise above that is written ?
Why should we not be thankful that a work is put upon
us which is so plainly within our power, to hold the
Gospel Truths, to count and note them, to feed upon
them, to hand them on ?   However, wilful and feverish
minds have not the wisdom to trust Divine teaching.
They persist in saying that Articles of Belief are mere
formalities ; and that to preach and transmit them is to
miss the conversion of the heart in faith and holiness.
They would rather rouse emotions, with the view (as
they hope) of changing the character.   Forgetful that
tempers and states of mind are things seen by God alone,
and when really spiritual are the work of His Unseen
Spirit, and beyond the power of man to insure or ascertain, they put upon themselves what a man cannot do.
They think it a light thing to be sowers of that heavenly
seed, which He shall make spring up in the hearer's
heart to life eternal.   They are willing to throw it aside
as something barren and worthless, as the sand of the
sea-shore ; and they desire to plant simply the flowers of
grace (or what appear such) in one another's hearts, as
though under their assiduous culture they could take
root therein.   Far different is the example set us in the
services of the Church !   In the Office for Baptism the
Articles of the Creed are recited one by one, that the
infant *Christian* may be put in charge of every jot and

tittle of the sacred Covenant, which he inherits.   In the
Communion Service, in the midst of its solemn praises
to the God of all grace, when Angels and Archangels
are to be summoned to join in the Thanksgiving, Articles
from the Creed are recited, as if by way of preparation,
with an exact doctrinal precision, according to the Festival celebrated,—as for instance on this day.   And in the
Visitation of the Sick, he whom God seems about to call
away, is asked, not whether he has certain spiritual
feelings within him (of which he cannot judge), but,
definitely and to his great comfort, whether he believes
those Articles of the Christian Faith, one by one, which
he received at Baptism, was catechized in during his
childhood, and confessed whenever he came to worship
God in Church.   It is in the same spirit that the most
precise and systematic of all the Creeds, the Athanasian,
is rather, as the form of it shows, a hymn of praise to
the Eternal Trinity; it being meet and right at festive
seasons to bring forth before our God every jewel of the
Mysteries entrusted to us, to show that those of which
He gave us we have lost none.

3. Lastly, the sacred character of our charge is shown
most forcibly by the sanction which attends it.   What
God has guarded by an Anathema, surely claims some
jealous custody on our part.   Christ says expressly,
" He that believeth and is baptized shall be saved; and
he that believeth not shall be damned.' [1]   It is quite
clear, that in our Lord's meaning, this belief included
the reception of a positive Creed, because He gave one
at the time,—that sovereign Truth, from which all

[1] Mark xvi. 16.

others flow, which we this day celebrate, the Faith of Father, Son, and Holy Ghost, Three Persons, One God. This doctrine then, at least, is necessary to be believed by every one in order to salvation: and that certain other doctrines are also necessary, is plain from other parts of Scripture; as, for instance, our Lord's Resurrection, from St. Paul's words to the Romans.[1] Now, this doctrine of the Resurrection, which closed our Lord's earthly mission, is evidently at a wide interval in the series of doctrines from that of the Trinity in Unity, which is the foundation of the whole Dispensation; so that a thoughtful mind, which fears to go wrong, will see reason to conclude even from hence, that perchance the doctrines which go between the two—the Incarnation, for instance, or the Crucifixion—are also essential parts of saving Faith. And, in fact, various passages of Scripture, as we have already seen, occur, in which these intermediate Articles are separately made the basis of the Gospel. Again, let St. Paul's language to the Galatians be well considered, who had departed from the Faith in what might have seemed but a subordinate detail, the abolition of the Jewish Law. "Though we, or an Angel from heaven," he says, " preach any other Gospel unto you, than that which· we have preached unto you, let him be Anathema. As we said before, so say I now again, If any man preach any other Gospel unto you than that ye have received, let him be Anathema."[2] The state of the case then is this:—we know that some doctrines are necessary to be believed; we are not told how many; and we have

---

[1] Rom. x. 9.   [2] Gal. i. 8, 9.

no powers of mind adequate to the task of solving the problem. We cannot give any sufficient reason, beside the revealed word, why the doctrine of the Trinity itself should be essential; and if it is essential nevertheless, why should not any other? How dangerous then is it to trifle with any portion of the message committed to us! Surely we are bound to guard what *may* be material in it, as carefully as if we knew it to be so; our not knowing it, so far from being a reason for indifference, becoming an additional motive for anxiety and watchfulness. And, while we do not dare anticipate God's final judgment by attaching the Anathema to individual unbelievers, yet neither do we dare conceal any part of the doctrines guarded by it, lest haply it should be found to lie against ourselves, who have " shunned to declare the whole counsel of God."

To conclude.—The error against which these remarks are directed, viz. that of systematizing and simplifying the Gospel Faith, making much of one or two articles of it, and disparaging or dismissing the rest, is not confined to this province of religion only. In the same spirit, sometimes the Ordinances, sometimes the Polity of the Church, are dishonoured and neglected; the Doctrine of Baptism contrasted with that of inward Sanctification, precepts of " decency and order " made light of before the command to evangelize the heathen, the injunction to " stand in the old ways " broken with a view to increase the so-called efficiency of our ecclesiastical institutions. In like manner, by one class of reasoners the Gospels are made everything, by another *the* Epistles. In all ages, indeed, consistent obedience is a very rare endowment; but in this cultivated age, we have undertaken to defend inconsistency on grounds of reason. On the other hand hear the words of Eternal Truth. "Whosoever shall break one of these *least* commandments, *and shall teach men so,* he shall be called the least in the Kingdom of Heaven; but whosoever shall do and teach them, the same shall be called great in the Kingdom of Heaven."[1]

[1] Matt. v. 19.

SERMON XXIII.

Tolerance of Religious Error.

(THE FEAST OF ST. BARNABAS THE APOSTLE.)

" He was a good man, and full of the Holy Ghost and of faith."—
ACTS xi. 24.

WHEN Christ came to form a people unto Himself
to show forth His praise, He took of every kind.
Highways and hedges, the streets and lanes of the city,
furnished guests for His supper, as well as the wilderness of Judea, or the courts of the Temple. His first
followers are a sort of type of the general Church, in
which many and various minds are as one. And this is
one use, if we duly improve it, of our Festivals; which
set before us specimens of the Divine Life under the
same diversity of outward circumstances, advantages,
and dispositions, which we discern around us. The
especial grace poured upon the Apostles and their
associates, whether miraculous or moral, had no tendency to destroy their respective peculiarities of temper
and character, to invest them with a sanctity beyond
our imitation, or to preclude failings and errors which
may be our warning. It left them, as it found them,

men. Peter and John, for instance, the simple fishers
on the lake of Gennesareth, Simon the Zealot, Matthew
the busy tax-gatherer, and the ascetic Baptist, how
different are these,—first, from each other,—then, from
Apollos the eloquent Alexandrian, Paul the learned
Pharisee, Luke the physician, or the Eastern Sages,
whom we celebrate at the Feast of the Epiphany; and
these again how different from the Blessed Virgin Mary,
or the Innocents, or Simeon and Anna, who are brought
before us at the Feast of the Purification, or the women
who ministered to our Lord, Mary the wife of Cleophas,
the Mother of James and John, Mary Magdalene,
Martha and Mary, sisters of Lazarus; or again, from the
widow with her two mites, the woman whose issue of
blood was staunched, from her who poured forth tears
of penitence upon His feet, and the ignorant Samaritan
at the well! Moreover, the definiteness and evident
truth of many of the pictures presented to us in
the Gospels serve to realize to us the history, and to
help our faith, while at the same time they afford us
abundant instruction. Such, for instance, is the imma-
ture ardour of James and John, the sudden fall of
Peter, the obstinacy of Thomas, and the cowardice of
Mark. St. Barnabas furnishes us with a lesson in his
own way; nor shall I be wanting in piety towards that
Holy Apostle, if on this his day I hold him forth, not
only in the peculiar graces of his character, but in those
parts of it in which he becomes our warning, not our
example.

The text says, that " he was a good man, full of the
Holy *Ghost and of faith.*" This praise of goodness is

explained by his very name, Barnabas, "the Son of Consolation," which was given him, as it appears, to mark his character of kindness, gentleness, considerateness, warmth of heart, compassion, and munificence.

His acts answer to this account of him. The first we hear of him is his selling some land which was his, and giving the proceeds to the Apostles, to distribute to his poorer brethren. The next notice of him sets before us a second deed of kindness, of as amiable, though of a more private character. "When Saul was come to Jerusalem, he assayed to join himself to the disciples; but they were all afraid of him, and believed not that he was a disciple. But Barnabas took him and brought him to the Apostles, and declared how he had seen the Lord in the way, and that He had spoken to him, and how he had preached boldly at Damascus, in the name of Jesus."[1] Next, he is mentioned in the text, and still with commendation of the same kind. How had he shown that "he was a good man?" by going on a mission of love to the first converts at Antioch. Barnabas, above the rest, was honoured by the Church with this work, which had in view the encouraging and binding together in unity and strength this incipient fruit of God's grace. "When he came, and had seen the grace of God, he was glad" (surely this circumstance itself is mentioned by way of showing his character); "and exhorted them all that with purpose of heart they would cleave unto the Lord." Thus he may even be accounted the founder of the Church of Antioch, being aided by St. Paul, whom he was successful

[1] Acts ix. 26, 27.

in bringing thither. Next, on occasion of an approaching famine, he is joined with St. Paul in being the minister of the Gentiles' bounty towards the poor saints of Judea. Afterwards, when the Judaizing Christians troubled the Gentile converts with the Mosaic ordinances, Barnabas was sent with the same Apostle and others from the Church of Jerusalem to relieve their perplexity. Thus the Scripture history of him does but answer to his name, and is scarcely more than a continued exemplification of his characteristic grace. Moreover, let the particular force of his name be observed. The Holy Ghost is called our Paraclete, as assisting, advocating, encouraging, comforting us; now, as if to put the highest honour upon the Apostle, the same term is applied to him. He is called " the Son of Consolation," or the Paraclete ; and in accordance with this honourable title, we are told, that when the Gentile converts of Antioch had received from his and St. Paul's hands the Apostles' decision against the Judaizers, " they rejoiced for the *consolation.*"

On the other hand, on two occasions his conduct is scarcely becoming an Apostle, as instancing somewhat of that infirmity which uninspired persons of his peculiar character frequently exhibit. Both are cases of indulgence towards the faults of others, yet in a different way ; the one, an over-easiness in a matter of doctrine, the other, in a matter of conduct. With all his tenderness for the Gentiles, yet on one occasion he could not resist indulging the prejudices of some Judaizing brethren, who came from Jerusalem to Antioch. *Peter* first was carried away; before they

came, " he did eat with the Gentiles, but when they were
come, he withdrew, and separated himself, fearing them
which were of the circumcision. And the other Jews
dissembled likewise with him; insomuch, that Barnabas
also was carried away with their dissimulation." The
other instance was his indulgent treatment of Mark, his
sister's son, which occasioned the quarrel between him
and St. Paul. " Barnabas determined to take with
them," on their Apostolic journey, " John, whose sur-
name was Mark. But Paul thought not good to take
him with them, who departed from them from Pam-
phylia, and went not with them to the work."[1]

Now it is very plain what description of character,
and what kind of lesson, is brought before us in the
history of this Holy Apostle. Holy he was, full of
the Holy Ghost and of faith; still the characteristics
and the infirmities of man remained in him, and thus
he is "unto us for an ensample," consistently with the
reverence we feel towards him as one of the foundations
of the Christian Church. He is an ensample and warning to us, not only as showing us what we ought to be,
but as evidencing how the highest gifts and graces are
corrupted in our sinful nature, if we are not diligent
to walk step by step, according to the light of God's
commandments. Be our mind as heavenly as it may
be, most loving, most holy, most zealous, most energetic,
most peaceful, yet if we look off from Him for a moment,
and look towards ourselves, at once these excellent
tempers fall into some extreme or mistake. Charity
becomes over-easiness, holiness is tainted with spiritual

----

[1] Gal. ii. 12, 13.   [2] Acts xv. 37, 38.

pride, zeal degenerates into fierceness, activity eats up the spirit of prayer, hope is heightened into presumption. We cannot guide ourselves. God's revealed word is our sovereign rule of conduct; and therefore, among other reasons, is faith so principal a grace, for it is the directing power which receives the commands of Christ, and applies them to the heart.

And there is particular reason for dwelling upon the character of St. Barnabas in this age, because he may be considered as the type of the better sort of men among us, and those who are most in esteem. The world itself indeed is what it ever has been, ungodly; but in every age it chooses some one or other peculiarity of the Gospel as the badge of its particular fashion for the time being, and sets up as objects of admiration those who eminently possess it. Without asking, therefore, how far men act from Christian principle, or only from the imitation of it, or from some mere secular or selfish motive, yet, certainly, this age, as far as appearance goes, may be accounted in its character not unlike Barnabas, as being considerate, delicate, courteous, and generous-minded in all that concerns the intercourse of man with man. There is a great deal of thoughtful kindness among us, of conceding in little matters, of scrupulous propriety of words, and a sort of code of liberal and honourable dealing in the conduct of society. There is a steady regard for the rights of individuals, nay, as one would fain hope in spite of misgivings, for the interest of the poorer classes, the stranger, the fatherless, and the widow. In such a country as ours, there must *always be numberless* instances of distress after all;

yet the anxiety to relieve it existing among the more
wealthy classes is unquestionable. And it is as unquestionable that we are somewhat disposed to regard
ourselves favourably in consequence; and in the midst
of our national trials and fears, to say (nay, sometimes
with real humility and piety) that we do trust that
these characteristic virtues of the age may be allowed
to come up as a memorial before God, and to plead for
us. When we think of the commandments, we know
Charity to be the first and greatest; and we are tempted
to ask with the young ruler, "What lack we yet?"

I ask, then, by way of reply, does not our kindness
too often degenerate into weakness, and thus become
not Christian Charity, but lack of Charity, as regards
the objects of it? Are we sufficiently careful to do
what is right and just, rather than what is pleasant?
do we clearly understand our professed principles, and
do we keep to them under temptation?

The history of St. Barnabas will help us to answer
this question honestly. Now I fear we lack altogether,
what he lacked in certain occurrences in it, firmness,
manliness, godly severity. I fear it must be confessed,
that our kindness, instead of being directed and braced
by principle, too often becomes languid and unmeaning;
that it is exerted on improper objects, and out of season,
and thereby is uncharitable in two ways, indulging those
who should be chastised, and preferring their comfort
to those who are really deserving. We are over-tender
in dealing with sin and sinners. We are deficient in
jealous custody of the revealed Truths which Christ
has left us. We allow men to speak against the Church,

its ordinances, or its teaching, without remonstrating with them. We do not separate from heretics, nay, we object to the word as if uncharitable; and when such texts are brought against us as St. John's command, not to show hospitality towards them, we are not slow to answer that they do not apply to us. Now I scarcely can suppose any one really means to say for certain, that these commands are superseded in the present day, and is quite satisfied upon the point; it will rather be found that men who so speak, merely wish to put the subject from them. For a long while they have forgotten that there were any such commands in Scripture; they have lived as though there were not, and not being in circumstances which immediately called for the consideration of them, they have familiar-ized their minds to a contrary view of the matter, and built their opinions upon it. When reminded of the fact, they are sorry to have to consider it, as they perhaps avow. They perceive that it interferes with the line of conduct to which they are accustomed. They are vexed, not as if allowing themselves to be wrong, but as feeling conscious that a plausible argu-ment (to say the least) may be maintained against them. And instead of daring to give this argument fair play, as in honesty they ought, they hastily satisfy themselves that objections may be taken against it, use some vague terms of disapprobation against those who use it, recur to, and dwell upon, their own habitual view of the benevolent and indulgent spirit of the Gospel, and then dismiss the subject altogether, as if it had *never been brought* before them.

[several lines illegible/struck through] of it: it is by com-
[illegible] of Christianity, which they
[illegible] whereas the very problem
[illegible] now [illegible] is to accomplish, is the
[illegible] opposite virtues. It is not
[illegible] speaking to cultivate single
[illegible] some one partial view of his
[illegible] whether of action or of
[illegible] with all his might, he
[illegible] and allows himself to
[illegible]. This is not difficult:
[illegible] virtue or self-denial in it. On
the contrary, there is a [illegible] often in thus sweeping
away [illegible] and especially in matters of giving
and [illegible]. Liberality is always popular, whatever
is the subject of it, and excites a glow of pleasure and
self-approbation in the giver, even though it involves
[illegible] upon the property of
others. Thus in the sacred province of religion, men
are [illegible]—without any bad principle, without that
[illegible] disbelief or ignorance of the Truth, or that self-
[illegible], which are chief instruments of Satan at this
day, not again from mere cowardice or worldliness, but
from thoughtlessness, a sanguine temper, the excitement of the moment, the love of making others happy,
[illegible] of flattery, and the habit of looking only
one way,—led on to give up Gospel Truths, to consent
to open the Church to the various denominations of
error which abound among us, or to alter our Services
so as to please the scoffer, the lukewarm, or the vicious.
To be kind is their one principle of action; and, when

they find offence taken at the Church's creed, they begin to think how they may modify or curtail it, under the same sort of feeling as would lead them to be generous in a money transaction, or to accommodate another at the price of personal inconvenience. Not understanding that their religious privileges are a trust to be handed on to posterity, a sacred property entailed upon the Christian family, and their own in enjoyment rather than in possession, they act the spendthrift, and are lavish of the goods of others. Thus, for instance, they speak against the Anathemas of the Athanasian Creed, or of the Commination Service, or of certain of the Psalms, and wish to rid themselves of them.

Undoubtedly, even the best specimens of these men are deficient in a due appreciation of the Christian Mysteries, and of their own responsibility in preserving and transmitting them; yet, some of them are such truly "good" men, so amiable and feeling, so benevolent to the poor, and of such repute among all classes, in short, fulfil so excellently the office of shining like lights in the world, and witnesses of Him "who went about doing good," that those who most deplore their failing, will still be most desirous of excusing them personally, while they feel it a duty to withstand them. Sometimes it may be, that these persons cannot bring themselves to think evil of others; and harbour men of heretical opinions or immoral life from the same easiness of temper which makes them fit subjects for the practices of the cunning and selfish in worldly matters. And sometimes they fasten on certain favourable points of character in the person *they should* discountenance, and cannot get themselves to attend to any but these; arguing that he is certainly pious and well-meaning, and that his errors plainly do himself no harm;—whereas the question is not about their effects on this or that individual, but simply whether they *are* errors; and again, whether they are not certain to be injurious to the mass of men, or on the long run, as it is called. Or they cannot bear to hurt another by the expression of their disapprobation, though it be that "his soul may be saved in the day of the Lord." Or perhaps they are deficient in keenness of intellectual perception as to the moral mischief of certain speculative opinions, as they consider them; and not knowing their ignorance enough to forbear the use of private judgment, nor having faith enough to acquiesce in God's word, or the decision of His Church, they incur the responsibility of serious changes. Or, perhaps they shelter themselves behind some confused notion, which they have taken up, of the peculiar character of our own Church, arguing that they belong to a tolerant Church, that it is but consistent as well as right in her members to be tolerant, and that they are but exemplifying tolerance in their own conduct, when they treat with indulgence those who are lax in creed or conduct. Now, if by the tolerance of our Church, it be meant that she does not countenance the use of fire and sword against those who separate from her, so far she is truly called a tolerant Church; but she is not tolerant of error, as those very formularies, which these men wish to remove, testify; and if she retains within her bosom proud *intellects*, and cold hearts, and unclean hands, and dispenses her blessings to those who disbelieve or are unworthy of them, this arises from other causes, certainly not from her principles; else were she guilty of Eli's sin, which may not be imagined.

Such is the defect of mind suggested to us by the instances of imperfection recorded of St. Barnabas; it will be more clearly understood by contrasting him with St. John. We cannot compare good men together in their points of excellence; but whether the one or the other of these Apostles had the greater share of the spirit of love, we all know that anyhow the Beloved Disciple abounded in it. His General Epistle is full of exhortations to cherish that blessed temper, and his name is associated in our minds with such heavenly dispositions as are more immediately connected with it, —contemplativeness, serenity of soul, clearness of faith. Now see in what he differed from Barnabas; in uniting charity with a firm maintenance of "the Truth as it is in Jesus." So far were his fervour and exuberance of charity from interfering with his zeal for God, that rather, the more he loved men, the more he desired to bring before them the great unchangeable Verities to which they must submit, if they would see life, and on which a weak indulgence suffers them to shut their eyes. He loved the brethren, but he "loved them in the Truth." [1] He loved them for the Living Truth's sake which had redeemed them, for the Truth which was in them, for the Truth which was the measure of their spiritual attainments. He loved the Church so honestly, that he was stern towards those who troubled

[1] 8 John 1.

her. He loved the world so wisely that he preached the Truth in it: yet, if men rejected it, he did not love them so inordinately as to forget the supremacy of the Truth, as the Word of Him who is above all. Let it never be forgotten then, when we picture to ourselves this saintly Apostle, this unearthly Prophet, who fed upon the sights and voices of the world of spirits, and looked out heavenwards day by day for Him whom he had once seen in the flesh, that this is he who gives us that command about shunning heretics, which whether of force in this age or not, still certainly in any age is (what men now call) severe; and that this command of his is but in unison with the fearful descriptions he gives in other parts of his inspired writings of the Presence, the Law, and the Judgments of Almighty God. Who can deny that the Apocalypse from beginning to end is a very fearful book; I may say, the most fearful book in Scripture, full of accounts of the wrath of God? Yet, it is written by the Apostle of love. It is possible, then, for a man to be at once kind as Barnabas, yet zealous as Paul. Strictness and tenderness had no "sharp contention" in the breast of the Beloved Disciple; they found their perfect union, yet distinct exercise, in the grace of Charity, which is the fulfilling of the whole Law.

I wish I saw any prospect of this element of zeal and holy sternness springing up among us, to temper and give character to the languid, unmeaning benevolence which we misname Christian love. I have no hope of my country till I see it. Many schools of Religion and Ethics are to be found among us, and they

all profess to magnify, in one shape or other, what they
consider the principle of love ; but what they lack is,
a firm maintenance of that characteristic of the Divine
Nature, which, in accommodation to our infirmity, is
named by St. John and his brethren, the wrath of God.
Let this be well observed. There are men who are
advocates of Expedience ; these, as far as they are religious at all, resolve conscience into an instinct of mere
benevolence, and refer all the dealings of Providence
with His creatures to the same one Attribute. Hence,
they consider all punishment to be remedial, a means
to an end, deny that the woe threatened against sinners
is of eternal duration, and explain away the doctrine
of the Atonement. There are others, who place religion in the mere exercise of the excited feelings ; and
these too, look upon their God and Saviour, as far (that
is) as they themselves are concerned, solely as a God
of love. They believe themselves to be converted from
sin to righteousness by the mere manifestation of that
love to their souls, drawing them on to Him ; and
they imagine that that same love, untired by any
possible transgressions on their part, will surely carry
forward every individual so chosen to final triumph.
Moreover, as accounting that Christ has already done
everything for their salvation, they do not feel that
a moral change is necessary on their part, or rather,
they consider that the Vision of revealed love works
it in them spontaneously ; in either case dispensing
with all laborious efforts, all " fear and trembling," all
self-denial in " working out their salvation," nay, looking upon such qualifications with suspicion, as leading

to a supposed self-confidence and spiritual pride. Once more, there are others of a mystical turn of mind, with untutored imaginations and subtle intellects, who follow the theories of the old Gentile philosophy. These, too, are accustomed to make love the one principle of life and providence in heaven and earth, as if it were a pervading Spirit of the world, finding a sympathy in every heart, absorbing all things into itself, and kindling a rapturous enjoyment in all who contemplate it. They sit at home speculating, and separate moral perfection from action. These men either hold, or are in the way to hold, that the human soul is pure by nature; sin an external principle corrupting it; evil, destined to final annihilation; Truth attained by means of the imagination; conscience, a taste; holiness, a passive contemplation of God; and obedience, a mere pleasurable work. It is difficult to discriminate accurately between these three schools of opinion, without using words of unseemly familiarity; yet I have said enough for those who wish to pursue the subject. Let it be observed then, that these three systems, however different from each other in their principles and spirit, yet all agree in this one respect, viz., in overlooking that the Christian's God is represented in Scripture, not only as a God of Love, but also as "a consuming fire." Rejecting the testimony of Scripture, no wonder they also reject that of conscience, which assuredly forebodes ill to the sinner, but which, as the narrow religionist maintains, is not the voice of God at all, —or is a mere benevolence, according to the disciple of *Utility*,—or, in the judgment of the more mystical sort, a kind of passion for the beautiful and sublime. Regarding thus "the goodness" only, and not "the severity of God," no wonder that they ungird their loins and become effeminate; no wonder that their ideal notion of a perfect Church, is a Church which lets every one go on his way, and disclaims any right to pronounce an opinion, much less inflict a censure on religious error.

But those who think themselves and others in risk of an eternal curse, dare not be thus indulgent. Here then lies our want at the present day, for this we must pray,—that a reform may come in the spirit and power of Elias. We must pray God thus "to revive His work in the midst of the years;" to send us a severe Discipline, the Order of St. Paul and St. John, "speaking the Truth in love," and "loving in the Truth,"—a Witness of Christ, "knowing the terror of the Lord," fresh from the presence of Him "whose head and hairs are white like wool, as white as snow, and whose eyes are as a flame of fire, and out of His mouth a sharp sword,"—a Witness not shrinking from proclaiming His wrath, as a real characteristic of His glorious nature, though expressed in human language for our sakes, proclaiming the narrowness of the way of life, the difficulty of attaining Heaven, the danger of riches, the necessity of taking up our cross, the excellence and beauty of self-denial and austerity, the hazard of disbelieving the Catholic Faith, and the duty of zealously contending for it. Thus only will the tidings of mercy come with force to the souls of men, with a constraining *power and with an* abiding impress, when hope and fear in together. Then only will Christians be successful in fight, ' quitting themselves like men,' conquering and ruling the fury of the world, and maintaining the Church in purity and power, when they condense their feelings by a severe discipline, and are living in the midst of firmness, strictness, and holiness. Then only can we prosper under the blessing and grace of Him who is the Spirit both of love and of truth, when the heart of Paul is vouchsafed to us, to withstand even Peter and Barnabas, if ever they are overcome by mere human feelings, to " know henceforth no man after the flesh," to put away from us sister's son, or nearer relative, to relinquish the sight of them, the hope of them, and the desire of them, when He commands, who raises up friends even to the lonely, if they trust in Him, and will give us " within His walls a name better than of sons and of daughters, an everlasting name that shall not be cut off."[1]

[1] Isa. lvi. 4, 5.

SERMON XXIV.

𝕽𝖊𝖇𝖚𝖐𝖎𝖓𝖌 𝕾𝖎𝖓.

(THE FEAST OF THE NATIVITY OF ST. JOHN BAPTIST.)

"John had said unto Herod, It is not lawful for thee to have thy
brother's wife."—MARK vi. 18.

IN the Collect of this day, we pray God to enable us
"boldly to rebuke vice" after the example of St.
John the Baptist, who died a Martyr in the faithful
discharge of this duty.

Herod the Tetrarch had taken his brother's wife.
John the Baptist protested against so heinous a sin;
and the guilty king, though he could not bring himself to
forsake it, yet respected the prophet, and tried to please
him in other ways; but Herodias, the proud and cruel
woman whom he had married, resented his interference,
and at length effected his death. I need not go through
the details of this atrocious history, which are well
known to every reader of the Gospels.

St. John the Baptist had a most difficult office to
fulfil; that of rebuking a king. Not that it is difficult
for a man of rude arrogant mind to say a harsh thing to

men in power,—nay, rather, it is a gratification to such
a one; but it is difficult to rebuke well, that is, at a
right time, in a right spirit, and a right manner. The
Holy Baptist rebuked Herod without making him
angry; therefore he must have rebuked him with
gravity, temper, sincerity, and an evident good-will
towards him. On the other hand, he spoke so firmly,
sharply, and faithfully, that his rebuke cost him his life.

We who now live have not that extreme duty put
upon us with which St. John was laden; yet every one
of us has a share in his office, inasmuch as we are all
bound "to rebuke vice boldly," when we have fit opportunities for so doing. I proceed then to make some
remarks upon the duty, as enforced upon us by to-day's
Festival.

Now, it is plain that there are two sorts of men in
the world; those who put themselves forward, and
speak much; and those who retire, and from indolence,
timidity, or fastidiousness, do not care to express an
opinion on what comes before them. Neither of these
classes will act the part of St. John the Baptist in their
intercourse with others: the retiring will not rebuke
vice at all; the bold and ill-mannered will take a
pleasure in giving their judgment, whether they are fit
judges or not, whether they ought to speak or not, and
at all times proper and improper.

These self-appointed censors of vice are not to be
countenanced or tolerated by any serious Christian.
The subjects of their attacks are often open to censure,
it is true; and should be censured, but not by them.
When these men take upon them, on their own authority,

to blame them; often, because those whose duty it is, neglect to do so; and then they flatter themselves with the notion that they are energetic champions of virtue, strenuous and useful guardians of public morals or popular rights. There is a multitude of such men in these days, who succeed the better, because they conceal their names; and are thus relieved of the trouble of observing delicacy in their manner of rebuking, escape the retaliation which the assailed party may inflict on an open assailant, and are able to dispense with such requisites of personal character and deportment as are ordinarily expected from those who assume the office of the Baptist. And, by speaking against men of note, they gratify the bad passions of the multitude; fond, as it ever is, of tales of crime, and malevolent towards the great; and thus they increase their influence, and come to be looked up to and feared.

Now such officious accusers of vice are, I say, to be disowned by all who wish to be really Christians. Every one has his place, one to obey, another to rule, a third to rebuke. It is not religious to undertake an office without a commission. John the Baptist was miraculously called to the duties of a reformer and teacher. Afterwards, an order of men was appointed for the performance of the same services; and this order remains to this day in an uninterrupted succession. Those who take upon them to rebuke vice without producing credentials of their authority, are intruding upon the office of God's Ministers. They may indeed succeed in their usurpation, they may become popular, be supported by the many, and be recognised even by the persons whom they attack; still the function of censor is from God, whose final judgment it precedes and shadows forth; and not a whole generation of self-willed men can bestow on their organ the powers of a divine ambassador. It is our part, then, anxiously to guard against the guilt of acquiescing in the claims of such false prophets, lest we fall under the severity of our Lord's prediction: "I am come in My Father's name," He says, "and ye receive Me not. If another shall come in his own name, him ye will receive."[1]

I notice this peculiarity of the Reprover's office, as founded on a Divine Commission, and the consequent sin of undertaking it without a call, for another reason. Besides these bad men, who clamour against vice for gain and envy's sake, I know there are others of a better stamp, who imagine that they ought to rebuke, when in truth they ought not; and who, on finding that they cannot do the office well, or on getting into trouble in attempting it, are perplexed and discouraged, or consider that they suffer for righteousness' sake. But our duty is commonly a far more straightforward matter than excited and over-sensitive minds are apt to suppose, that is, as far as concerns our *knowing* it; and, when we find ourselves perplexed to ascertain it, we should ask ourselves, whether we have not embarrassed our course by some unnecessary or self-willed conduct of our own. For instance, when men imagine it to be their duty to rebuke their superiors, they get into difficulties, for the simple reason, that it is and ever will be difficult to do another man's duty. When the young

[1] John v. 43.

take upon them to set right their elders, private Christians speak against the Clergy, the Clergy attempt to direct their Bishops, or servants their masters, they will find that, generally speaking, the attempt does not succeed; and perhaps they will impute their failure to circumstances,—whereas, the real reason is, that there was no call on them to rebuke at all. There is ever, indeed, a call on them to keep from sin themselves in all things, which itself is a silent protest against whatever is wrong in high places,—and this they cannot avoid, and need not wish to avoid; but very seldom, only in extreme cases, for instance, as, when the Faith is in jeopardy, or in order to protect or rescue the simple-minded, is a man called upon in the way of duty, directly to blame or denounce his superiors.

And in truth we have quite enough to do in the way of rebuking vice, if we confine our censure to those who are the lawful subjects of it. These are our equals and our inferiors. Here, again, it is easy to use violent language towards those who are below us in station, to be arrogant, to tyrannize; but such was not St. John the Baptist's manner of reproving. He reproved under the prospect of suffering for his faithfulness; and we should never use a strong word, however true it be, without being willing to acquiesce in some penalty or other, should it so happen, as the seal of our earnestness. We must not suppose, that our inferiors are without power to annoy us, because they are inferior. We depend on the poor as well as on the rich. Nor, by inferiors, do I mean those merely who are in a lower rank of society. Herod was St. John's inferior; the greatest

king is, in one sense, inferior to God's ministers, and
is to be approached by them, with all honour indeed
and loyal service, but without trepidation of mind or
cowardice, without forgetting that they are servants of
the Church, gifted with their power by a divine appointment. And what is true even in the instance of the
King himself is much more applicable in the case of
the merely wealthy or ennobled. But is it a light
matter to reprove such men? And can we do so
without the risk of suffering for it? Who is sufficient
for these things, without the guidance and strength of
Him who died to purchase for His Church this high
authority?

Again, parents are bound to rebuke their children;
but here the office is irksome for a different reason. It
is misplaced affection, not fear, which interferes here
with the performance of our duty. And besides, parents
are indolent as well as overfond. They look to their
home as a release from the world's cares, and cannot
bear to make duties in a quarter where they would
find a recreation. And they have their preferences and
partialities about their children; and being alternately
harsh and weakly indulgent, are not respected by them,
even when they seasonably rebuke them.

And as to rebuke those who are inferior to us in
the temporal appointments of Providence, is a serious
work, so also, much more, does it require a ripeness in
Christian holiness to rebuke our equals suitably;—and
this, first, because we fear their ridicule and censure;
next, because the failings of our equals commonly lie
in the same line as our own, and every considerate

person is aware, that, in rebuking another, he is binding himself to a strict and religious life, which we naturally shrink from doing. Accordingly, it has come to pass, that Christians, by a sort of tacit agreement, wink at each other's faults, and keep silence; whereas, if each of us forced himself to make his neighbour sensible when he did wrong, he would both benefit another, and, through God's blessing, would bind himself also to a more consistent profession. Who can say how much harm is done by thus countenancing the imperfections of our friends and equals? The standard of Christian morals is lowered; the service of God is mixed up with devotion to Mammon; and thus society is constantly tending to a heathen state. And this culpable toleration of vice is sanctioned by the manners of the present age, which seems to consider it a mark of good breeding not to be solicitous about the faith or conduct of those around us, as if their private views and habits were nothing to us; which would have more pretence of truth in it, were they merely our fellow-creatures, but is evidently false in the case of those who all the while profess to be Christians, who imagine that they gain the privileges of the Gospel by their profession, while they bring scandal on it by their lives.

Now, if it be asked, what rules can be given for rebuking vice?—I observe, that, as on the one hand to perform the office of a censor requires a maturity and consistency of principle seen and acknowledged, so is it also the necessary result of possessing it. They who reprove with the greatest propriety, from their weight of character, are generally the very men who are also best qualified for reproving. To rebuke well is a gift which grows with the need of exercising it. Not that any one will gain it without an effort on his part; he must overcome false shame, timidity, and undue delicacy, and learn to be prompt and collected in withstanding evil; but after all, his mode of doing it will depend mainly on his *general* character. The more his habitual temper is formed after the law of Christ, the more discreet, unexceptionable, and graceful will be his censures, the more difficult to escape or to resist.

What I mean is this: cultivate in your general deportment a cheerful, honest, manly temper; and you will find fault well, because you will do so in a natural way. Aim at viewing all things in a plain and candid light, and at calling them by their right names. Be frank, do not keep your notions of right and wrong to yourselves, nor, on some conceit that the world is too bad to be taught the Truth, suffer it to sin in word or deed without rebuke. Do not allow friend or stranger in the familiar intercourse of society to advance false opinions, nor shrink from stating your own, and do this in singleness of mind and love. Persons are to be found, who tell their neighbours of their faults in a strangely solemn way, with a great parade, as if they were doing something extraordinary; and such men not only offend those whom they wish to set right, but also foster in themselves a spirit of self-complacency Such a mode of finding fault is inseparably connected with a notion that they themselves are far better than *the* parties they blame; whereas the single-hearted

Christian will find fault, not austerely or gloomily, but in love; not stiffly, but naturally, gently, and as a matter of course, just as he would tell his friend of some obstacle in his path which was likely to throw him down, but without any absurd feeling of superiority over him, because he was able to do so. His feeling is, "I have done a good office to you, and you must in turn serve me." And though his advice be not always taken as he meant it, yet he will not dwell on the pain occasioned to himself by such a result of his interference; being conscious, that in truth there ever is much to correct in his mode of doing his duty, knowing that his intention was good, and being determined any how to make light of his failure, except so far as to be more cautious in future against even the appearance of rudeness or intemperance in his manner.

These are a few suggestions on an important subject. We daily influence each other for good or evil; let us not be the occasion of misleading others by our silence, when we ought to speak. Recollect St. Paul's words:— "Be not partaker of other men's sins: keep thyself pure."[1]

[1] 1 Tim. v. 22.

SERMON XXV.

𝕿𝖍𝖊 𝕮𝖍𝖗𝖎𝖘𝖙𝖎𝖆𝖓 𝕸𝖎𝖓𝖎𝖘𝖙𝖗𝖞.

(THE FEAST OF ST. PETER THE APOSTLE.)

" I say unto you, Among those that are born of women there is not a greater prophet than John the Baptist; but he that is least in the Kingdom of God is greater than he."—LUKE vii. 28.

ST. PETER'S day suitably follows the day of St. John the Baptist; for thus we have a striking memento, as the text suggests, of the especial dignity of the Christian Ministry over all previous Ministries which Almighty God has appointed. St. John was "much more than a Prophet;" he was as great as any messenger of God that had ever been born; yet the least in the Kingdom of heaven, the least of Christ's Ministers, is greater than he. And this, I observe, is a reflection especially fitted for this Festival, because the Apostle Peter is taken in various parts of the Gospel, as the appropriate type and representative of the Christian ministry.[1]

Now, let us consider in what the peculiar dignity of the Christian Minister consists. Evidently in this, that

---

[1] *Vide* Matt. xvi. 18, 19. Luke xxii. 29, 30. John xxi. 15—17.

he is the representative of Christ; for, as Christ is infinitely above all other messengers from God, he who stands in His stead, must be superior, beyond compare, to all Ministers of religion, whether Prophets, Priests, Lawgivers, Judges, or Kings, whom Almighty God ever commissioned. Moses, Aaron, Samuel, and David, were shadows of the Saviour; but the Minister of the Gospel is His present substitute. As a type or prophecy of Grace is less than a pledge and means, as a Jewish sacrifice is less than a Gospel sacrament, so are Moses and Elias less by office than the representatives of Christ. This I consider to be evident, as soon as stated; the only question being, whether there is reason for thinking, that Christ *has*, in matter of fact, left representatives behind Him; and this, as I proceed to show, Scripture enables us to determine in the affirmative.

Now, in the first place, as we all know, Christ chose twelve out of His disciples, whom He called Apostles, to be His representatives even during His own ministry. And He gave them the power of doing the wonderful works which He did Himself. Of course I do not say He gave them equal power (God forbid!); but He gave them a certain sufficient portion of His power. " He gave them power," says St. Luke, " and authority over all devils, and to cure diseases; and He sent them to preach the Kingdom of God, and to heal the sick."[1] And He expressly made them His substitutes to the world at large; so that to receive them was to receive Himself. "He that receiveth you, receiveth Me."[2] Such was their principal power before His passion, similar to

---

[1] *Luke* ix. 1, 2.　　[2] *Matt.* x. 40.

that which He principally exercised, viz. the commission to preach and to perform bodily cures. But when He had wrought out the Atonement for human sin upon the Cross, and purchased for man the gift of the Holy Ghost, then He gave them a higher commission; and still, be it observed, parallel to that which He Himself then assumed. "*As My Father hath sent Me, even so send I you.* And when He had said this, He breathed on them, and saith unto them, Receive ye the Holy Ghost. Whose soever sins ye remit, they are remitted unto them; and whose soever sins ye retain, they are retained."[1] Here, then, the Apostles became Christ's representatives] in the power of His Spirit, for the remission of sins, as before they were His representatives as regards miraculous cures, and preaching His Kingdom.

The following texts supply additional evidence that the Apostles were commissioned in Christ's stead, and inform us likewise in detail of some of the particular offices included in their commission. "Let a man so account of us, as of the *Ministers* of Christ, and *Stewards of the Mysteries* of God." "Ye received me as an *Angel'* or heavenly Messenger "of God, even *as Christ Jesus.*" "We *are Ambassadors* for Christ, as though God did beseech you by us; we pray you *in Christ's stead,* be ye reconciled to God."[2]

The Apostles then, standing in Christ's place, were consequently exalted by office far above any divine Messengers before them. We come to the same *conclusion* from considering the sacred treasures committed

[1] John xx. 21—23.   [2] 1 Cor. iv. 1.   Gal. iv. 14.   2 Cor. v. 20.

to their custody, which (not to mention their miraculous powers, which is beside our present purpose) were those peculiar spiritual blessings which flow from Christ as a Saviour, as a Prophet, Priest, and King.

These blessings are commonly designated in Scripture as "the Spirit," or "the gift of the Holy Ghost." John the Baptist said of himself and Christ; "I indeed baptize you with water unto repentance; but He shall baptize you with the Holy Ghost, and with fire."[1] In this respect, Christ's ministrations were above all that had ever been before Him, in bringing with them the gift of the Holy Ghost, that one gift, one, yet multiform, sevenfold in its operation, in which all spiritual blessedness is included. Accordingly, our Lord was solemnly anointed with the Holy Ghost Himself, as an initiation into His Ministerial office. He was manifested as receiving, that He might be believed on as giving. He was thus commissioned, according to the Prophet, "to preach good tidings," "to heal the broken-hearted," "to give the oil of joy for mourning." Therefore, in like manner, the Apostles also were anointed with the same heavenly gift for the same Ministerial office. "He breathed on them, and saith unto them, Receive ye the Holy Ghost." Such as was the consecration of the Master, such was that of the Disciples; and such as His, were the offices to which they were thereby admitted.

Christ is a Prophet, as authoritatively revealing the will of God and the Gospel of Grace. So also were the Apostles; "He that heareth you, heareth Me; and he that despiseth you, despiseth Me: and he that despiseth

---

[1] Matt. iii. 11.

Me, despiseth Him that sent Me;" "He that despiseth, despiseth not man, but God, who hath also given unto us His Holy Spirit."[1]

Christ is a Priest, as forgiving sin, and imparting other needful divine gifts. The Apostles, too, had this power; "Whose soever sins ye remit, they are remitted unto them; and whose soever sins ye retain, they are retained." "Let a man so account of us as . . . Stewards of the Mysteries of God."

Christ is a King, as ruling the Church; and the Apostles rule it in His stead. " I appoint unto you a Kingdom, as My Father hath appointed unto Me ; that ye may eat and drink at My table in My Kingdom, and sit on thrones judging the twelve tribes of Israel."[2]

The gift, or office, cannot be named, which belongs to our Lord as the Christ, which He did not in its degree transfer to His Apostles by the communication of that Spirit, through which He Himself wrought; one of course excepted, the One great work, which none else in the whole world could sustain, of being the Atoning Sacrifice for all mankind. So far no one can take His place, and "His glory He does not give to another." His Death upon the Cross is the sole Meritorious Cause, the sole Source of spiritual blessing to our guilty race; but as to those offices and gifts which flow from this Atonement, preaching, teaching, reconciling, absolving, censuring, dispensing grace, ruling, ordaining, these all are included in the Apostolic Commission, which is instrumental and representative in His absence. "As My Father hath sent Me, so send I you." His gifts are

[1] *Luke* x. 16. 1 Thess. iv. 8.   [2] *Luke* xxi. 29, 30.

uot confined to Himself. "The whole house is filled with the odour of the ointment."

This being granted, however, as regards the Apostles themselves, some one may be disposed to inquire, whether their triple office has descended to Christian Ministers after them. I say their *triple* office, for few persons will deny that some portion of their commission still remains among us. The notion that there is no divine appointment of one man above another for Ministerial duties is not a common one, and we need not refute it. But it is very common for men to believe only as far as they can see and understand; and, because they are witnesses of the process and effects of instructing and ruling, and not of (what may be called) "the ministry of reconciliation," to accept Christ's Ministers as representatives of His Prophetic and Regal, not of His Priestly authority. Assuming then their claim to inherit two portions of His Anointing, I shall confine myself to the question of their possessing the third likewise: not however with a view of proving it, but rather of removing such antecedent difficulties as are likely to prejudice the mind against it.

By a Priest, in a Christian sense, is meant an appointed channel by which the peculiar Gospel blessings are conveyed to mankind, one who has power to apply to individuals those gifts which Christ has promised us generally as the fruit of His mediation. This power was possessed by the Apostles; I am now to show that it is possessed by their successors likewise.

1. Now, first, that there is a strong line of distinction between *the Apostles* and other Christian Ministers, I

readily grant; nay, rather I would maintain it to be so clearly marked that there is no possibility of confusing together those respects in which they resemble with those in which they differ from their brethren. The Apostles were not only Ministers of Christ, but first founders of His Church; and their gifts and offices, so far forth as they had reference to this part of their commission, doubtless were but occasional and extraordinary, and ended with themselves. They were organs of Revelation, inspired Teachers, in some respects infallible, gifted with divers tongues, workers of miracles; and none but they are such. The duration of any gift depends upon the need which it supplies; that which has answered its purpose ends, that which is still necessary is graciously continued. Such at least seems to be the rule of a Merciful Providence. Therefore it is, that the Christian Ministry still includes in it the office of teaching, for education is necessary for every soul born into the world; and the office of governing, for " decency and order" are still necessary for the quiet and union of the Christian brotherhood. And, for the same reason, it is natural at first sight to suppose that the office of applying the gifts of grace should be continued also, while there is guilt to be washed away, sinners to be reconciled, believers to be strengthened, matured, comforted. What warrant have we from the nature of the case, for making any distinction between the ministry of teaching and the ministry of reconciliation? if one is still committed to us, why not the other also?

And it will be observed, that the only real antecedent difficulty which attaches to the doctrine of the Christian

Priesthood, is obviated by Scripture itself. It might be thought that the power of remitting and retaining sins was too great to be given to sinful man over his fellows; but in matter of fact it was committed to the Apostles without restriction, though they were not infallible in what they did. "*Whose soever* sins ye remit they are remitted unto them; and *whose soever* sins ye retain, they are retained." The grant was in the very form of it unconditional, and left to their Christian discretion. What has once been given, may be continued. I consider this remark to be of weight in a case like the present, where the very nature of the professed gift is the only considerable reason against the fact of its bestowal.

2. But all this is on the bare antecedent view of the case. In fact, our Lord Himself has decided the question, by declaring that His presence, by means of His Apostles, *should* be with the Church to the end of the world. He promised this on the solemn occasion of His leaving them; He declared it when He bade them make converts, baptize, and teach. As well may we doubt whether it is our duty to preach and make proselytes, and prepare men for Heaven, as that His Apostolic Presence is with us, for those purposes. His words then at first sight even go to include *all* the gifts vouchsafed to His first Ministers; far from having a scanty grant of them, so large is the promise, that we are obliged to find out seasons to justify us in considering the Successors of the Apostles in any respects less favoured than themselves. Such reasons we know are to be found, and lead us to distinguish the extraordinary gifts from the

ordinary, a distinction which the event justifies; but what is there either in Scripture or in Church History to make us place the commission of reconciliation among those which are extraordinary?

3. In the next place, it is deserving of notice that this distinction between ordinary and extraordinary gifts, is really made in Scripture itself, and that among the extraordinary there is no mention made of the sacerdotal power. No one can doubt, that on the day of Pentecost the formal inauguration of the Apostles took place into their high and singular office of building the Church of Christ. They were "wise Master-builders, according to the grace given them;" and that grace was extraordinary. However, among those gifts, "tongues and visions, prophecies and wonders," their priestly power is not enumerated. On the contrary, that power had been previously conferred, according to the passage already cited, when Christ breathed on them, and gave them, through the Holy Ghost, the authority to remit and retain sins.[1] And

[1] The following passage supplies a corroboration of the above argument, and carries it on to the doctrine of the Apostolical Succession:—
"The very first act of the Apostles after Christ was gone out of their sight, was the ordination of Matthias in the room of the traitor Judas. That ordination is related very minutely. Every particular of it is full of instruction; but at present I wish to draw attention to one circumstance more especially: namely, the *time* when it occurred. It was contrived (if one may say so) exactly to fall within *the very short interval* which elapsed between the departure of our Lord, and the arrival of the Comforter in His place: on that 'little while,' during which the Church was comparatively left alone in the world. Then it was that St. Peter rose and declared with authority, that the time was come for supplying the vacancy which Judas had made. 'One,' said he, 'must be ordained;' and without delay they proceeded to the ordination. Of course, St. Peter must have had from our Lord express

further, I would remind you, that this is certainly our Church's deliberate view of the subject: for she expressly puts into the Bishop's mouth at ordination the very words here used by our Saviour to His Apostles. "Receive the Holy Ghost;" "Whose soever sins ye remit, they are remitted to them; and whose soever sins ye retain, they are retained;" words, which it were inexpressibly profane for man to use to man, except by a plain divine commission to do so.

4. But again, has not the Gospel Sacraments? and have not Sacraments, as pledges and means of grace, a priestly nature? If so, the question of the existence of a Christian Priesthood is narrowed at once to the simple

authority for this step. Otherwise it would seem most natural to defer a transaction so important until the unerring Guide, the Holy Ghost, should have come among them, as they knew He would in a few days On the other hand, since the Apostles were eminently Apostles of our Incarnate Lord, since their very being, *as* Apostles, depended entirely on their personal mission from Him (which is the reason why catalogues are given of them, with such scrupulous care, in many of the holy books): in that regard one should naturally have expected that He Himself before His departure would have supplied the vacancy by personal designation. But we see it was not His pleasure to do so. As the Apostles afterwards brought on the ordination sooner, so He had deferred it longer than might have been expected. Both ways it should seem as if there were a purpose of bringing the event within those ten days, *during which,* as I said, *the church was left to herself;* left to exercise her faith and hope, much as Christians are left now, without any *miraculous* aid or extraordinary illumination from above. Then, at that moment of the New Testament history in which the circumstances of believers corresponded most nearly to what they have been since miracles and inspiration ceased,—just at that time it pleased our Lord that a fresh Apostle should be consecrated, with authority and commission as ample as the former enjoyed. In a word, it was His will that the eleven Disciples alone, not Himself personally, should name the successor of Judas; and that they chose the right person, He gave testimony very soon after, by sending His Holy Spirit on St. *Matthias,* as richly as on St. John, St. James, or St. Peter."—*Tracts for the Times,* vol. ii. No. 52.

question whether it is or is not probable that so precious
an ordinance as a channel of grace would be committed
by Providence to the custody of certain guardians.   The
tendency of opinions at this day is to believe that
nothing more is necessary, for acceptance than faith in
God's promise of mercy; whereas it is certain from
Scripture, that the gift of reconciliation is not conveyed
to individuals except through appointed ordinances.
Christ has interposed something between Himself and
the soul; and if it is not inconsistent with the liberty
of the Gospel that a Sacrament should interfere, there is
no antecedent inconsistency in a keeper of the Sacrament attending upon it.   Moreover, the very circumstance that a standing Ministry has existed from the
first, leads on to the inference that that Ministry was
intended to take charge of the Sacraments; and thus
the facts of the case suggest an interpretation of our
Lord's memorable words, when He committed to St.
Peter "the *keys* of the Kingdom of Heaven."

I would have this Scripture truth considered attentively; viz. that Sacraments are the channels of the
peculiar Christian privileges, and not merely (as many
men think, and as the rite of Confirmation really is)
seals of the covenant.   A man may object, indeed, that
in St. Paul's Epistle to the Romans nothing is said
about channels and instruments; that faith is represented as the sole medium of justification.   But I will
refer him, by way of reply, to the same Apostle's speech
to Festus and Agrippa, where he describes Christ as
saying to him on his miraculous conversion, " Rise and
stand upon thy feet ; for I have appeared unto thee for

this purpose, to make thee a Minister and a Witness," sending him forth, as it might appear, to preach the Gospel, without instrumentality of Ordinance or Minister. Had we but this account of his conversion, who would not have supposed, that he who was "to open men's eyes, and turn them from darkness to light," had been pardoned and accepted at once upon his faith, without rite or form? Yet from other parts of the history, we learn what is here omitted, viz. that an especial revelation was made to Ananias, lest Saul should go without baptism; and that, so far from his being justified immediately on his faith, he was bid not to tarry, but "to arise and be baptized, and *to wash away his sins,* calling on the name of the Lord."[1] So dangerous is it to attempt to prove a negative from insulated passages of Scripture.

Here then we have a clear instance in St. Paul's own case, that there are priestly Services between the soul and God, even under the Gospel; that though Christ has purchased inestimable blessings for our race, yet that it is still necessary ever to apply them to individuals by visible means; and if so, I confess, that to me at least it seems more likely antecedently, that such services should have, than that they should lack, an appropriate minister. But here again we are not left to mere conjecture, as I proceed to show.

5. You well know that the benefits of the Atonement are frequently represented in Scripture under the figure of spiritual food, bread from heaven, the water that never faileth, and in more sacred language, as the

---

[1] *Acts* xxvi. 16—18; xxii. 16; ix. 17. Vide also xiii. 2, 3.

communion of the Body and Blood of the Divine Sacrifice. Now, this special Christian benefit is there connected, as on the one hand with an outward rite, so on the other with certain appointed Dispensers. So that the very context of Scripture leads us on from the notion of a priestly service to that of a priesthood.

" Who then is that faithful and wise *Steward,*" says Christ, " whom his Lord shall make ruler over His household, to give them their *portion of food* in due season ? Blessed is that servant, whom his Lord when He cometh shall find so doing."[1] Now, I infer from this passage; first, that there are, under the Gospel, especial Dispensers of the Christian's spiritual food, in other words (if the word " food "[2] may be interpreted from the parallel of the sixth chapter of St. John), Dispensers of invisible grace, or Priests ;—next, that they are to continue to the Church in every age till the end, for it is said, " Blessed is he, whom his Lord, *when He cometh*, shall find so doing;"—further, that the Minister mentioned is also " Ruler over His household," as in the case of the Apostles, uniting the Regal with the Sacerdotal office ;—lastly, the word " Steward," which incidentally occurs in the passage, a title applied by St. Paul to the Apostles, affords an additional reason for supposing that other like titles, such as " Ambassadors of Christ," given to the Apostles, do also belong in a true and sufficient sense to their Successors.

6. These considerations in favour of the existence of a Christian Priesthood, are strengthened by observing that the office of intercession, which though not a

[1] Luke xii. 43.   [2] σιτομέτριον.

peculiarity, is ever characteristic of the Priestly Order, is spoken of in Scripture as a sort of prerogative of the Gospel Ministry. For instance, Isaiah, speaking of Christian times, says, " I have set watchmen upon thy walls, O Jerusalem, which shall never hold their peace day nor night. Ye that make mention of the Lord, keep not silence ; and give Him no rest, till He establish, and till He make Jerusalem a praise in the earth."[1] In the Acts of the Apostles, we find Christ's ministers engaged in this sacred service, according to the prophecy. " There were in the Church that was at Antioch certain prophets and teachers, as Barnabas, and Simeon called Niger, and Lucius of Cyrene, and Manaen, foster brother to Herod the Tetrarch, and Saul. As they *ministered* to the Lord, and fasted,"[2] the Holy Ghost separated two of them for His work. This " ministering " to the Lord with fasting was surely some solemn intercessory service. And this agrees with a passage in St. James's Epistle, which seems to invest the Elders of the Church with this same privilege of the priesthood. " Is any sick among you ? Let him call for the Elders of the Church, *and let them pray over him* (not pray *with* him merely), anointing him with oil in the name of the Lord ; and *the prayer of faith* (not the oil merely) shall save the sick, and the Lord shall raise him up." In like manner St. Paul speaks of Epaphras as " our dear fellow-servant, who is *for* you," that is, for the Colossians to whom he is writing, " a faithful minister of Christ." Presently he explains what was the service which Epaphras did for them : " always *labouring*

[1] Isa. lxii. 6, 7.   [2] Acts xiii. 1, 2.

fervently for you in prayer, that ye may stand perfect and complete in all the will of God."[1]

7. We may end these remarks by recurring to the instances of St. Peter and St. John the Baptist; who, as types of God's ordained servants, before and after His Son's coming, may serve to explain the office of ordinary Christian Ministers. Even the lowest of them is "greater than John." Now what was it that he wanted? Was it the *knowledge of Gospel doctrine?* No, surely; no words can be clearer than his concerning the New covenant. "Behold the Lamb of God, which taketh away the sin of the world." "He that cometh from above, is above all . . . He whom God hath sent speaketh the words of God, for God giveth not the Spirit by measure unto Him. The Father loveth the Son, and hath given all things into His hand. He that believeth on the Son hath everlasting life, and he that believeth not the Son shall not see life, but the wrath of God abideth on him."[2] Therefore, the Baptist lacked not the full Christian *doctrine;* what he did lack was (as he says himself) the Baptism of *the Spirit*, conveying a commission from Christ the Saviour, in all His manifold gifts, ordinary and extraordinary, Regal and Sacerdotal. John was not inferior to us Gospel Ministers in knowledge, but in power.

On the other hand, if, as I have made appear, St. Peter's ministerial office continues as regards ordinary purposes, in the persons of those who come after him, we are bound to understand our Lord's blessing, pronounced in the first instance upon him, as descending

[1] *James* v. 14, 15. Col. i. 7; iv. 12.　[2] John i. 29; iii. 31—36.

in due measure on the least of us His ministers who
"keep the faith," Peter being but the representative
and type of them all. "Blessed art thou, Simon Bar-
jona; for flesh and blood hath not revealed it unto
thee, but My Father, which is in heaven. And I say
also unto thee, that thou art Peter, and upon this rock
I will build My Church, and the gates of hell shall not
prevail against it. And I will give unto thee the keys
of the Kingdom of Heaven; and whatsoever thou shalt
bind on earth shall be bound in heaven, and whatsoever
thou shalt loose on earth shall be loosed in heaven."
August and glorious promise! Can it be, that it is all
expended on St. Peter, how great soever that noble
Apostle? Is it inserted in the "everlasting Gospel,"
to witness merely of one long since departed? Is it
the practice of the inspired word to exalt individuals?
Does not the very exuberance of the blessing resist any
such niggardly use of it? Does it not flow over in
spite of us, till our unbelief is vanquished by the
graciousness of Him who spoke it? Is it, in short,
anything but the prejudices of education, which prevent
so many of us from receiving it in that fulness of grace
in which it was poured out?

I say our *prejudices*,—for these surely are the cause
of our inconsistency in faith; adopting, as we do, a rule
of Scripture interpretation, which carries us a certain
way, and stops short of the whole counsel of God, and
should teach us nothing, or a great deal more. If the
promises to Christ's Apostles are not fulfilled in the
Church for ever after, why should the blessing attaching
to the *Sacraments* extend after the first age? Why

should the Lord's Supper be now the Cómmunion of
the Lord's Body and Blood? Why should Baptism
convey spiritual privileges? Why should any part of
Scripture afford permanent instruction? Why should
the way of life be any longer narrow? Why should
the burden of the Cross be necessary for every disciple
of Christ? Why should the Spirit of adoption any
longer be promised us? Why should separation from
the world be now a duty? Happy indeed it is for men
that they *are* inconsistent; for then, though they lose
some part of a Christian's faith, at least they keep a
portion. This will happen in quiet times, and in the
case of those who are of mature years, and whose minds
have been long made up on the subject of religion. But
should a time of controversy arise, then such inconsistencies become of fearful moment as regards the
multitude called Christian, who have not any decided
convictions to rest upon. Inconsistency of creed is
sure to attract the notice of the intellect, unless habit
has reconciled the heart to it. Therefore, in a speculative age, such as our own, a religious education
which involves such inconsistency, is most dangerous
to the unformed Christian, who will set straight his
traditionary creed by unlearning the portion of truth
it contains, rather than by adding that in which it is
deficient. Hence, the lamentable spectacle, so commonly
seen, of men who deny the Apostolic commission proceeding to degrade the Eucharist from a Sacrament to
a bare commemorative rite; or to make Baptism such
a mere outward form, and sign of profession, as it would
childish or fanciful to revere. And reasonably; for

they who think it superstitious to believe that particular persons are channels of grace, are but consistent in denying virtue to particular ordinances. Nor do they stop even here; for denying the grace of baptism, they proceed to deny the doctrine of original sin, for which that grace is the remedy.[1] Further, denying the doctrine of original sin, they necessarily impair the doctrine of the Atonement, and so prepare a way for the denial of our Lord's Divinity. Again, denying the power of the Sacraments on the ground of its *mysteriousness*, demanding from the very text of Scripture the fullest proof of it conceivable, and thinking little of the blessedness of " not seeing, and yet believing," they naturally proceed to object to the doctrine of the Trinity as obstructing and obscuring the simplicity (as they consider it) of the Gospel, and but indirectly deducible from the extant documents of inspiration. Lastly, after they have thus divested the divine remedies of sin, and the treatment necessary for the sinner, of their solemnity and awe, having made the whole scheme of salvation of as intelligible and ordinary a character as the repair of any accident in the works of man, having robbed Faith of its mysteries, the Sacraments of their virtue, the Priesthood of its commission, no wonder that sin itself is soon considered a venial matter, moral evil as a mere imperfection, man as involved in no great peril or misery, his duties of no very arduous or anxious nature. In a word, religion, as such, is in the way to disappear from

---

[1] *E. g.* A Dissenting Catechism has lately been published in the country for popular use, in which the doctrine of original sin is denied, by way of meeting the charge of cruelty towards children, as involved in *the omission of infant baptism.*

the mind altogether; and in its stead a mere cold worldly morality, a decent regard to the claims of society, a cultivation of the benevolent affections, and a gentleness and polish of external deportment, will be supposed to constitute the entire duties of that being, who is conceived in sin, and the child of wrath, is redeemed by the precious blood of the Son of God, is born again and sustained by the Spirit through the invisible strength of Sacraments, and called, through self-denial and sanctification of the inward man, to the Eternal Presence of the Father, Son, and Holy Ghost.

Such is the course and issue of unbelief, though beginning in what the world calls trifles. Beware then, O my Brethren, of entering a way which leads to death. Fear to question what Scripture says of the Ministers of Christ, lest the same perverse spirit lead you on to question its doctrine about Himself and His Father. "Little children, it is the last time; and as ye have heard that Antichrist shall come, even now are there many Antichrists. . . . They went out from us, but they were not of us."[1] "Ye shall know them by their fruits."[2] If any man come to you, bringing any scoff against the power of Christ's Ministers, ask him what he holds concerning the Sacraments, or concerning the Blessed Trinity; look narrowly after his belief as regards the Atonement, or Original Sin. Ascertain whether he holds with the Church's doctrine in these points; see to it whether at very best he does not try to evade the question, has recourse to explanations, or professes to ve no opinion at all upon it. Look to these things,

[1] John ii. 18, 19.   [2] Matt. vii. 16.

that you may see whither you are invited. Be not robbed of your faith blindfold. Do what you do with a clear understanding of the consequences. And if the arguments which he uses against you tend to show that your present set of opinions is in some measure inconsistent, and force you to see in Scripture more than you do at present, or else less, be not afraid to add to it, rather than to detract from it. Be quite sure that, go as far as you may, you will never, through God's grace, be led to see more in it than the early Christians saw; that, however you enlarge your creed, you will but carry yourselves on to Apostolic perfection, equally removed from the extremes of presumption and of unbelief, neither intruding into things not seen as yet, nor denying, on the other hand, what you cannot see.

SERMON XXVI.

Human Responsibility.

(THE FEAST OF ST. JAMES THE APOSTLE.)

" To sit on My right hand and on My left is not Mine to give; but it shall be given to them for whom it is prepared of My Father."—MATT. xx. 23.

IN these words, to which the Festival of St. James the Greater especially directs our minds, our Lord solemnly declares that the high places of His Kingdom are not His to give,—which can mean nothing else, than that the assignment of them does not simply and absolutely depend upon Him; for that He will actually dispense them at the last day, and moreover is the meritorious cause of any being given, is plain from Scripture. I say, He avers most solemnly that something besides His own will and choice is necessary, for obtaining the posts of honour about His throne; so that we are naturally led on to ask, *where* it is that this awful prerogative is lodged. Is it with His Father? He proceeds to speak of His Father; but neither does He assign it to Him, "It shall be given to them for whom it is *prepared* of My Father." The Father's foreknowledge and design

are announced, not His choice. "Whom He did foreknow, them He did predestinate." He prepares the
reward, and confers it, but upon whom ? No answer is
given us, unless it is conveyed in the words which
follow,—upon the humble :—" Whosoever will be great
among you, let him be your minister ; and whosoever
will be chief among you, let him be your servant."

Some parallel passages may throw some further light
upon the question. In the description our Lord gives
us of the Last Judgment, He tells us He shall say to
them on His right hand, "Come, ye blessed of My
Father, inherit the kingdom *prepared* for you from the
foundation of the world." Here we have the same expression. Who then are the heirs for whom the Kingdom is prepared ? He tells us expressly, those who fed
the hungry and thirsty, lodged the stranger, clothed the
naked, visited the sick, came to the prisoners, for His
sake. Consider again an earlier passage in the same
chapter. To whom is it that He will say, "Enter thou
into the joy of thy Lord ?"—to those whom He can
praise as " good and faithful servants," who have been
" faithful over a few things." These two passages
then carry our search just to the very point which is
suggested by the text. They lead us *from* the thought
of God and Christ, and throw us upon human agency
and responsibility, for the solution of the question ; and
they finally lodge us there, *unless* indeed other texts of
Scripture can be produced to lead us on further still.
We know for certain that they for whom the Kingdom
is prepared are the humble, the charitable, and the diligent in the improvement of their gifts ; to which another

11]   Y

text (for instance) adds the spiritually-minded :—"Eye hath not seen the things which God hath *prepared* for them that *love* Him."[1] Is this as far as we can go? Does it now depend ultimately on ourselves, or on any one else, that we come to be humble, charitable, diligent, and lovers of God?

Now, in answering this question, religious men have for many centuries differed in opinion; not indeed in the first and purest ages of the Church, but when corruptions began to steal in. In the primitive times it was always considered that, though God's grace was absolutely necessary for us from first to last,—before we believed, in order to our believing, and while we obeyed and worked righteousness, in order to our obeying,—so that not a deed, word, or thought could be pleasing to Him without it; yet, that after all the human mind had also from first to last a power of resisting grace, and thus (as the foregoing texts imply) had the ultimate determination of its own fate committed to it, whether to be saved or rejected, the responsibility of its conduct, and, if it was rejected, the whole blame of it. However, at the beginning of the fifth century, when shadows were coming over the Church, a celebrated Doctor arose, whose name must ever be honoured by us, for his numberless gifts, his diligence, and his extended usefulness, whatever judgment may be passed on certain of his opinions. He is known in the Theological Schools as the first to have given some sort of sanction to two doctrines hitherto unknown in the Church, and apparently far removed from each other, as indeed are the

---

[1] Matt. xxv. 21, 34—36. 1 Cor. ii. 9.

modern Systems in which they are found. The one is the Predestinarian Hypothesis; viz. that, in spite of the text, it is God and Christ with whom the ultimate decision concerning the individual's state depends; that His grace does not merely suggest, influence, precede, and follow, but forms in the soul a new character, not by the soul's instrumentality, but immediately by Himself, and is effectual with some, not with others, at His own will, not at the individual's. The one, I say, is this Predestinarian Doctrine; and the other is the doctrine of Purgatory. With this latter I am not now concerned; and I mention it, only as a remarkable fact, that the same Teacher, highly to be venerated except where he deviates from Catholic doctrine, should have first sanctioned certain characteristics of two Systems, which lie on either side, as of the primitive, so of the present Anglican Church. Dismissing the coincidence with this remark, I proceed to make some brief observations on the ground of argument on which the Predestinarian Doctrine rests.

It is doubtless a great mystery, how it is that one man believes, and another rejects the Gospel. It is altogether a mystery; we cannot get at all beyond the fact, and must be content with our ignorance. But men of reasoning, subtle, and restless minds, have within them a temptation to inquisitiveness; they cannot acquiesce in the limits of God's revelation, and go on to assume a cause for the strange things they see, when they are not told one. Thus they argue that a man's self cannot be the ultimate cause of his faith or unbelief, *else there* would be more first causes than

God in the world: as if the same reasoning would not show that God is the Author of evil; or as if it were more intelligible, why the Divine Will should choose this man and reject that, than why an individual man should choose or reject good or evil. When then they see, as is constantly seen in life, two persons, in education the same, in circumstances the same, both baptized, both admitted to full Church privileges, one turning out well, the other ill, astonished at the mystery, they hastily say, "Here is God's secret election! God has decreed life to one, and has passed over the other; else why this difference of conduct?" when they should bow the head, and wait till the day of the revelation of all secrets. Again, they assume that the will is subjected to the influence of the reason, affections, and the like, in the same uniform way in which material bodies obey the laws of matter;—that certain inducements or a certain knowledge being presented, the mind can but act in one way; so that, its movements varying, on a given rule, according to influences from without (whether from the world or from God), every one's doom must be determined, either by the mere chance of external circumstances (which is irrational), or else certainly by the determination of God. Such are their reasonings; and it is remarkable that they should trust to reasoning, and in so special a way, considering they are commonly the men who speak against human reason as fallible and corrupt, when it is brought to oppose their opinions. Such grounds of argument, then, we may dismiss at once, except in philosophical discussions; certainly when we speak as Christians.

Next, let us inquire whether there be any Scripture reason for breaking the chain of doctrine which the text suggests. Christ gives the Kingdom to those for whom it is prepared of the Father; the Father prepares it for those who love and serve Him. Does Scripture warrant us in reversing this order, and considering that any are chosen to love Him by His irreversible decree? The disputants in question maintain that it does.

1. Scripture is supposed expressly to *promise* perseverance, when men once savingly partake of grace; as where it is said, " He which hath begun a good work in you, will perform it until the day of Jesus Christ;"[1] and hence it is inferred that the salvation of the individual rests ultimately with God, and not with himself. But here I would object in the outset to applying to individuals promises and declarations made to bodies, and of a general nature. The question in debate is, not whether God carries forward bodies of men, such as the Christian Church, to salvation, but whether He has accorded any promise of indefectibility to given individuals? Those who differ from us say, that individuals are absolutely chosen to eternal life; let them then reckon up the passages in Scripture where perseverance is promised to individuals. Till they can satisfy this demand, they have done nothing by producing such a text as that just cited; which, being spoken of the body of Christians, does but impart that same kind of encouragement, as is contained in other general declarations, such as the statement about God's

[1] Phil. i. 6.

willingness to save, His being in the midst of us, and the like.

But let us suppose, for argument's sake, that such passages may be applied to individuals; for instance, as when Christ says, that no one " shall pluck His sheep out of His Father's hand." Now, I would maintain that here a condition is understood, as is constantly the case in Scripture, as in other writings; viz. that while the sheep " follow " Christ, and keep within the fold, none can pluck them thence. God proclaims his name to Moses, as " forgiving iniquity, and transgression, and sin, and that will by no means clear the guilty;"[1] but what would be thought of a commentator who hence inferred that the impenitent might be forgiven, and the repenting sinner fail of pardon?

Again, " It is God which worketh in you both to will and to do of His good pleasure."[2] What is this but a declaration, that on the whole all our sanctification is from first to last God's work? how does it interfere with this, to say that we may effectually resist that work? Might it not truly be said that the cure of a sick person was wholly attributable to the physician, without denying that the former, had he so chosen, might have obstinately rejected the medicine, or that there might have been (though there was not) some malignant habit of body, which completely baffled the medical art? Does the chance of failure make it less the physician's work when there is not failure?

In truth, the two doctrines of the sovereign and

---

[1] John x. 28. Exod. xxxiv. 7. [2] Phil. ii. 13

overruling power of Divine grace, and man's power of resistance, need not at all interfere with each other. They lie in different provinces, and are (as it were) incommensurables. Thus St. Paul evidently accounted them; else he could not have introduced the text in question with the exhortation, "Work out" or accomplish "your own salvation with fear and trembling, *for* it is God which worketh" or acts "in you." So far was he from thinking man's distinct working inconsistent with God's continual aiding, that he assigns the knowledge of the latter as an encouragement to the former. Let me challenge then a Predestinarian to paraphrase this text. We, on the contrary, find no insuperable difficulty in it, considering it to enjoin upon us a deep awe and reverence, while we engage in those acts and efforts which are to secure our salvation from the belief that God is in us and with us, inspecting and succouring our every thought and deed. Would not the Jewish High Priest, on the Great Day of Atonement, when going through his several acts of propitiation in God's presence, without and within the Veil, "exceedingly fear and quake," lest he should fail in aught put upon him? and shall not we, in our more blessed Covenant, knowing that God himself is within us, and in all we do, fear the more from the thought that, after all, we have our own part in the work, and must do it well, if we are to be saved? What, on the other hand, is the meaning of saying with the Predestinarian, "Work anxiously, because, in reality, you have no work to do?"

I say this, not so much by way of argument against

... is to show that a text which might be addressed in one small circumstance or so say to be implicated with an exhortation ... as proves that it ... and therefore similar passages ... readily be examined as he would have ... proven that his argument from it. "The whole work of salvation is of God, therefore man has no real part in securing it;" is not this contrary to the Apostle's own argument from his own words, "Man must exert himself because God is present with him." It is quite certain that a modern Predestinarian never could have written such a sentence.

Another instructive passage of this kind is our Lord's declaration with St. John's comment upon it, in the sixth chapter of his Gospel. "There are some of you that believe not. For Jesus knew from the beginning who they were that believed not, and who should betray Him. And He said, Therefore said I unto you, that no man can come unto Me, unless it were given unto him of My Father." Here in the plain meaning of the words, God's foreknowledge of the issue of free will in individuals is made compatible though the manner how is not told us) with electing grace. "Whom He did foreknow, He also did predestinate."

Take again another passage. "I obtained mercy, because I did it ignorantly;" "I obtained mercy, that in me first Jesus Christ might show forth all long suffering."[1] It appears that the Apostle saw no inconsistency in preaching that no sinner can claim forgiveness, yet that those who are less guilty than others obtain it. These two doctrines do not seem to have come into

[1] John vi. 64, 65.   1 Tim. i. 13, 16.

collision in his mind, any more than in our own; but it is quite plain that a Predestinarian never would have introduced the first while descanting on the second.

2. In the next place, there are many passages of the following kind, which are sometimes taken to favour the Predestinarian view, and require explanation. " God hath blessed us with all spiritual blessings in heavenly places in Christ, according as He hath chosen us in Him before the foundation of the world, that we should be holy and without blame before Him in love, having predestinated us unto the adoption of children by Jesus Christ to Himself, according to the good pleasure of His will." Here certainly an election is spoken of, irrespective of the conduct of the individuals who are subjects of it. Again, " By grace are ye saved through faith; and that salvation not of yourselves, it is the gift of God :"[1] and the like. But in such passages let it be observed, neither heaven nor the grace of sanctification is spoken of, but the present privilege, high indeed and peculiar to the Gospel, but only a privilege, of regeneration. This great Christian gift of course includes in it the communication of a sanctifying grace; but such a grace may be, and under circumstances has been, given without it. The Jews were aided by the Spirit of Sanctification, not of Regeneration. They were not the sons of God, as we are; whereas in every age " the just have lived by faith," and the like fruits of Sanctification. Now, where are we told that this sanctifying Grace is irrespective of the free-will of individuals? for this is the point. On the other hand,

---

[1] Eph. i. 3—5; ii. 8.

we readily grant that the grace of Regeneration is such; indeed, we grant that it is more than all that certain teachers hold Sanctification to be. It is a definite and complete gift conveyed, not gradually, but at once; or at least it has not more than a second degree, in the rite of Confirmation, wherein what is given in Baptism is sealed and secured; and moreover, it is a state distinct from every other, consisting in the Sacred Presence of the Spirit of Christ in soul and body; and lastly, it is bestowed on this man, or that, not by any rule which we can discover, but at the inscrutable decree of Him who calls into His Church whom He will. But faith, together with the other gifts of Sanctification, is not thus bestowed. In its nature it is independent of Regeneration, and, in the formal scheme of the Gospel, it is antecedent to it. It is the antecedent condition for receiving the Ordinances which convey and seal Regeneration,—Baptism and Confirmation. Hence, St. John says, "*As many as received Him*, to them gave He power to become the sons of God, even to them that believe on His Name, which were born, not of blood, nor of the will of the flesh, nor of the will of man, but of God." And St. Paul, "*Believing* in Christ, ye were *sealed with that Holy Spirit of promise*, which is the earnest of our inheritance, until the redemption of the purchased possession."[1]

It avails not, therefore, to enlarge upon the characteristics of the Christian Election, with a view of proving the irreversible decrees of God concerning the *final* salvation of individuals.

---

[1] John i. 12, 13. Eph. i. 13, 14.

3. Lastly, there are passages which speak of God's *judicial* dealings with the heart of man; in which, doubtless, He does act absolutely at His sole will,—yet not in the beginning of His Providence towards us, but at the close. Thus He is said "to send" on men "strong *delusion* to believe a lie;" but only on those who "received not the love of the truth that they might be saved."[1] Such irresistible influences do but presuppose, instead of superseding, our own accountableness.

These three explanations then being allowed their due weight,—the compatibility of God's sovereignty over the soul, with man's individual agency; the distinction between Regeneration and faith and obedience; and the judicial purpose of certain Divine influences upon the heart,—let us ask what does there remain of Scripture evidence in behalf of the Predestinarian doctrines? Are we not obliged to leave the mystery of human agency and responsibility as we find it? as truly a mystery in itself as that which concerns the Nature and Attributes of the Divine Mind.

Surely it will be our true happiness thus to conduct ourselves; to use our reason, in getting at the true sense of Scripture, not in making a series of deductions from it; in unfolding the doctrines therein contained, not in adding new ones to them; in acquiescing in what is told, not in indulging curiosity about the "secret things" of the Lord our God.

I conclude with the following text, which, while it is a solemn warning to us all to turn to God with a true heart, states with a force not to be explained

[1] 2 Thess. ii. 10, 11.

away, what the revealed Will is, and what we are to
hold respecting it. "*As I live*, saith the Lord God, I
have no pleasure in the death of the wicked; but that
the wicked turn from his way and live. Turn ye,
turn ye from your evil ways: for why will ye die,
O House of Israel?"[1]

[1] Ezek. xxxiii. 11.

SERMON XXVII.

Guilelessness.

(THE FEAST OF ST. BARTHOLOMEW THE APOSTLE.)

" Jesus saw Nathanael coming to Him, and saith of him, Behold an Israelite indeed, in whom is no guile !"—JOHN i. 47.

ST. BARTHOLOMEW, whose Festival we celebrate to-day, has been supposed to be the same as the Nathanael mentioned in the text. Nathanael was one of Christ's first converts, yet his name does not occur again till the last chapter of St. John's Gospel, where he is mentioned in company with certain of the Apostles, to whom Christ appeared after His resurrection. Now, why should the call of Nathanael have been recorded in the opening of the Gospel, among the acts of Christ in the beginning of His Ministry, unless he was an Apostle? Philip, Peter, and Andrew, who are mentioned at the same time, were all Apostles ; and Nathanael's name is introduced without preface, as if familiar to a Christian reader. At the end of the Gospel it appears again, and there too among Apostles. Besides, the Apostles were the special witnesses of Christ, when He was risen.

He manifested Himself, "not to all the people," says Peter, "but unto witnesses chosen before of God, even to us, who did eat and drink with Him after He rose from the dead."[1] Now, the occasion on which Nathanael is mentioned, was one of these manifestations. "This is now the third time," says the Evangelist, "that Jesus was manifested to His disciples, after that He was risen from the dead." It was in the presence of Nathanael, that He gave St. Peter his commission, and foretold his martyrdom, and the prolonged life of St. John. All this leads us to conjecture that Nathanael is one of the Apostles under another name. Now, he is not Andrew, Peter, or Philip, for they are mentioned in connexion with him in the first chapter of the Gospel; nor Thomas, James, or John, in whose company he is found in the last chapter; nor Jude (as it would seem), because the name of Jude occurs in St. John's fourteenth chapter. Four Apostles remain, who are not named in his Gospel,—St. James the Less, St. Matthew, St. Simon, and St. Bartholomew; of whom St. Matthew's second name is known to have been Levi, while St. James, being related, was not at any time a stranger to our Lord, which Nathanael evidently was. If then Nathanael were an Apostle, he was either Simon or Bartholomew. Now it is observable, that, according to St. John, Philip brought Nathanael to Christ; therefore Nathanael and Philip were friends: while in the other Gospels, in the list of Apostles, Philip is associated with Bartholomew; "Simon and Andrew, James and John, Philip and Bartholomew."[2] This is some evidence that

---

[1] Acts x. 41.   [2] Matt. x. 3.

Bartholomew and not Simon is the Nathanael of St. John. On the other hand, Matthias has been suggested instead of either, his name meaning nearly the same as Nathanael in the original language. However, since writers of some date decide in favour of Bartholomew, I shall do the like in what follows.

What then do we learn from his recorded character and history? It affords us an instructive lesson.

When Philip told him that he had found the long-expected Messiah of whom Moses wrote, Nathanael (that is, Bartholomew) at first doubted. He was well read in the Scriptures, and knew the Christ was to be born in Bethlehem; whereas Jesus dwelt at Nazareth, which Nathanael supposed in consequence to be the place of His birth,—and he knew of no particular promises attached to that city, which was a place of evil report, and he thought no good could come out of it. Philip told him to come and see; and he went to see, as a humble single-minded man, sincerely desirous to get at the truth. In consequence, he was vouchsafed an interview with our Saviour, and was converted.

Now, from what occurred in this interview, we gain some insight into St. Bartholomew's character. Our Lord said of him, " Behold an Israelite indeed, in whom is no guile!" and it appears, moreover, as if, before Philip called him to come to Christ, he was engaged in meditation or prayer, in the privacy which a fig-tree's shade afforded him. And this, it seems, was the life of one who was destined to act the busy part of an Apostle; quietness without, guilelessness within. This was the tranquil *preparation* for great dangers and sufferings\

We see who make the most heroic Christians, and are the most honoured by Christ!

An even, unvaried life is the lot of most men, in spite of occasional troubles or other accidents ; and we are apt to despise it, and to get tired of it, and to long to see the world,—or, at all events, we think such a life affords no great opportunity for religious obedience. To rise up, and go through the same duties, and then to rest again, day after day,—to pass week after week, beginning with God's service on Sunday, and then to our worldly tasks,—so to continue till year follows year, and we gradually get old,—an unvaried life like this is apt to seem unprofitable to us when we dwell upon the thought of it. Many indeed there are, who do not think at all ;—but live in their round of employments, without care about God and religion, driven on by the natural course of things in a dull irrational way like the beasts that perish. But when a man begins to feel he has a soul, and a work to do, and a reward to be gained, greater or less, according as he improves the talents committed to him, then he is naturally tempted to be anxious from his very wish to be saved, and he says, " What must I *do* to please God ?" And sometimes he is led to think he ought to be useful on a large scale, and goes out of his line of life, that he may be doing something worth doing, as he considers it. Here we have the history of St. Bartholomew and the other Apostles to recall us to ourselves, and to assure us that we need not give up our usual manner of life, in order to serve God; that the most humble and quietest station *is* acceptable to Him, if improved duly,—nay, affords means for maturing the highest Christian character, even that of an Apostle. Bartholomew read the Scriptures and prayed to God; and thus was trained at length to give up his life for Christ, when He demanded it.

But, further, let us consider the particular praise which our Saviour gives him. "Behold an Israelite indeed, in whom is no guile!" This is just the character which (through God's grace) they may attain most fully, who live out of the world in the private way I have been describing,—which is made least account of by man, and thought to be in the way of success in life, though our Saviour chose it to make head against all the power and wisdom of the world. Men of the world think an ignorance of its ways is a disadvantage or disgrace; as if it were somehow unmanly and weak to have abstained from all acquaintance with its impieties and lax practices. How often do we hear them say that a man must do so and so, unless he would be singular and absurd; that he must not be too strict, or indulge high-flown notions of virtue, which may be good to talk about, but are not fit for this world! When they hear of any young person resolving on being consistently religious, or being strictly honest in trade, or observing a noble purity in language and demeanour, they smile and think it very well, but that it will and must wear off in time. And they are ashamed of being innocent, and pretend to be worse than they really are. Then they have all sorts of little ways—are mean, jealous, suspicious, censorious, cunning, insincere, selfish; and think *others* as low-minded as themselves, only proud, or in some sense hypocritical, unwilling to confess their real motives and feelings.

To this base and irreligious multitude is opposed the Israelite indeed, in whom there is no guile. David describes his character in the fifteenth Psalm; and, taken in all its parts, it is a rare one. He asks, " Lord, who shall abide in Thy tabernacle? who shall dwell in Thy holy hill? He that walketh uprightly, and worketh righteousness, and speaketh the truth in his heart. He that backbiteth not with his tongue, nor doeth evil to his neighbour, nor taketh up a reproach against his neighbour. In whose eyes a vile person is contemned; but he honoureth them that fear the Lord. He that sweareth to his own hurt, and changeth not."

I say, it is a difficult and rare virtue, to mean what we say, to love without dissimulation, to think no evil, to bear no grudge, to be free from selfishness, to be innocent and straightforward. This character of mind is something far above the generality of men; and when realized in due measure, one of the surest marks of Christ's elect. And the instances which we may every now and then discover of it among Christians, will be an evidence to us, if evidence be wanting, that, in spite of all that grovelling minds may say about the necessity of acquaintance with the world and with sin, in order to get on well in life, yet after all, inexperienced guilelessness carries a man on as safely and more happily. For, first, it is in itself a great privilege to a rightly disposed mind, not to be sensible of the moral miseries of the world; and this is eminently the lot of the simple-hearted. They take everything in good part

which happens to them, and make the best of every
one; thus they have always something to be pleased
with, not seeing the bad, and keenly sensible of the
good. And communicating their own happy peace to
those around them, they really diminish the evils of
life in society at large, while they escape from the
knowledge of them themselves. Such men are cheerful
and contented; for they desire but little, and take
pleasure in the least matters, having no wish for riches
and distinction. And they are under the tyranny of no
evil or base thoughts, having never encouraged what in
the case of other men often spreads disorder and un-
holiness through their whole future life. They have no
phantoms of former sins, such as remain even to the
penitent, when he has subdued their realities, rising up
in their minds, harassing them, for a time domineering,
and leaving a sting behind them. Guileless persons are,
most of all men, skilful in shaming and silencing the
wicked;—for they do not argue, but take things for
granted in so natural a way, that they throw back the
sinner upon the recollection of those times of his youth,
when he was pure from sin, and thought as they do now;
and none but very hardened men can resist this sort of
appeal. Men of irreligious lives live in bondage and
fear; even though they do not acknowledge it to themselves. Many a one, who would be ashamed to own it,
is afraid of certain places or times, or of solitude, from a
sort of instinct that he is no company for good spirits,
and that devils may then assail him. But the guileless
man has a simple boldness and a princely heart; he
overcomes *dangers* which others shrink from, merely

...

...among the poor and lowly that this ...character of mind is found to exist. Secular ...ing and ...very ... countless in their respective ... a powerful ... to ... the ... of its ...ness and purity ... even in kings' courts, and the ...ols of philosophy Nathanaels may be discovered. ...like the Apostles, they have been subjected to the world's ...ings, they have been thwarted in their day, lived in anxiety, and seemingly lost by their ...esty, yet without being foiled either of its present comfort or its ultimate ... Such was our great Arch-bishop and Martyr, to whom perchance we owe it, that we who now live are still members of a branch of the Church Catholic; one of whose "greatest unpopular infirmities," according to the historian of his times, was "that he believed innocence of heart, and integrity of manners, was a guard strong enough to secure any man in his voyage through this world, in what company soever he travelled, and through what ways soever he was to pass. And sure," he adds, "never any man was better supplied with that provision."

I have in these remarks spoken of guileless men as members of society, because I wished to show that, even in that respect in which they seem deficient, they possess a hidden strength, an unconscious wisdom, which makes them live above the world, and sooner or later triumph over it. The weapons of their warfare are not carnal; and they are fitted to be Apostles, though they seem to be ordinary men. Such is the blessedness of the innocent, that is, of those who have never given way to evil, or formed themselves to habits of sin; who in consequence literally do not know its power or its misery, who have thoughts of truth and peace ever before them, and are able to discern at once the right and wrong in conduct, as by some delicate instrument which tells truly because it has never been ill-treated. Nay, such may be the portion (through God's mercy) even of those who have at one time departed from Him, and then repented; in proportion as they have learned to love God, and have purified themselves, not only from sin, but from the recollections of it.

Lastly, more is requisite for the Christian, even than guilelessness such as Bartholomew's. When Christ sent forth him and his brethren into the world, He said, "Behold, I send you forth as sheep in the midst of wolves; be ye therefore wise as serpents and harmless as doves." Innocence must be joined to prudence, discretion, self-command, gravity, patience, perseverance in well-doing, as Bartholomew doubtless learned in due season under his Lord's teaching; but innocence is the beginning. Let us then pray God to fulfil in us "all the good pleasure of His goodness, and the work of faith with power;" that if it should please Him suddenly to bring us forward to great trials, as He did His Apostles, we may not be taken by surprise, but be found to have made a private or domestic life a preparation for the achievements of Confessors and Martyrs.

SERMON XXVIII.

The Danger of Riches.

(THE FEAST OF ST. MATTHEW THE APOSTLE.)

" Woe unto you that are rich ! for ye have received your consolation."—
LUKE vi. 24.

UNLESS we were accustomed to read the New Testament from our childhood, I think we should be very much struck with the warnings which it contains, not only against the love of riches, but the very possession of them; we should wonder with a portion of that astonishment which the Apostles at first felt, who had been brought up in the notion that they were a chief reward which God bestowed on those He loved. As it is, we have heard the most solemn declarations so continually, that we have ceased to attach any distinct meaning to them; or, if our attention is at any time drawn more closely to them, we soon dismiss the subject on some vague imagination, that what is said in Scripture had a reference to the particular times when Christ came, without attempting to settle its exact application to us, or whether it has any such application at all,—as if the circumstance, that the interpretation requires care and thought, were an excuse for giving no thought or care whatever to the settling of it.

But, even if we had ever so little concern in the Scripture denunciations against riches and the love of riches, the very awfulness of them might have seemed enough to save them from neglect; just as the flood, and the judgment upon Sodom and Gomorrah, are still dwelt upon by Christians with solemn attention, though we have a promise against the recurrence of the one, and trust we shall never be so deserted by God's grace as to call down upon us the other. And this consideration may lead a man to suspect that the neglect in question does not entirely arise from unconcern, but from a sort of misgiving that the subject of riches is one which cannot be safely or comfortably discussed by the Christian world at this day; that is, which cannot be discussed without placing the claims of God's Law and the pride of life into visible and perplexing opposition.

Let us then see what the letter of Scripture says on the subject. For instance, consider the text. "Woe unto you that are rich! for ye have received your consolation." The words are sufficiently clear (it will not be denied), as spoken of rich persons in our Saviour's day. Let the full force of the word "consolation" be observed. It is used by way of contrast to the comfort which is promised to the Christian in the list of Beatitudes. Comfort, in the fulness of that word, as including help, guidance, encouragement, and support, is the peculiar promise of the Gospel. The Promised Spirit,

---

[1] Matt. v. 4.

who has taken Christ's place, was called by Him "the Comforter." There is then something very fearful in the intimation of the text, that those who have riches thereby receive their portion, such as it is, in full, instead of the Heavenly Gift of the Gospel. The same doctrine is implied in our Lord's words in the parable of Dives and Lazarus: "Son, remember thou in thy lifetime receivedst *thy* good things, and likewise Lazarus evil things; but *now* he is *comforted*, and thou art tormented." At another time He said to His disciples, "How hardly shall they that have riches enter into the kingdom of God! for it is easier for a camel to go through a needle's eye, than for a rich man to enter into the kingdom of God." [1]

Now, it is usual to dismiss such passages with the remark, that they are directed, not against those who have, but against those who trust in, riches; as if forsooth they implied no *connexion* between the having and the trusting, no warning *lest* the possession led to the idolatrous reliance on them, no necessity of fear and anxiety in the possessors, lest they should become castaways. And this irrelevant distinction is supposed to find countenance in our Lord's own language on one of the occasions above referred to, in which He first says, "How hardly shall they that *have* riches," then, "How hard is it for them that *trust* in riches, to enter into the kingdom of God;" whereas surely, He only removes His disciples' false impression, that the bare circumstance of possessing wealth was inconsistent with a state of salvation, and no more interprets *having* by *trusting* than

[1] Luke xvi. 25; xviii. 24, 25.

makes ...... essential to .... He comments he
... without identifying, without explaining away; and
the simple question which lies for our determination is
this:—whether, considering that they who had riches
when Christ came were likely in His judgment idolatrous to trust in them, there is or is not reason for
thinking that this likelihood varies materially in different
ages: and according to the solution of this question,
must we determine the application of the woe pronounced in the text to these .... And, at all events,
... to be observed, it is for those who would make out
that these passages do not apply now to give their
reasons for their opinion: the burden of proof is with
them. Till they draw their clear and reasonable distinctions between the first and the nineteenth century,
the denunciation hangs over the world—that is, as
much is over the Pharisees and Sadducees at our
Lord's coming.

But, in truth, that our Lord meant to speak of riches
as being in some sense a calamity to the Christian, is
plain, not only from such texts as this foregoing, but
from His praises and recommendation on the other
hand of poverty. For instance, "Sell that ye have
and give alms; provide yourselves bags which wax
not old." "If thou wilt be perfect, go sell that thou
hast, and give to the poor, and thou shalt have treasure
in heaven." "Blessed be ye poor: for yours is the
kingdom of God." "When thou makest a dinner or a
supper, call not thy friends, nor thy brethren, neither
thy kinsmen, nor thy rich neighbours .... but .... call
...... poor, the maimed, the lame, the blind." And in

like manner, St. James: "Hath not God chosen the poor of this world rich in faith, and heirs of that kingdom which He hath promised to them that love Him?"[1] Now, I cite these texts in the way of doctrine, not of precept. Whatever be the line of conduct they prescribe to this or that individual (with which I have nothing to do at present), so far seems clear, that according to the rule of the Gospel, the absence of wealth is, as such, a more blessed and a more Christian state than the possession of it.

The most obvious danger which worldly possessions present to our spiritual welfare is, that they become practically a substitute in our hearts for that One Object to which our supreme devotion is due. They are present; God is unseen. They are means at hand of effecting what we want: whether God will hear our petitions for those wants is uncertain; or rather I may say, certain in the negative. Thus they minister to the corrupt inclinations of our nature; they promise and are able to be gods to us, and such gods too as require no service, but, like dumb idols, exalt the worshipper, impressing him with a notion of his own power and security. And in this consist their chief and most subtle mischief. Religious men are able to repress, nay extirpate sinful desires, the lust of the flesh and of the eyes, gluttony, drunkenness, and the like, love of amusements and frivolous pleasures and display, indulgence in luxuries of whatever kind; but as to wealth, they cannot easily rid themselves of a secret feeling that

[1] Luke xii. 33. Matt. xix. 21. Luke vi. 20; xiv. 12, 13. James ii. 5.

it gives them a footing to stand upon, an importance, a superiority; and in consequence they get attached to this world, lose sight of the duty of bearing the Cross, become dull and dim-sighted, and lose their delicacy and precision of touch, are numbed (so to say) in their fingers' ends, as regards religious interests and prospects. To risk all upon Christ's word seems somehow unnatural to them, extravagant, and evidences a morbid excitement; and death, instead of being a gracious, however awful release, is not a welcome subject of thought. They are content to remain as they are, and do not contemplate a change. They desire and mean to serve God, nay actually do serve Him in their measure; but not with the keen sensibilities, the noble enthusiasm, the grandeur and elevation of soul, the dutifulness and affectionateness towards Christ which become a Christian, but as Jews might obey, who had no Image of God given them except this created world, "eating their bread with joy, and drinking their wine with a merry heart," caring that "their garments be always white, and their head lacking no ointment, living joyfully with the wife whom they love all the days of the life of their vanity," and "enjoying the good of their labour."[1] Not, of course, that the due use of God's temporal blessings is wrong, but to make them the object of our affections, to allow them to beguile us from the "One Husband" to whom we are espoused, is to mistake the Gospel for Judaism.

This, then, if we may venture to say so, was some part of our Saviour's meaning, when He connects together

1 Eccles. ix. 7—9 ; v. 18.

the having with the trusting in riches; and it is especially suitable to consider it upon this day, when we commemorate an Apostle and an Evangelist, whose history is an example and encouragement for all those who have, and fear lest they should trust. But St. Matthew was exposed to an additional temptation, which I shall proceed to consider; for he not only possessed, but he was engaged also in the pursuit of wealth. Our Saviour seems to warn us against this further danger in His description of the thorns in the parable of the Sower, as being "the care of this world and the deceitfulness of riches;" and more clearly in the parable of the Great Supper, where the guests excuse themselves, one, as having "bought a piece of ground," another "five yoke of oxen." Still more openly does St. Paul speak in his First Epistle to Timothy : "They that desire to be rich, fall into temptation and a snare, and into many foolish and hurtful lusts, which drown men in destruction and perdition. For the love of money is the root of all evil; which, while some coveted after, they have erred from the Faith, and pierced themselves through with many sorrows."[1]

The danger of *possessing* riches is the carnal security to which they lead; that of "*desiring*" and *pursuing* them, is, that an object of this world is thus set before us as the aim and end of life. It seems to be the will of Christ that His followers should have no aim or end, pursuit or business, merely of this world. Here, again, I speak as before, not in the way of precept, but of doctrine. I am looking at His holy religion as at a

[1] Matt. xiii. 22. Luke xiv. 18, 19. 1 Tim. vi. 9, 10.

distance, and determining what is its general character and spirit, not what may happen to be the duty of this or that individual who has embraced it. It is His will that all we do should be done, not unto men, or to the world, or to self, but to His glory; and the more we are enabled to do this simply, the more favoured we are. Whenever we act with reference to an object of this world, even though it be ever so pure, we are exposed to the temptation—(not irresistible, God forbid!) still to the temptation—of setting our hearts upon obtaining it. And therefore, we call all such objects *excitements*, as stimulating us incongruously, casting us out of the serenity and stability of heavenly faith, attracting us aside by their proximity from our harmonious round of duties, and making our thoughts converge to something short of that which is infinitely high and eternal. Such excitements are of perpetual occurrence, and the mere undergoing them, so far from involving guilt in the act itself or its results, is the great business of life and the discipline of our hearts. It is often a sin to withdraw from them, as has been the case of some perhaps who have gone into monasteries to serve God more entirely. On the other hand, it is the very duty of the Spiritual Ruler to labour for the flock committed to him, to suffer and to dare; St. Paul was encompassed with excitements hence arising, and his writings show the agitating effect of them on his mind. He was like David, a man of war and blood; and that for our sakes. Still it holds good that the essential spirit of the Gospel is "quietness and confidence;" that the possession of these is the *highest gift*, and to gain them perfectly our main aim.

Consequently, however much a duty it is to undergo excitements when they are sent upon us, it is plainly unchristian, a manifest foolishness and sin, to seek out any such, whether secular or religious. Hence gaming is so great an offence; as being a presumptuous creation on our part of a serious, if not an overpowering temptation to fix the heart upon an object of this world. Hence, the mischief of many amusements, of (what is called) the fashion of the day; which are devised for the very purpose of taking up the thoughts, and making time pass easy. Quite contrary is the Christian temper, which is in its perfect and peculiar enjoyment when engaged in that ordinary, unvaried course of duties which God assigns, and which the world calls dull and tiresome. To get up day after day to the same employments, and to feel happy in them, is the great lesson of the Gospel; and, when exemplified in those who are alive to the temptation of being busy, it implies a heart weaned from the love of this world. True it is that illness of body, as well as restlessness of mind, may occasionally render such a life a burden; it is true also that indolence, self-indulgence, timidity and other similar bad habits, may adopt it by preference, as a pretext for neglecting more active duties. Men of energetic minds and talents for action are called to a life of trouble; they are the compensations and antagonists of the world's evils: still let them never forget their place; they are men of war, and we war that we may obtain peace. They are but men of war, honoured indeed by God's choice, and, in spite of all momentary excitements, resting in the depth of their hearts upon

the One true Vision of Christian faith; still after all
they are but soldiers in the open field, not builders of
the Temple, nor inhabitants of those "amiable" and
specially blessed "Tabernacles" where the worshipper
lives in praise and intercession, and is militant amid the
unostentatious duties of ordinary life. "Martha, Martha,
thou art anxious and troubled about many things; but
one thing is needful, and Mary has chosen that good
part which shall not be taken away from her."[1]   Such
is our Lord's judgment, showing that our true happiness
consists in being at leisure to serve God without excitements.   For this gift we especially pray in one of our
Collects: "Grant, O Lord, that the course of this world
may be so peaceably ordered by Thy governance, that
Thy Church may joyfully serve Thee in all godly quietness."[2]   Persecution, civil changes, and the like break
in upon the Church's calm.   The greatest privilege of a
Christian is to have nothing to do with worldly politics,
—to be governed and to submit obediently; and though
here again selfishness may creep in, and lead a man to
neglect public concerns in which he is called to take his
share, yet, after all, such participation must be regarded
as a duty, scarcely as a privilege, as the fulfilment of
trusts committed to him for the good of others, not as
the enjoyment of rights (as men talk in these days of
delusion), not as if political power were in itself a good.

To return to the subject immediately before us; I
say then, that it is a part of Christian caution to see
that our engagements do not become pursuits.   Engagements are our portion, but pursuits are for the most

[1] Luke x. 41, 42.   [2] Vide 1 Tim. ii. 2.

part of our own choosing. We may be engaged in worldly business, without pursuing worldly objects; "not slothful in business," yet "serving the Lord." In this then consists the danger of the pursuit of gain, as by trade and the like. It is the most common and widely extended of all excitements. It is one in which every one almost may indulge, nay, and will be praised by the world for indulging. And it lasts through life; in that differing from the amusements and pleasures of the world, which are short-lived, and succeed one after another. Dissipation of mind, which these amusements create, is itself indeed miserable enough : but far worse than this dissipation is the concentration of mind upon some worldly object, which admits of being constantly pursued,—and such is the pursuit of gain. Nor is it a slight aggravation of the evil, that anxiety is almost sure to attend it. A life of money-getting is a life of care; from the first there is a fearful anticipation of loss in various ways to depress and unsettle the mind; nay to haunt it, till a man finds he can think about nothing else, and is unable to give his mind to religion, from the constant whirl of business in which he is involved. It is well this should be understood. You may hear men talk as if the pursuit of wealth was the business of life. They will argue, that by the law of nature a man is bound to gain a livelihood for his family, and that he finds a reward in doing so, an innocent and honourable satisfaction, as he adds one sum to another, and counts up his gains. And perhaps they go on to argue, that it is the very duty of man since Adam's fall, "in the sweat of his face," by effort and anxiety, "to eat bread." How strange it is that they do not remember Christ's gracious promise, repealing that original curse, and obviating the necessity of any real pursuit after "the meat that perisheth!" In order that we might be delivered from the bondage of corruption, He has expressly told us that the necessaries of life shall never fail His faithful follower, any more than the meal and oil the widow-woman of Sarepta; that, while he is bound to labour for his family, he need not be engrossed by his toil,—that while he is busy, his heart may be at leisure for his Lord. "Be not anxious, saying, what shall we eat? or what shall we drink? or wherewithal shall we be clothed? For after all these things do the Gentiles seek; for your heavenly Father knoweth that ye have need of all these things. But seek ye first the kingdom of God and His righteousness; and all these things shall be added unto you." Here is revealed to us at once our privilege and our duty, the Christian portion of having engagements of this world without pursuing objects. And in accordance with our Divine Teacher are the words of the Apostle, introductory of a passage already cited. "We brought nothing into this world, and it is certain we can carry nothing out. And having food and raiment, let us therewith be content."[1] There is no excuse then for that absorbing pursuit of wealth, which many men indulge in as if a virtue, and expatiate upon as if a science. "After all these things do the Gentiles seek!" Consider how different is the rule of life left us by the Apostles. "I speak this for your own profit," says St. Paul, "that ye may attend upon the

[1] Matt. vi. 1 Tim. vi. 7, 8.

Lord, without distraction." "This I say, brethren, the
time is short; it remaineth, that both they that have
wives be as though they had none, and they that weep
as though they wept not, and they that rejoice as though
they rejoiced not, and they that buy as though they
possessed not, and they that use this world as not
abusing it, for the fashion of this world passeth away."
"Be anxious for nothing; but in everything, by
prayer and supplication with thanksgiving, let your
requests be made known unto God." And St. Peter,
"Casting all your anxiety upon Him, for He careth
for you."[1]

I have now given the main reason why the pursuit
of gain, whether in a large or small way, is prejudicial
to our spiritual interests, that it fixes the mind upon an
object of this world; yet others remain behind. Money
is a sort of creation, and gives the acquirer, even more
than the possessor, an imagination of his own power;
and tends to make him idolize self. Again, what we
have hardly won, we are unwilling to part with; so that
a man who has himself made his wealth will commonly
be penurious, or at least will not part with it except in
exchange for what will reflect credit upon himself, or
increase his importance. Even when his conduct is
most disinterested and amiable (as in spending for the
comfort of those who depend upon him), still this indulgence of self, of pride and worldliness, insinuates itself.
Very unlikely therefore is it that he should be liberal
towards God; for religious offerings are an expenditure
without sensible return, and that upon objects for which

[1] *1 Cor. vii. 29—31, 35. Phil. iv. 6. 1 Pet. v. 7.*

A A 2

the very pursuit of wealth has indisposed his mind. Moreover, if it may be added, there is a considerable tendency in occupations connected with gain to make a man unfair in his dealings,—that is, in a subtle way. There are so many conventional deceits and prevarications in the details of the world's business, so much intricacy in the management of accounts, so many perplexed questions about justice and equity, so many plausible subterfuges and fictions of law, so much confusion between the distinct yet approximating outlines of honesty and civil enactment, that it requires a very straightforward mind to keep firm hold of strict conscientiousness, honour, and truth, and to look at matters in which he is engaged, as he would have looked on them, supposing he now came upon them all at once as a stranger.

And if such be the effect of the pursuit of gain on an individual, doubtless it will be the same on a nation; and if the peril be so great in the one case, why should it be less in the other? Rather, considering that the tendencies of things are sure to be brought out, where time and numbers allow them fair course, is it not certain that any multitude, any society of men, whose object is gain, will on the whole be actuated by those feelings, and moulded into that character, which has been above described? With this thought before us, it is a very fearful consideration that we belong to a nation which in good measure subsists by making money. I will not pursue it; nor inquire whether the especial political evils of the day have not their root in that *principle*, which St. Paul calls the root of all evil, the love of money. Only let us consider the fact, that we *are* money-making people, with our Saviour's declarations before us against wealth, and trust in wealth : and we shall have abundant matter for serious thought.

Lastly, with this dreary view before us of our condition and prospects as a nation, the pattern of St. Matthew is our consolation; for it suggests that we, Christ's ministers, may use great freedom of speech, and state unreservedly the peril of wealth and gain, without aught of harshness or uncharitableness towards individuals who are exposed to it. They may be brethren of the Evangelist, who left all for Christ's sake. Nay, such there have been (blessed be God!) in every age ; and in proportion to the strength of the temptation which surrounds them, is their blessedness and their praise, if they are enabled amid the " wares of the seas" and the " great wisdom of their traffic" to hear Christ's voice, to take up their cross, and follow Him.

SERMON XXIX.

The Powers of Nature.

(THE FEAST OF ST. MICHAEL AND ALL ANGELS.)

" Who maketh His Angels spirits, His ministers a flaming fire."—
PSALM civ. 4.

ON to-day's Festival it well becomes us to direct our minds to the thought of those Blessed Servants of God, who have never tasted of sin; who are among us, though unseen, ever serving God joyfully on earth as well as in heaven; who minister, through their Maker's condescending will, to the redeemed in Christ, the heirs of salvation.

There have been ages of the world, in which men have thought too much of Angels, and paid them excessive honour; honoured them so perversely as to forget the supreme worship due to Almighty God. This is the sin of a dark age. But the sin of what is called an educated age, such as our own, is just the reverse: to account slightly of them, or not at all; to ascribe all *we* see around us, not to their agency, but to certain *assumed* laws of nature. This, I say, is likely to be our

sin, in proportion as we are initiated into the learning
of this world;—and this is the danger of many (so
called) philosophical pursuits, now in fashion, and
recommended zealously to the notice of large portions
of the community, hitherto strangers to them,—che-
mistry, geology, and the like; the danger, that is, of
resting in things seen, and forgetting unseen things, and
our ignorance about them.

I will attempt to say what I mean more at length
The text informs us that Almighty God makes His
Angels spirits or winds, and His Ministers a flame of
fire. Let us consider what is implied in this.

1. What a number of beautiful and wonderful objects
does Nature present on every side of us! and how little
we know concerning them! In some indeed we see
symptoms of intelligence, and we get to form some idea
of what they are. For instance, about brute animals we
know little, but still we see they have sense, and we
understand that their bodily form which meets the eye
is but the index, the outside token of something we do
not see. Much more in the case of men: we see them
move, speak, and act, and we know that all we see takes
place in consequence of their will, because they have a
spirit within them, though we do not see it. But why
do rivers flow? Why does rain fall? Why does the
sun warm us? And the wind, why does it blow?
Here our natural reason is at fault; we know, I say,
that it is the *spirit* in man and in beast that makes man
and beast move, but reason tells us of no spirit abiding
in what is commonly called the natural world, to make
it perform its ordinary duties. Of course, it is God's

will which *sustains* it all ; so does God's will enable *us* to move also, yet this does not hinder, but, in one sense we may be truly said to move ourselves : but how do the wind and water, earth and fire, move ? Now here Scripture interposes, and seems to tell us, that all this wonderful harmony is the work of Angels. Those events which we ascribe to chance as the weather, or to nature as the seasons, are duties done to that God who maketh His Angels to be winds, and His Ministers a flame of fire. For example, it was an Angel which gave to the pool at Bethesda its medicinal quality ; and there is no reason why we should doubt that other health-springs in this and other countries are made such by a like unseen ministry. The fires on Mount Sinai, the thunders and lightnings, were the work of Angels ; and in the Apocalypse we read of the Angels restraining the four winds. Works of vengeance are likewise attributed to them. The fiery lava of the volcanoes, which (as it appears) was the cause of Sodom and Gomorrah's ruin, was caused by the two Angels who rescued Lot. The hosts of Sennacherib were destroyed by an Angel, by means (it is supposed) of a suffocating wind. The pestilence in Israel when David numbered the people, was the work of an Angel. The earthquake at the resurrection was the work of an Angel. And in the Apocalypse the earth is smitten in various ways by Angels of vengeance.[1]

Thus, as far as the Scripture communications go, we

[1] John v. 4. Exod. xix. 16—18. Gal. iii. 19. Acts vii. 53. Rev. vii. 1. Gen. xix. 13. 2 Kings xix. 35. 2 Sam. xxiv. 15—17. *Matt.* xxviii. 2. Rev. viii., ix., xvi.

learn that the course of Nature, which is so wonderful, so beautiful, and so fearful, is effected by the ministry of those unseen beings. Nature is not inanimate; its daily toil is intelligent; its works are *duties.* Accordingly, the Psalmist says, " The heavens declare the glory of God, and the firmament showeth His handy-work." " O Lord, Thy word endureth for ever in heaven. Thy truth also remaineth from one generation to another; Thou hast laid the foundation of the earth, and it abideth. They continue this day according to Thine ordinance, for *all things serve Thee.*"[1]

I do not pretend to say, that we are told in Scripture what Matter is; but I affirm, that as our souls move our bodies, be our bodies what they may, so there are Spiritual Intelligences which move those wonderful and vast portions of the natural world which seem to be inanimate; and as the gestures, speech, and expressive countenances of our friends around us enable us to hold intercourse with them, so in the motions of universal Nature, in the interchange of day and night, summer and winter, wind and storm, fulfilling His word, we are reminded of the blessed and dutiful Angels. Well then, on this day's Festival, may we sing the hymn of those Three Holy Children whom Nebuchadnezzar cast into the fiery furnace. The Angels were bid to change the nature of the flame, and make it harmless to them; and they in turn called on all the creatures of God, on the Angels especially, to glorify Him. Though many hundreds of years have passed since that time, and the world now vainly thinks it knows more than it did, and

[1] Ps. xix. 1; cxix. 89—91.

that it has found the real causes of the things it sees, still may we say, with grateful and simple hearts, " O all ye works of the Lord, O ye Angels of the Lord, O ye sun and moon, stars of heaven, showers and dew, winds of God, light and darkness, mountains and hills, green things upon the earth, bless ye the Lord, praise Him, and magnify Him for ever." Thus, whenever we look abroad, we are reminded of those most gracious and holy Beings, the servants of the Holiest, who deign to minister to the heirs of salvation. Every breath of air and ray of light and heat, every beautiful prospect, is, as it were, the skirts of their garments, the waving of the robes of those whose faces see God in heaven. And I put it to any one, whether it is not as philosophical, and as full of intellectual enjoyment, to refer the movements of the natural world to them, as to attempt to explain them by certain theories of science; useful as these theories certainly are for particular purposes, and capable (in subordination to that higher view) of a religious application.

2. And thus I am led to another use of the doctrine under consideration. While it raises the mind, and gives it a matter of thought, it is also profitable as a humbling doctrine, as indeed I have already shown. Vain man would be wise, and he curiously examines the works of Nature, as if they were lifeless and senseless; as if he alone had intelligence, and they were base inert matter, however curiously contrived at the first. So he goes on, tracing the order of things, seeking for Causes in that order, giving names to the wonders he meets with, and thinking he understands what he has

given a name to. At length he forms a theory, and recommends it in writing, and calls himself a philosopher. Now all these theories of science, which I speak of, are useful, as classifying, and so assisting us to *recollect*, the works and ways of God and of His ministering Angels. And again, they are ever most useful, in enabling us to *apply* the course of His providence, and the ordinances of His will, to the benefit of man. Thus we are enabled to enjoy God's gifts; and let us thank Him for the knowledge which enables us to do so, and honour those who are His instruments in communicating it. But if such a one proceeds to imagine that, because he knows something of this world's wonderful order, he therefore knows *how* things really go on, if he treats the miracles of Nature (so to call them) as mere mechanical processes, continuing their course by themselves,—as works of man's contriving (a clock, for instance) are set in motion, and go on, as it were, of themselves,—if in consequence he is, what may be called, irreverent in his conduct towards Nature, thinking (if I may so speak) that it does not hear him, and see how he is bearing himself towards it; and if, moreover, he conceives that the Order of Nature, which he partially discerns, will stand in the place of the God who made it, and that all things continue and move on, not by His will and power, and the agency of the thousands and ten thousands of His unseen Servants, but by fixed laws, self-caused and self-sustained, what a poor weak worm and miserable sinner he becomes! Yet such, I fear, is the condition of many men nowadays, who *talk loudly*, and appear to themselves and others to

... we can ... hence ... and ... in a time instead of ... nor can we know much more about the operations of Nature than we do.

... now let us consider what the real state of the case is ... supposing we discover, as we are describing, when examining a flower, a stem, or a pebble, or a ... fragment, which it was, as something so beneath ... of its existence suddenly discovered that ... was the presence of some powerful being who was hidden behind the visible things he was inspecting, who though concealing his visible hand, was giving them their beauty, grace and perfection in being God's instrument for his purposes, by whose rule and ornaments those wondrous objects were which he was so eager to examine, what would be his thoughts? Should we but accidentally show a rudeness of manner towards our fellow-man, tread on the hem of his garment, or brush roughly against him, are we not vexed, not as if we had met him, but from the fear we may have been disrespectful? David had watched the awful pestilence three days tombless not with curious eyes but with indescribable terror and remorse; but when at length he 'lifted up his eyes and saw the Angel of the Lord' ('who caused the pestilence') 'stand between the earth and the heaven, having a drawn sword in his hand stretched out over Jerusalem, then David and the elders, who were clothed in sackcloth, fell upon their faces.'[1] The mysterious, irresistible pestilence became still more fearful when the cause was known;—and what is true of the terrible, is true on the other hand of the pleasant

[1] 1 Chron. xxi. 16.

and attractive operations of Nature. When then we walk abroad, and "meditate in the field at the eventide," how much has every herb and flower in it to surprise and overwhelm us! For, even did we know as much about them as the wisest of men, yet there are those around us, though unseen, to whom our greatest knowledge is as ignorance; and, when we converse on subjects of Nature scientifically, repeating the names of plants and earths, and describing their properties, we should do so religiously, as in the hearing of the great Servants of God, with the sort of diffidence which we always feel when speaking before the learned and wise of our own mortal race, as poor beginners in intellectual knowledge, as well as in moral attainments.

Now I can conceive persons saying all this is fanciful; but if it appears so, it is only because we are not accustomed to such thoughts. Surely we are not told in Scripture about the Angels for nothing, but for practical purposes; nor can I conceive a use of our knowledge more practical than to make it connect the sight of this world with the thought of another. Nor one more consolatory; for surely it is a great comfort to reflect that, wherever we go, we have those about us, who are ministering to all the heirs of salvation, though we see them not. Nor one more easily to be understood and felt by all men; for we know that at one time the doctrine of Angels was received even too readily. And if any one would argue hence against it as dangerous, let him recollect the great principle of our Church, that the abuse of a thing does not supersede the use of it; and let him explain, if he can, St. Paul's exhorting Timothy

...

Lastly, it is a motive to our exertions in doing the will of God, to think that, if we attain to heaven, we shall become the fellows of the blessed Angels. Indeed, what do we know of the courts of heaven, but as peopled by them? and therefore doubtless they are presented to us, that we may have something to fix our thoughts on, when we look heavenwards. Heaven indeed is the palace of Almighty God, and of Him doubtless we must think in the first place; and again of His Son our Saviour, who died for us, and who is manifested in the Gospels, in order that we may have something definite to look forward to : for the same cause, surely, the Angels also are revealed to us, that heaven may be as little as possible an unknown place in our imaginations.

Let us then entertain such thoughts as these of the Angels of God ; and while we try to think of them worthily, let us beware lest we make the contemplation of them a mere feeling, and a sort of luxury of the imagination. This world is to be a world of practice and labour; God reveals to us glimpses of the Third Heaven for our comfort; but if we indulge in these as the end of our present being, not trying day by day to purify ourselves for the future enjoyment of the fulness of them, they become but a snare of our enemy. The Services of religion, day by day, obedience to God in our calling and in ordinary matters, endeavours to imitate our Saviour Christ in word and deed constant prayer to Him, and dependence on Him, these are the due preparation for receiving and profiting by His revelations; whereas many a man can write and talk beautifully about them, who is not at all better or nearer heaven for all his excellent words.

SERMON XXX.

The Danger of Accomplishments.

(THE FEAST OF ST. LUKE THE EVANGELIST.)

"In the hearts of all that are wise hearted, I have put wisdom."—
EXODUS xxxi. 6.

ST. LUKE differed from his fellow-evangelists and
fellow-disciples in having received the advantages
of (what is called) a liberal education. In this respect he
resembled St. Paul, who, with equal accomplishments,
appears to have possessed even more learning. He is said
to have been a native of Antioch, a city celebrated for
the refined habits and cultivated intellect of its inhabitants ; and his profession was that of a physician or
surgeon, which of itself evidences him to have been in
point of education something above the generality of
men. This is confirmed by the character of his writings,
which are superior in composition to any part of the
New Testament, excepting some of St. Paul's Epistles.

There are persons who doubt whether what are called
" accomplishments," whether in literature or in the fine
arts, can be consistent with deep and practical serious-

ness of mind. They think that attention to these argues a lightness of mind, and, at least, takes up time which might be better employed; and, I confess, at first sight they seem to be able to say much in defence of their opinion. Yet, notwithstanding, St. Luke and St. Paul were accomplished men, and evidently took pleasure in their accomplishments.

I am not speaking of human *learning;* this also many men think inconsistent with simple uncorrupted faith. They suppose that learning must make a man proud. This is of course a great mistake; but of it T am not speaking, but of an over-jealousy of *accomplishments,* the elegant arts and studies, such as poetry, literary composition, painting, music, and the like; which are considered (not indeed to make a man *proud,* but) to make him *trifling.* Of this opinion, how far it is true, and how far not true, I am going to speak: being led to the consideration of it by the known fact, that St. Luke was a polished writer, and yet an Evangelist.

Now, that the accomplishments I speak of have a *tendency* to make us trifling and unmanly, and therefore are to be viewed by each of us with suspicion as far as regards himself, I am ready to admit, and shall presently make clear. I allow, that in matter of fact, refinement and luxury, elegance and effeminacy, go together. Antioch, the most polished, was the most voluptuous city of Asia. But the *abuse* of good things is no argument against the things themselves; mental cultivation *may* be a divine gift, though it is abused. All God's gifts are *perverted* by man; health, strength, intellectual power, are all turned by sinners to bad purposes, yet they are not evil in themselves: therefore an acquaintance with the elegant arts may be a gift and a good, and intended to be an instrument of God's glory, though numbers who have it are rendered thereby indolent, luxurious, and feeble-minded.

But the account of the building of the Tabernacle in the wilderness, from which the text is taken, is decisive on this point. It is too long to read to you, but a few verses will remind you of the nature of it. "Thou shalt speak unto all that are wise hearted, whom I have filled with the spirit of wisdom, that they may make Aaron's garments to consecrate him, that he may minister unto me in the priest's office." "See I have called by name Bezaleel . . . and have filled him with the Spirit of God, in wisdom and in understanding, and in knowledge, and in all manner of workmanship, to devise cunning works, to work in gold, and in silver, and in brass, and in cutting of stones, to set them, and in carving of timber, to work all manner of workmanship." "Take ye from among you an offering unto the Lord; whosoever is of a willing heart let him bring it, an offering of the Lord, gold, and silver, and brass, and blue, and purple, and scarlet and fine linen, and goats' hair, and rams' skins dyed red, and badgers' skins, and shittim wood, and oil for the light, and spices for anointing oil, and for the sweet incense, and onyx stones, and stones to be set for the ephod, and for the breast-plate. And every wise hearted among you shall come and make all that the Lord hath commanded."[1]

---

[1] Exod. xxviii. 3; xxxi. 2—6; xxxv. 5—19.

How then is it, that what in itself is of so excellent, and (I may say) divine a nature, is yet so commonly perverted? I proceed to state what is the danger, as it appears to me, of being accomplished, with a view to answer this question.

Now the *danger* of an elegant and polite education is, that it separates feeling and acting; it teaches us to think, speak, and be affected aright, without forcing us to practise what is right. I will take an illustration of this, though somewhat a familiar one, from the effect produced upon the mind by reading what is commonly called a romance or novel, which comes under the description of polite literature, of which I am speaking. Such works contain many good sentiments (I am taking the better sort of them) : characters too are introduced, virtuous, noble, patient under suffering, and triumphing at length over misfortune. The great truths of religion are upheld, we will suppose, and enforced; and our affections excited and interested in what is good and true. But it is all fiction; it does not exist out of a book which contains the beginning and end of it. *We* have nothing *to do ;* we read, are affected, softened or roused, and that is all; we cool again,—nothing comes of it. Now observe the effect of this. God has made us feel in order that we may *go on to act* in consequence of feeling; if then we allow our feelings to be excited without acting upon them, we do mischief to the moral system within us, just as we might spoil a watch, or other piece of mechanism, by playing with the wheels of it. We weaken its springs, and they cease to act truly. *Accordingly,* when we have got into the habit of amusing ourselves with these works of fiction, we come at length to feel the excitement without the slightest thought or tendency to act upon it; and, since it is very difficult to begin any duty *without* some emotion or other (that is, to begin on mere principles of dry reasoning), a grave question arises, how, after destroying the connexion between feeling and acting, how shall we get ourselves to act when circumstances make it our duty to do so? For instance, we will say we have read again and again, of the heroism of facing danger, and we have glowed with the thought of its nobleness. We have felt how great it is to bear pain, and submit to indignities, rather than wound our conscience; and all this, again and again, when we had no opportunity of carrying our good feelings into practice. Now, suppose at length we actually come into trial, and let us say, our feelings become roused, as often before, at the thought of boldly resisting temptations to cowardice, shall we therefore do our duty, quitting ourselves like men? rather, we are likely to talk loudly, and then run from the danger. Why?—rather let us ask, why *not?* what is to keep us from yielding? Because we *feel* aright? nay, we have again and again felt aright, and thought aright, without accustoming ourselves to act aright, and, though there was an original connexion in our minds between feeling and acting, there is none now; the wires within us, as they may be called, are loosened and powerless.

And what is here instanced of fortitude, is true in all cases of duty. The refinement which literature gives, is that of thinking, feeling, knowing and speaking, right, *not of* acting right; and thus, while it makes the manners amiable, and the conversation decorous and agreeable, it has no tendency to make the conduct, the practice of the man *virtuous*.

Observe, I have supposed the works of fiction I speak of to inculcate right sentiments ; though such works (play-books for example) are often vicious and immoral. But even at best, supposing them well principled, still after all, at best, they are, I say, dangerous, in them-selves ;—that is, if we allow refinement to stand in the place of hardy, rough-handed obedience. It follows, that I am much opposed to certain *religious* novels, which some persons think so useful : that they some-times do good, I am far from denying ;—but they do more harm than good. They do harm on the whole ; they lead men to cultivate the religious affections sepa-. rate from religious practice. And here I might speak of that entire religious system (miscalled religious) which makes Christian faith consist, not in the honest and plain practice of what is right, but in the luxury of excited religious feeling, in a mere meditating on our Blessed Lord, and dwelling as in a reverie on what He has done for us ;—for such indolent contemplation will no more sanctify a man *in fact*, than reading a poem or listening to a chant or psalm-tune.

The case is the same with the arts last alluded to, poetry and music. These are especially likely to make us unmanly, if we are not on our guard, as exciting emotions without insuring correspondent practice, and so destroying the connexion between feeling and acting ; for I here mean by unmanliness the inability to do with ourselves *what we wish*,—the saying fine things and yet lying slothfully on our couch, as if we could not get up, though we ever so much wished it.

And here I must notice something besides in elegant accomplishments, which goes to make us over-refined and fastidious, and falsely delicate. In books, everything is made beautiful in its way. Pictures are drawn of *complete* virtue; little is said about failures, and little or nothing of the drudgery of ordinary, every-day obedience, which is neither poetical nor interesting. True faith teaches us to do numberless disagreeable things for Christ's sake, to bear petty annoyances, which we find written down in no book. In most books Christian conduct is made grand, elevated, and splendid; so that any one, who only knows of true religion from books, and not from actual endeavours to be religious, is sure to be offended at religion when he actually comes upon it, from the roughness and humbleness of his duties, and his necessary deficiencies in doing them. It is beautiful in a picture to wash the disciples' feet; but the sands of the real desert have no lustre in them to compensate for the servile nature of the occupation.

And further still, it must be observed, that the art of composing, which is a chief accomplishment, has in itself a tendency to make us artificial and insincere. For to be ever attending to the fitness and propriety of our words, is (or at least there is the risk of its being) a kind of acting; and knowing what can be said on both sides of a subject, is a main step towards thinking the one side as good as the other. Hence men in ancient times, who cultivated polite literature, went by the name of "Sophists;" that is, men who wrote elegantly, and talked eloquently, on any subject whatever, right or wrong. St. Luke perchance might have been such a Sophist, had he not been a Christian.

Such are some of the dangers of elegant accomplishments; and they beset more or less all educated persons; and of these perhaps not the least such females as happen to have no very direct duties, and are above the drudgery of common life, and hence are apt to become fastidious and fine,—to love a luxurious ease, and to amuse themselves in mere elegant pursuits, the while they admire and profess what is religious and virtuous, and think that they really possess the character of mind which they esteem.

With these thoughts before us, it is necessary to look back to the Scripture instances which I began by adducing, to avoid the conclusion that accomplishments are positively dangerous, and unworthy a Christian. But St. Luke and St. Paul show us, that we may be sturdy workers in the Lord's service, and bear our cross manfully, though we be adorned with all the learning of the Egyptians; or rather, that the resources of literature, and the graces of a cultivated mind, may be made both a lawful source of enjoyment to the possessor, and a means of introducing and recommending the Truth to others; while the history of the Tabernacle shows that all the cunning arts and precious possessions of this world may be consecrated to a religious service, and be made to speak of the world to come.

I conclude then with the following cautions, to which the foregoing remarks lead. First, we must avoid giving too much time to lighter occupations; and next, we must never allow ourselves to read works of fiction or poetry, or to interest ourselves in the fine arts for the mere sake of the things themselves: but keep in mind all along that we are Christians and accountable beings, who have fixed principles of right and wrong, by which all things must be tried, and have religious habits to be matured within them, towards which all things are to be made subservient. Nothing is more common among accomplished people than the habit of reading books so entirely for reading's sake, as to praise and blame the actions and persons described in a random way, according to their fancy, not considering whether they are really good or bad according to the standard of moral truth. I would not be austere; but when this is done habitually, surely it is dangerous. Such too is the abuse of poetical talent, that sacred gift. Nothing is more common than to fall into the practice of uttering fine sentiments, particularly in letter writing, as a matter of course, or a kind of elegant display. Nothing more common in singing than to use words which have a light meaning, or a bad one. All these things are hurtful to seriousness of character. It is for this reason (to put aside others) that the profession of stage-players, and again of orators, is a dangerous one. They learn to say good things, and to excite in themselves vehement feelings, about nothing at all.

If we are in earnest, we shall let nothing lightly pass by which may do us good, nor shall we dare to trifle with such sacred subjects as morality and religious duty. We shall apply all we read to ourselves; and this almost without intending to do so, from the mere sincerity and honesty of our desire to please God. We shall be suspicious of all such good thoughts and wishes, and we shall shrink from all such exhibitions of our principles, as fall short of action. We shall aim at doing right, and so glorifying our Father, and shall exhort and constrain others to do so also ; but as for talking on the appropriate subjects of religious meditation, and *trying* to show piety, and to excite corresponding feelings in another, even though our nearest friend, far from doing this, we shall account it a snare and a mischief. Yet this is what many persons consider the highest part of religion, and call it spiritual conversation, the test of a spiritual mind ; whereas, putting aside the incipient and occasional hypocrisy, and again the immodesty of it, I call all formal and intentional expression of religious emotions, all studied passionate discourse, *dissipation,*—dissipation the same in nature, though different in subject, as what is commonly so called ; for it is a drain and a waste of our religious and moral strength, a general weakening of our spiritual powers (as I have already shown); and all for what ? —for the pleasure of the immediate excitement. Who can deny that this religious disorder is a parallel case to that of the sensualist? Nay, precisely the same as theirs, from whom the religionists in question think themselves very far removed, of the fashionable world I mean, who read works of fiction, frequent the public shows, are ever on the watch for novelties, and affect a pride of manners and a " mincing "[1] deportment, and are ready with all kinds of good thoughts and keen emotions on all occasions.

¹ Isa. iii. 16.

Of all such as abuse the decencies and elegancies of moral truth into a means of luxurious enjoyment, what would a prophet of God say? Hear the words of the holy Ezekiel, that stern rough man of God, a true Saint in the midst of a self-indulgent, high-professing people: "Thou son of man, the children of thy people still are talking against thee by the walls and in the doors of the houses, and speak one to another, every one to his brother, saying, Come, I pray you, and hear what is the word that cometh forth from the Lord. And they come unto thee as the people cometh, and they sit before thee as My people, and they hear thy words, but they will not do them: for with their mouth they show much love, but their heart goeth after their covetousness. And, lo, thou art unto them as a very lovely song of one that hath a pleasant voice, and can play well on an instrument: for they hear thy words, but they do them not." [1]

Or, consider St. Paul's words; which are still more impressive, because he was himself a man of learning and accomplishments, and took pleasure, in due place, in the pursuits to which these give rise:

"Preach the word; be instant in season, out of season; reprove, rebuke, exhort, with all long-suffering and doctrine. For the time will come when they will not endure sound doctrine; but after their own lusts shall they heap to themselves teachers, having itching ears. And they shall turn away their ears from the Truth, and shall be turned unto fables." "Watch ye, stand fast in the faith, quit you like men, be strong." [2]

[1] *Ezek.* xxxiii. 30—32.   [2] 2 Tim. iv. 2—4. 1 Cor. xvi. 18.

SERMON XXXI.

Christian Zeal.

(THE FEAST OF ST. SIMON AND ST. JUDE THE APOSTLES.)

" The zeal of Thine house hath eaten Me up."—JOHN ii. 17.

THE Apostles commemorated on this Festival direct
our attention to the subject of Zeal, which I
propose to consider, under the guidance of our Saviour's
example, as suggested by the text. St. Simon is called
Zelotes, which means the Zealous; a title given him (as
is supposed) from his belonging before his conversion to
the Jewish sect of Zealots, which professed extraordinary
Zeal for the law. Anyhow, the appellation marks him
as distinguished for this particular Christian grace. St.
Jude's Epistle, which forms part of the service of the
day, is almost wholly upon the duty of manifesting Zeal
for Gospel Truth, and opens with a direct exhortation
to " contend earnestly for the Faith once delivered to
the Saints." The Collect also indirectly reminds us of
the same duty, for it prays that all the members of
the Church may be united in spirit by the Apostles'

doctrine; and what are these but the words of Zeal, viz. of a love for the Truth and the Church so strong as not to allow that man should divide what God hath joined together?

However, it will be a more simple account of Zeal, to call it the earnest desire for God's honour, leading to strenuous and bold deeds in His behalf; and that in spite of all obstacles. Thus when Phinehas stood up and executed judgment in Israel, he was zealous for God. David also, in his punishment of the idolaters round about, and in preparing for the building of the Temple, showed his Zeal, which was one of his especial virtues. Elijah, when he assembled the Israelites upon Mount Carmel, and slew the prophets of Baal, was "very zealous for the Lord God of Hosts." Hezekiah besides, and Josiah, were led to their reformations in religious worship by an admirable Zeal; and Nehemiah too, after the captivity, who with the very fire and sweetness of Gospel Love set the repentant nation in order for the coming of Christ.

1. Now, Zeal is one of the elementary religious qualifications; that is, one of those which are essential in the very notion of a religious man. A man cannot be said to be in earnest in religion, till he magnifies his God and Saviour; till he so far consecrates and exalts the thought of Him in his heart, as an object of praise, and adoration, and rejoicing, as to be pained and grieved at dishonour shown to Him, and eager to avenge Him. In a word, a religious temper is one of loyalty towards God; and we all know what is meant by being loyal from the experience of civil matters. To be loyal is not

merely to obey; but to obey with promptitude, energy dutifulness, disinterested devotion, disregard of consequences. And such is Zeal, except that it is ever attended with that reverential feeling which is due from a creature and a sinner towards his Maker, and towards Him alone. It is the main principle in *all* religious service to love God above all things; now, Zeal is to love Him above all men, above our dearest and most intimate friends. This was the especial praise of the Levites, which gained for them the reward of the Priesthood, viz. their executing judgment on the people in the sin of the golden calf. " Let Thy Thummim and Thy Urim be with Thy Holy One, whom Thou didst prove at Massah, and with whom Thou didst strive at the waters of Meribah. Who said unto his father and to his mother, I have not seen him; neither did he acknowledge his brethren, nor knew his own children; for they have observed Thy word, and kept Thy covenant. They shall teach Jacob Thy Judgments, and Israel Thy Law; they shall put incense before Thee, and whole burnt sacrifice upon Thine Altar. Bless, Lord, his substance, and accept the work of his hands; smite through the loins of them that rise against him, and of them that hate him, that they rise not again." Phinehas was rewarded in like manner, after executing judgment. " Behold, I give unto him My covenant of peace. And he shall have it, and his seed after him, even the covenant of an everlasting Priesthood, because he was zealous for his God."[1] Zeal is the very consecration of God's Ministers to their office. Accordingly

[1] Deut. xxxiii. 8—11. Numb. xxv. 12, 13.

our Blessed Saviour, the One Great High Priest, the Antitype of all Priests who went before Him and the Lord and Strength of all who come after, began His manifestation of Himself by two acts of Zeal. When twelve years old he deigned to put before us in representation the sacredness of this duty, when He remained in the Temple "while His father and mother sought Him sorrowing," and on their finding Him, returned answer, "Wist ye not that I must be about My Father's business?" And again, at the opening of His public Ministry, He went into the Temple, and "made a scourge of small cords, and drove out the sheep and oxen, and overthrew the changers' tables"[1] that profaned it: thus fulfilling the prophecy contained in the text, "The Zeal of Thine house hath eaten Me up."

Being thus consumed by Zeal Himself, no wonder He should choose His followers from among the Zealous. James and John, whom He called Boanerges, the sons of Thunder, had warm hearts, when He called them, however wanting in knowledge ; and felt as if an insult offered to their Lord should have called down fire from Heaven. Peter cut off the right ear of one of those who seized Him. Simon was of the sect of the Zealots. St. Paul's case is still more remarkable. He, in his attachment to the elder Covenant of God, had even fought against Christ ; but he did so from earnestness, from being "zealous towards God," though blindly. He "verily thought with himself, that he *ought to do* many things contrary to the name of Jesus of Nazareth," and acted "in ignorance ;"[2] so he was spared. With

[1] Luke ii. 48, 49. John ii. 15.   [2] Acts xxvi. 9. 1 Tim. i. 13.

a sort of heavenly compassion his persecuted Lord told him, that it was " hard for him to kick against the pricks ;" and turned his ignorant zeal to better account. On the same ground rests the commendation which that Apostle bestows in turn upon his countrymen, while he sorrowfully condemns their unpardonable obstinacy. ' My heart's desire and prayer to God for Israel," he says, " is, that they might be saved; for I bear them record. that they have a Zeal of God, but not according to knowledge."[1] They were guilty, because they might have known what they did not know ; but so far as they were zealous, they claimed from him a respectful notice, and were far better surely than those haughty scorners, the Romans, who felt no concern whether there was a God or no, worshipped one idol as readily as another, and spared the Apostles from contemptuous pity. Of these was Gallio, who "cared for none of those things" which either Jews or Christians did. Such men are abominated by our Holy Lord, who "honours them that honour Him," while "they that despised Him are lightly esteemed."[2] He signifies this judgment on the lukewarm and disloyal, in His message to the Church of Laodicea : " I know thy works, that thou art neither cold nor hot. I would thou wert cold or hot. So then, because thou art lukewarm and neither cold nor hot, I will cast thee forth out of My mouth."[3] Thus positive misbelief is a less odious state of mind than the temper of those who are indifferent to religion, who say that one opinion is as good as the other, and contemn or ridicule those who

[1] *Rom. x. 1.* [2] *1 Sam. ii. 30.* [3] *Rev. iii. 15, 16.*

are in earnest. Surely, if this world be a scene of contest between good and evil, as Scripture declares, "he that is not with Christ, is against Him;" and Angels who witness what is going on, and can estimate its seriousness, may well cry out, "Curse ye Meroz, curse ye bitterly the inhabitants thereof; because they came not to the help of the Lord, to the help of the Lord against the mighty." [1]

I do not deny that this view of the subject is different from that which certain principles and theories now current in the world would lead us to adopt; but this surely is no reason that it should not be true, unless indeed, amid the alternate successes of good and evil, there be any infallible token given us to ascertain the superior illumination of the present century over all those which have preceded it. In fact we have no standard of Truth at all but the Bible, and to that I would appeal. "To the Law and to the Testimony;" if the opinions of the day are conformable to it, let them remain in honour, but if not, however popular they may be at the moment, they will surely come to nought. It is the present fashion to call Zeal by the name of intolerance, and to account intolerance the chief of sins; that is, any earnestness for one opinion above another concerning God's nature, will, and dealings with man,—or, in other words, any earnestness for the Faith once delivered to the Saints, any earnestness for Revelation as such. Surely, in this sense, the Apostles were the most intolerant of men : what is it but intolerance in this sense of the word to declare, that " he that hath the

[1] Judges v. 23.

Son hath life, and he that hath not the Son of God hath not life;" that "they that obey not the Gospel of our Lord Jesus Christ, shall be punished with everlasting destruction from the presence of the Lord;" that "neither fornicators, nor idolaters, nor adulterers, nor covetous, nor revilers, nor extortioners, shall inherit the kingdom of God;" that we must not even "eat" with a brother who is one of such; that we may not "receive into our houses," or "bid God speed" to any one who comes to us without the "doctrine of Christ"? Has not St. Paul, whom many seem desirous of making an Apostle of less rigid principles than his brethren, said, even about an individual, "The Lord reward him according to his works!"[1] and though we of this day have not the spiritual discernment which alone can warrant such a form of words about this man or that, have we not here given us a clear evidence, that there are cases in which God's glory is irreconcilable with the salvation of sinners, and when, in consequence, it is not unchristian to acquiesce in His judgments upon them? These words were deliberately written by St. Paul, in the closing days of his life, when his mind was most calm and heavenly, his hope most assured, his reward immediately in view: circumstances which render it impossible for any one who even reverences St. Paul as a man of especial holiness, to explain them away, not to insist on the argument from his inspiration.

Such is Zeal, a Christian grace to the last, while it is also an elementary virtue; equally belonging to the

---

[1] 1 John v. 12.   2 Thess. i. 8, 9.   1 Cor. vi. 9, 10 ; v. 11, 2 John 10, 11.   2 Tim. iv. 14.

young convert and the matured believer; displayed by
Moses at the first, when he slew the Egyptian, and by
St. Paul in his last hours, while he was reaching forth
his hand for his heavenly crown.

2. On the other hand, Zeal is an imperfect virtue;
that is, in our fallen state, it will ever be attended by
unchristian feelings, if it is cherished by itself. This is
the case with many other tempers of mind which yet
are absolutely required of us. Who denies that it is a
duty in the returning sinner to feel abhorrence of his
past offences, and a dread of God's anger? yet such
feelings, unless faith accompany them, lead to an un-
fruitful remorse, to despair, to hardened pride; or again,
to perverse superstitions. Not that humiliation is
wrong in any sense or degree, but it induces collateral
weaknesses or sins, from unduly exciting one side of
our imperfect nature. Mercy becomes weakness, when
unattended by a sense of justice and firmness : the
wisdom of the serpent becomes craft, unless it be received into the harmlessness of the dove. And Zeal,
in like manner, though an essential part of a Christian temper, is but a part; and is in itself imperfect,
even for the very reason that it is elementary. Hence
it appropriately fills so prominent a place in the
Jewish Dispensation, which was intended to lay the
foundations, as of Christian Faith, so of the Christian
character. Whether we read the injunctions delivered
by Moses against idolatry and idolaters, or trace
the actual history of God's chosen servants, such as
Phinehas, Samuel, Elijah, and especially David, we find
that the Law was peculiarly a Covenant of Zeal. On

the other hand, the Gospel brings out into its full proportions, that perfect temper of mind, which the Law enjoined indeed, but was deficient both in enforcing and creating,—Love; that is, Love or Charity, as described by St. Paul in his first Epistle to the Corinthians, which is not merely brotherly-love (a virtue ever included in the notion of Zeal itself), but a general temper of gentleness, meekness, sympathy, tender consideration, openheartedness towards all men, brother or stranger, who come in our way. In this sense, Zeal is of the Law, and Love of the Gospel: and Love perfects Zeal, purifying and regulating it. Thus the Saints of God go on unto perfection. Moses ended his life as "the meekest of men," though he began it with undisciplined Zeal, which led him to a deed of violence. St. John, who would call down fire from heaven, became the Apostle of Love; St. Paul, who persecuted Christ's servants, "was made all things to all men;" yet neither of them lost their Zeal, though they trained it to be spiritual.

Love, however, is not the only grace which is necessary to the perfection of Zeal; Faith is another. This, at first sight, may sound strange; for what is Zeal, it may be asked, but a result of Faith? who is zealous for that in which he does not trust and delight? Yet, it must be kept in mind, that we have need of Faith, not only that we may direct our actions to a right object, but that we may perform them rightly; it guides us in choosing the means, as well as the end. Now, Zeal is very apt to be self-willed; it takes upon *itself to serve* God in its own way. This is evident from the very nature of it; for, in its ruder form, it manifests itself in sudden and strong emotions at the sight of presumption or irreverence, proceeding to action almost as a matter of feeling, without having time to inquire which way is best. Thus, when our Lord was seized by the officers, Peter forthwith "drew his sword, and struck a servant of the High Priest's, and smote off his ear."[1] Patience, then, and resignation to God's will, are tempers of mind of which Zeal especially stands in need,—that dutiful Faith, which will take nothing for granted on the mere suggestion of nature, looks up to God with the eyes of a servant towards his master, and, as far as may be, ascertains His will before it acts. If this heavenly corrective be wanting, Zeal, as I have said, is self-willed in its temper: while, by using sanctions, and expecting results of this world, it becomes (what is commonly called) political. Here, again, we see the contrast between the Jewish and the Christian Dispensations. The Jewish Law being a visible system, sanctioned by temporal rewards and punishments, necessarily involved the duty of a political temper on the part of those who were under it. They were bound to aim at securing the triumph of Religion here; realizing its promises, enjoying its successes, enforcing its precepts, with the sword. This, I say, was their duty; and, as fulfilling it, among other reasons, David is called "a man after God's own heart." But the Gospel teaches us to "walk by Faith, not by sight;" and Faith teaches us so to be *zealous,* as still to forbear anticipating the next world,

---

[1] Matt. xxvi. 51.

but to wait till the Judge shall come. St. Peter drew his sword, in order (as he thought) to realize at once that good work on which his heart was set, our Lord's deliverance; and, on this very account, he met with that Saviour's rebuke, who presently declared to Pilate, that His Kingdom was not of this world, else would His servants fight. Christian Zeal, therefore, ever bears in mind that the Mystery of Iniquity is to continue on till the Avenger solves it once for all; it renounces all hope of hastening His coming, all desire of intruding upon His work. It has no vain imaginings about the world's real conversion to Him, however men may acknowledge Him outwardly, knowing that "the world lies in wickedness." It has recourse to no officious modes of propagating or strengthening His truth. It does not flatter and ally itself with Samaria, in order to repress Syria. It does not exalt an Idumæan as its king, though he be willing to beautify the Temple, or has influence with the Emperors of the World. It plans no intrigues; it recognises no parties; it relies on no arm of flesh. It looks for no essential improvements or permanent reformations, in the dispensation of those precious gifts, which are ever pure in their origin, ever corrupted in man's use of them. It acts according to God's will, this time or that, as it comes, boldly and promptly; yet letting each act stand by itself, as a sufficient service to him, not connecting them in one, or working them into system, further than He commands. In a word, Christian Zeal is not political.

Two reflections arise from considering this last

characteristic of the virtue in question; and with a brief notice of these I will conclude.

1. First, it is too evident how grievously the Roman Schools have erred in this part of Christian duty. Let their doctrines be as pure as they would represent, still they have indisputably made their Church an instrument of worldly politics by a "zeal not according to knowledge," and failed in this essential duty of a Christian Witness, viz. in preserving the spiritual character of Christ's kingdom.[1] In saying this, I would not willingly deny the great debt we owe to that Church for her faithful custody of the Faith itself through so many centuries; nor seem unmindful of the circumstances of other times, the gradual growth of religious error, and the external dangers which appeared to place the cause of Christianity itself in jeopardy, and to call for extraordinary measures of defence. Much less would I speak disrespectfully of the great men, who were the agents under Providence in various stages of that mysterious Dispensation, and whom, however our Zeal may burn, we must in very Charity believe to be, what their works and sufferings betoken, single-minded, self-denying servants of their God and Saviour.

2. The Roman Church then has become political; but let us of the present day beware of running into the other extreme, and of supposing that, because Christ's Kingdom is not based upon this world, that

---

[1] Among the principles referred to are the following, which occur among the Dictatus Hildebrandi : "Quod liceat illi [Papæ] imperatores *deponere;*" "Quod à fidelitate iniquorum subditos potest absolvere." *Vide* Laud against Fisher, p. 181.

it is not connected with it. Surely it was established here for the sake of this world, and must ever act in it, as if a part of it, though its origin is from above. Like the Angels which appeared to the Patriarchs, it is a Heavenly Messenger in human form. In its Polity, its Public Assemblies, its Rules and Ordinances, its Censures, and its Possessions, it is a visible body, and, to appearance, an institution of this world. It is no faulty zeal to labour to preserve it in the form in which Christ gave it.

And further, it should ever be recollected, that, though the Church is not of this world, yet we have assurance from God's infallible word, that there *are* in the world temporal and present Dispensers of His Eternal Justice. We are expressly told, that "the powers that be are ordained of God;" that they "bear not the sword in vain, but are ministers of God, revengers to execute wrath upon the evil-doer," and bestow "praise" on those who do well. Hence, as being gifted with a portion of God's power, they hold an office of a priestly nature,[1] and are armed with the fearful sanction, that "they that resist them, shall receive to themselves Judgment." On this ground, religious Rulers have always felt it to be their duty to act as in God's place for the promulgation of the Truth; and the Church, on the other hand, has seen her obligation not only to submit to them, in things temporal, but zealously to co-operate with them in her own line, towards those sacred objects which they have both in common. And thus has been happily fulfilled

---

[1] λειτουργοὶ Θεοῦ. Rom. xiii. 1—8.

for fifteen hundred years, Isaiah's prophecy, that " kings should be nursing fathers to the Church, and queens her nursing mothers." Yet, clearly, there is nothing here, either of a self-willed zeal, or political craft, in the conduct of the Church; inasmuch as she has but submitted herself thereby to the guidance of the revealed Word.

May Almighty God, for His dear Son's sake, lead us safely through these dangerous times; so that, while we never lay aside our Zeal for His honour, we may sanctify it by Faith and Charity, neither staining our garments by wrath or violence, nor soiling them with the dust of a turbulent world!

SERMON XXXII.

Use of Saints' Days.

(THE FEAST OF ALL SAINTS.)

" Ye shall be Witnesses unto Me, both in Jerusalem, and in all Judea, and in Samaria, and unto the uttermost part of the earth."—ACTS i. 8.

SO many were the wonderful works which our Saviour did on earth, that not even the world itself could have contained the books recording them. Nor have His marvels been less since He ascended on high;— those works of higher grace and more abiding fruit, wrought in the souls of men, from the first hour till now,—the captives of His power, the ransomed heirs of His kingdom, whom He has called by His Spirit work- ing in due season, and led on from strength to strength till they appear before His face in Zion. Surely not even the world itself could contain the records of His love, the history of those many Saints, that "cloud of Witnesses," whom we to-day celebrate, His purchased possession in every age! We crowd these all up into one day; we mingle together in the brief remembrance of an hour all the choicest deeds, the holiest lives, the

noblest labours, the most precious sufferings, which the
sun ever saw. Even the least of those Saints were the
contemplation of many days,—even the names of them,
if read in our Service, would outrun many settings and
risings of the light,—even one passage in the life of one
of them were more than sufficient for a long discourse.
" Who can count the dust of Jacob, and the number of
the fourth part of Israel?"[1] Martyrs and Confessors,
Rulers and Doctors of the Church, devoted Ministers
and Religious brethren, kings of the earth and all
people, princes and judges of the earth, young men and
maidens, old men and children, the first fruits of all
ranks, ages, and callings, gathered each in his own time
into the paradise of God. This is the blessed company
which to-day meets the Christian pilgrim in the Services
of the Church. We are like Jacob, when, on his journey
homewards, he was encouraged by a heavenly vision.
" Jacob went on his way, and the Angels of God met
him; and when Jacob saw them, he said, This is
God's host: and he called the name of that place
Mahanaim."[2]

And such a host was also seen by the favoured
Apostle, as described in the chapter from which the
Epistle of the day is taken. " I beheld, and lo, a great
multitude, which no man could number, of all nations,
and kindreds, and people, and tongues, stood before the
Lamb, clothed with white robes, and palms in their
hands. . . . These are they which came out of great
tribulation, and have washed their robes, and made
them white in the blood of the Lamb."[3]

[1] *Numb. xxiii.* 10.   [2] Gen. xxxii. 1, 2.   [3] Rev. vii. 9, 14.

This great multitude, which no man could number, is gathered into this one day's commemoration, the goodly fellowship of the Prophets, the noble army of Martyrs, the Children of the Holy Church Universal, who have rested from their labours.

The reason of this disposition of things is as follows:—Some centuries ago there were too many Saints' days; and they became an excuse for idleness. Nay, worse still, by a great and almost incredible perverseness, instead of glorifying God in His Saints, Christians came to pay them an honour approaching to Divine worship. The consequence was, that it became necessary to take away their Festivals, and to commemorate them all at once in a summary way. Now men go into the contrary extreme. These Holydays, few though they be, are not duly observed. Such is the way of mankind, ever contriving to slip by their duty, and fall into one or other extreme of error. Idle or busy, they are in both cases wrong: idle, and so neglecting their duties towards man; busy, and so neglecting their duties towards God. We have little to do, however, with the faults of others;—let us then, passing by the error of idling time under pretence of observing many Holydays, rather speak of the fault of our own day, viz. of neglecting to observe them, and that, under pretence of being too busy.

Our Church abridged the number of Holydays, thinking it right to have but a few; but we account any as too much. For, taking us as a nation, we are bent on gain; and grudge any time which is spent without reference to our worldly business. We should seriously reflect whether this neglect of the appointments of religion be not a great national sin. As to individuals, I can easily understand how it is that they pass them over. A considerable number of persons (for instance) have not their time at their own disposal. They are in service or business, and it is their duty to attend to the orders of their masters or employers,—which keep them from church. Or they have particular duties to keep them at home, though they are their own masters. Or, it even may be said, that the circumstances under which they find their calling, the mode in which it is exercised by others, may be a sort of reason for doing as others do. It may be such a worldly loss to them to leave their trade on a Saint's day and go to church, as to appear to them a reason in conscience for their not doing so? I do not wish to give an opinion upon this case or that, which is a matter for the individual immediately concerned. Still, I say, *on the whole,* that state of society must be defective, which renders it necessary for the Ordinances of religion to be neglected. There must be a fault *somewhere;* and it is the duty of every one of us to clear himself of his own portion of the fault, to avoid partaking in other men's sins, and to do his utmost that others may extricate themselves from the blame too.

I say this neglect of religious Ordinances is an especial fault of these latter ages. There was a time when men openly honoured the Gospel; and when, consequently, they had each of them more means of becoming religious. The institutions of the Church were impressed upon the face of society. Dates were reckoned not so much by months and seasons, as by sacred Festivals. The world kept pace with the Gospel; the arrangements of legal and commercial business were regulated by a Christian rule. Something of this still remains among us; but such customs are fast vanishing. Mere grounds of utility are considered sufficient for re-arranging the order of secular engagements. Men think it waste of time to wait upon the course of the Christian year; and they think they gain more by a business-like method, and the neatness, dispatch, and clearness in their worldly transactions consequent upon it (and this perhaps they really *do* gain, but they think they gain *more* by it), than they lose by dropping the Memorials of religion. These they really do lose; they lose those regulations which at stated times brought the concerns of another life before their minds; and, if the truth must be spoken, they often rejoice in losing what officiously interfered, as they consider, with their temporal schemes, and reminded them they were mortal.

Or view another part of the subject. It was once the custom for the churches to be open through the day, that at spare times Christians might enter them, —and be able to throw off for some minutes the cares of the world in religious exercises. Services were appointed for separate hours in the day, to allow of the attendance in whole or part of those who happened to be at hand. Those who could not come, still might keep their service-book with them; and at least repeat at times the prayers in private which were during the passing hour offered in church. Thus provision was made for the spiritual sustenance of Christians day by *day; for that* daily-needed bread which far exceeds "the bread that perisheth." All this is now at an end. We dare not open our churches, lest men should profane them instead of worshipping. As for an accurately arranged Ritual, too many of us have learned to despise it, and to consider it a form. Thus the world has encroached on the Church; the lean kine have eaten up the fat. We are threatened with years of spiritual famine, with the triumph of the enemies of the Truth, and with the stifling, or at least enfeebling of the Voice of Truth;—and why? All because we have neglected those religious observances through the year which the Church commands, which we are bound to observe; while, by neglecting them, we have provided a sort of argument for those who have wished to do them away altogether. No party of men can keep together without stated meetings; assemblings are, we know, the very life of political associations. Viewing, then, the institutions of the Church merely in a human point of view, how can we possess power as Christians, if we do *not*, and on the other hand, what great power we should have, if we *did*, flock to the Ordinances of religion, present a bold face to the world, and show that Christ has still servants true to Him? That we come to church on Sundays is a help this way, doubtless; but it would be a vastly more powerful evidence of our earnestness for the Truth, if we testified for Christ at some worldly inconvenience to ourselves, which would be the case with some of us on other Holy-days. Can we devise a more powerful mode of preach-*ing* to men at large, and one in which the most unlearned and most timid among us might more easily partake, of preaching Christ as a warning and a remembrance, than if all who loved the Lord Jesus Christ in sincerity made it a practice to throng the churches on the week-day Festivals and various Holy Seasons, allowing less religious persons the while to make the miserable gains which greater keenness in the pursuit of this world certainly does secure?

I have not yet mentioned the peculiar benefit to be derived from the observance of Saints' days: which obviously lies in their setting before the mind patterns of excellence for us to follow. In directing us to these, the Church does but fulfil the design of Scripture. Consider how great a part of the Bible is historical; and how much of the history is merely the lives of those men who were God's instruments in their respective ages. Some of them are no patterns for us, others show marks of the corruption under which human nature universally lies:—yet the chief of them are specimens of especial faith and sanctity, and are set before us with the evident intention of exciting and guiding us in our religious course. Such are, above others, Abraham, Joseph, Job, Moses, Joshua, Samuel, David, Elijah, Jeremiah, Daniel, and the like; and in the New Testament the Apostles and Evangelists. First of all, and in His own incommunicable glory, our Blessed Lord Himself gives us an example; but His faithful servants lead us on towards Him, and confirm and diversify His pattern. Now it has been the aim of our Church in her Saints' days to maintain the principle, and set a pattern, of this peculiarly Scriptural teaching. And we, at the present day, have particular need of the discipline of such commemorations as Saints' days, to recall us to ourselves. It is a fault of these times (for we have nothing to do with the faults of other times) to despise the past in comparison of the present. We can scarce open any of the lighter or popular publications of the day without falling upon some panegyric on ourselves, on the illumination and humanity of the age, or upon some disparaging remarks on the wisdom and virtues of former times. Now it is a most salutary thing under this temptation to self-conceit to be reminded, that in all the highest qualifications of human excellence, we have been far outdone by men who lived centuries ago; that a standard of truth and holiness was then set up which we are not likely to reach, and that, as for thinking to become wiser and better, or more acceptable to God than they were, it is a mere dream. Here we are taught the true value and relative importance of the various gifts of the mind. The showy talents, in which the present age prides itself, fade away before the true metal of Prophets and Apostles. Its boasted " knowledge " is but a shadow of " power " before the vigorous strength of heart which they displayed, who could calmly work moral miracles, as well as speak with the lips of inspired wisdom. Would that St. Paul or St. John could rise from the dead! How would the minute philosophers who now consider intellect and enlightened virtue all their own, shrink into nothing before those well-tempered, sharp-edged weapons of the Lord! Are not we come to this, is it not our shame as a nation, that, if not the Apostles themselves, at least the Ecclesiastical System they devised, and the Order they founded, are viewed with coldness and disrespect? How few are there who look with reverent interest upon the Bishops of the Church as the Successors of the Apostles; honouring them, if they honour, merely because they like them as individuals, and not from any thought of the peculiar sacredness of their office! Well, let it be! the End must one time come. It cannot be that things should stand still thus. Christ's Church is indestructible; and, lasting on through all the vicissitudes of this world, she *must* rise again and flourish, when the poor creatures of a day who opposed her, have crumbled into dust. "No weapon that is formed against her shall prosper." "Rejoice not against me, O mine enemy! when I fall, I shall arise; when I sit in darkness, the Lord shall be a light unto me."[1] In the meantime let us not forget our duty; which is, after the example of Saints, to take up our cross meekly, and pray for our enemies.

These are thoughts suitably to be impressed on us, on ending (as we do now) the yearly Festivals of the Church. Every year brings wonders. We know not any year, what wonders shall have happened before the circle of Festivals has run out again, from St. Andrew's to All Saints'. Our duty then is, to wait for the Lord's coming, to prepare His way before Him, to pray that when He comes we may be found watching; to pray for our country, for our King and all in authority under him, that God would vouchsafe to enlighten the understandings and change the hearts of men in power, and make them act in His faith and fear, for all orders

[1] Isa. liv. 17. Micah vii. 8.

... and temptations of ... and especially for those ... of the church which He has planted here. Let us not forget ... as evil men ... and that they knew not what they did ... the truth. Let us not forget ... as well as they, ... and ... obedience ... their will. Let us not forget that as we are called to ... a ... to suffer ... and if we suffer ... not think it strange concerning the ... that is to try us ... but to ... in ... the privilege of suffering, nor long suffering ... in order to make us ... we have suffered in Christ ... we have but suffered ... May God give us grace to ... them ... as well as to adore and admire them, and to say nothing for saying's sake but to do much and say little.

MORRIN AND GIBB, PRINTERS, EDINBURGH.

CPSIA information can be obtained
at www.ICGtesting.com
Printed in the USA
LVHW082140190619
621796LV00008B/357/P

9 780342 265046